BREAKING THE CYCLES OF PAIN:

Soul Secrets

Queen Shamala Bessie Davis Smith

ISBN 978-1-956001-57-0 (paperback)
ISBN 978-1-956001-58-7 (eBook)

Copyright © 2022 by Queen Shamala Bessie Davis Smith

All rights reserved. No part of this publication may be reproduced, distributed, or transmitted in any form or by any means, including photocopying, recording, or other electronic or mechanical methods without the prior written permission of the publisher.

Permission for libation epigraph

Permission Donna Kozik, founder Write a Book in a Weekend
All art on the book cover and the chapter parts are painted by the author.

Printed in the United States of America

IN THE TRADITION OF THE ANCESTORS
A Libation

For African people
Nothing important happens without a libation
An honoring of the ancestors who came before us
And made it possible for us to be
For this very important offering.
It is my pleasure to provide a libation.

To our first ancestors, that creative energy, the hidden one, who, though hidden, manifests in all things as all things, that God-force in the universe by any and all names…

> We pour libation. Ase!

To our ancestors of the African interior who entered the realm as the first people on the planet, flash point of the human family, children of creation itself, mothers and fathers of all mankind…

> We pour libation. Ase!

To our ancestors of ancient Kemet, earliest proponents of "Know thyself", who left unmistakable evidence of that high culture, who left a legacy of thousands of years of autonomy…

> We pour libation. Ase!

To our ancestors of the first exodus who took language, logic, effective speech, geometry, astronomy, music and spiritual principles out of Africa and peopled the world…

We pour libation. Ase!

To our ancestors of indomitable spirit who lived through legislated amnesia, who, despite loss of language, loss of culture, retained in the very fiber of their being's remnants of our story…

We pour libation. Ase!

To our elders, our teachers, our historians, our scholars, who work tenaciously to restore our collective memory, to recover, reconstruct and resurrect our culture, to re-wing the phoenix…

We pour libation. Ase!

To all of you, who are privileged to experience this offering, to read the words, to vibrate at their frequency, to absorb the light and love that they are…

We pour libation. Ase!

To our children and those yet to be born, our cultural and spiritual heirs, the repositories of our wisdom and our creative energies, who will also stand on the shoulders of the ancestors, and who must sit at their feet to learn again and for the first time the wonder of the African way…

We pour libation.
Ase! Ase! Aseo!
Thelma Cameron
2014

Dedication

First, I dedicate this book to the creative spirit of the ancestors, the ancient ones who came before us and left us with a purpose and passion for our lives. Not only did they give me the inspiration, but they also left me with valuable spiritual and academic teachers who provide positive influences on my life. Most of my early teachers and guides were women. As a young girl, I called them 'sheheroes' to include girls in the role modeling. My journey has been marked by inspired sheheroes who recognized my talents when I couldn't. *Breaking the Cycles of Pain: Soul Secrets* is dedicated to my teachers, healers, coaches and heroes/sheheroes/sheroes who progressively evoke the soul learning that I was seeking.

My mother, Mamie Lee Miller Davis, is my first teacher, beauty queen and heart encourager. The 'Colored' schools in Kinston, North Carolina refined my reading and writing. My first and second grade teacher Miss Fletcher encouraged me to read, read, read. The librarian in the 'Colored' library gave me discarded textbooks, old magazines and writing pads. My 11th grade English composition teacher, Miss Clark, and Mrs. Lenhart, my senior English teacher, were recognized and respected for their demand of excellence in reading, writing, speaking English, and exploring and analyzing its literature.

The teacher with the longest direct effect over my life development is my high school French teacher, Miss Carolyn Gray (Thompson Taylor). A mixture of an elegant Audrey Hepburn and a regal Queen Nefertiti, her theories about teaching, fashion and personal relationships inspired me to strive for more than society had laid out for me. What is especially poignant about Miss Gray was her gentle spirit, healing voice and wise, contemplative eyes. Her loving classroom demeanor evoked a desire within me to be a teacher and a counselor. Miss Gray understood me; she got me. I understood her as much as she allowed.

Mrs. Gray Thompson married, moved to upstate New York and I married and moved to Southern California. We communicated through the craft of letter writing. Years later, through Classmates.com, I connected with her sister Thelma and received Mrs. Carolyn Gray Thompson Taylor's phone number. For the last several years, Mrs. Taylor and I continued our divine conversation over the telephone. Living in Butler, Alabama, she was now Mrs. Taylor, but the same, open, loving person with a spacious heart. When I discovered that she was only five years older than me, I still was not able to call her Carolyn. A deep sense of respect and reverence always assailed the thought. For me she was never a commoner. She was a light that illuminated my path. Importantly, for us Black girls, she was an exemplary role model.

The last time I talked with my longtime friend was in 2019. I finally shared the secret that I had been afraid to tell my favorite teacher in 1961 in French 1A. This secret is the basis of this book, *Breaking the Cycles of Pain: Soul Secrets*. Important scenes in the book deal with our teacher/student interactions. She responded, "I knew there was something there, but I couldn't pinpoint it. You never looked defeated. I'm so glad that you continued on your path."

I also informed Mrs. Taylor how she had unwittingly influenced me to use my autobiographical voice for writing. I often strive to bring the clarity of her speech and thought to my writings. Mrs. Carolyn Gray Thompson Taylor was so humbled when I told her about the book dedication. She said, "Thank you for always finding me." We laughed.

My real life favorite shero made her transition about two months later. Both of us understood that our divine connection continues. Years. Time. Distance. Space cannot separate that which is eternal. Oprah Winfrey has been on my list of heroes/sheheroes/sheroes since the 80's when she made sexual abuse a public issue. Queen Carolyn Gray Thompson Taylor has been on my list of sheheroes for over 60 years. I will share this super shehero's tale with my granddaughter, Malika Power Shakir.

Foreword

I'd like to introduce a new African American writer, Reverend Dr. Queen Shamala Bessie Davis Smith, who captures the heart of what it was like to grow up in the Jim Crow South in the 40s, 50s and 60s. Her memoir, *Breaking the Cycles of Pain: Soul Secrets,* is an unapologetic, in-your-face tour de force. This is her second book; the first one being, *Black Butterfly Soul Song,* a collection of poems and short anecdotes about spiritual awakening. Dr. Queen Shamala's new book, *Breaking the Cycles of Pain: Soul Secrets* explores subject matters that aren't talked about much in the Black community. The author tackles the family secrets of Doris Love—infidelity, depression and voodoo. What is so powerful about her memoir is that, among many other inequalities suffered because of racism, the young child Doris also had to deal with childhood sexual molestation.

We now have a #Metoo movement for women, (mainly white), saying they have been molested or raped at some point in their lives. Yet very few have known the pains that Black women and Black men have endured due to odious involuntary sexual assault. Beginning with the Middle Passage up until now, Black men and women have been the victims of sexual abuse at a deplorably high rate. This has been one of America's dirty little secrets. But even more egregious, is when this sexual abuse happens in the nuclear family system. This is one of the most tabooed, insidious dysfunctions known to man.

Follow the irrepressible heroine, Doris, whose nickname is "Rabbit", as she, a budding writer/artist, tries to make sense of her home life and the larger segregated society. Observe the corrupted agent of change, Reverend Abraham Love, who simultaneously wreaks havoc in the family and stirs admiration in the community. Sit and bear witness with the author as she re-writes her painful reality.

Continue the saga of the ironic Love family in Queen Shamala's second memoir, *The Journey Let Us Cheer the Weary Traveler* in which Doris confronts the larger story of the intersectionality of sex, gender and racism in her adult experiences. Kimberle Crenshaw, a civil right leader and a social advocate, uses this term to aptly describe the overlapping dynamics of being Black and female in a system of male domination, oppression and discrimination.

Rev. Dr. Queen Shamala Fayemi Smith, a retired high school principal/counselor, was inspired to become a counselor during her first year of teaching English. Many high school students disclosed their secrets about incest, rape and abuse to her. One day a group of students left a letter in her office that disclosed a child abuse situation. As she read the letter, the terror, isolation and brokenness expressed in the writer made the counselor realized that child abuse/incest/molestation was a type of 'soul murder'. The issue was an untapped, unexplored, unspoken counseling situation in school, the community and life.

The next week Queen Shamala started a sexual abuse support group during lunch. The three students with the letter were part of the roster. Written and oral exercises opened the members to hidden and unspoken feelings.

According to Queen Shamala, "It was at this point I decided to write my whole life out. As they told their lives, they were telling mine. I knew writing would help me untangle it."

The counseling groups launched her into her raison d'etre and lifework-healing and writing.

Breaking the Cycles of Pain: Soul Secrets will stimulate some to positive action, like this author and serve as a catalyst to bring about much healing to others. This book is an important memoir that must be read!

Dr. Maxine Thompson 2020
http://www.maxinethompsonbooks.com
http://www.maxinethompson.com

Acknowledgements

This project begins with acknowledging the ancestors and all the paths they have led me down. I give thanks to life, its experiences, and its many opportunities for coming to know myself. I also acknowledge my family who has provided the perfect cauldron for extracting life's lessons. I want to thank my mama for telling 'my nosy self' one day, "The questions will lead you to your answers." That suggestion still motivates my research and writing today.

I pay tribute to all the Harlem Renaissance writers, scholarly researchers, spiritual leaders and committed teacher who enlightened my path. My personal sheheroes include Maya Angelou, Angela Davis, Dwayne Dyer, Baba Obafemi Fayemi, Dr. Faye V. Harrision, bell hooks, Dr. Martin Luther King, Queen Mother Shaw, Dr. Wade Nobles, Rev. Meri Ka Ra, Sensei Eugene, Lisa Sprinkles RScP (Religious Science Practitioner), Ophrah Winfrey and Malcolm X.

A special thanks to my daughter, Chef Yealang Odutola Fayemi Smith Shakir, who has accompanied me on the long, circuitous journey of writing. Yealang grew up seeing me shrouded in books, tablets and learning. At any point of a family or social gathering, I would eventually sequester myself in a corner with a book and a pen. I alternated between interfacing with loved ones and the inner world of ideas. Her appreciation of my writing has expanded to the point that we are finishing a joint book project together. *The Making of Soul* explores Yealang's interest in the alchemy of food and its preparation, especially Soul food.

A heartfelt recognition goes to my husband 'Jimmy' Kaliph Sahin Fayemi Smith, who agrees that "the second time around is cool." I appreciate his love and enthusiasm, especially his coming to the marriage and the writing with a joyous attitude and a keen intellect. His excellent wordsmithery, fact-checking ability and double extenders contributed invaluable support.

I give special acknowledgements to Dr. Maxine Thompson of Dr. Thompson's Literary Service for content-editing *Breaking the Cycles of Pain: Soul Secrets*. It is because of her persistent formula to 'expand, reduce and re-write' that the book's reader engagement, tension, suspense, structure and pacing are fully developed. Her expertise and insightful suggestions made me laugh and cry at the difficulty and intricacy of characters and theme development. I acknowledge Brahmashatiki Fudail for proofreading the manuscript and her supportive comments about the project.

Other people I wish to express my deep gratitude include the facilitator of the Saturday Literary Workshop, Lorine Calhoun and all the writing students who share glimpses of their lives with me in poetry, story and script. A shout out goes to Harry Phelps who encouraged me weekly, "Write your books right now! I want to publish one for you." Harry, who had written five books and a film, made his transition in 2017.

I appreciate the sharp eye and red pencil of my counselor colleague/writing buddy Susan Dorsey who helped me to eliminate pages of minutiae and liberties in my writings. I also acknowledge Alicia Seshat Sekhmet Randolph, my research consultant, who assisted me on several writing projects. My deep appreciation goes to Yuri Hinson, the daughter of the libationist, Thelma Cameron, for allowing me the continued use of her mother's evocative libations in my books. I salute, Thelma Cameron who made her transition in November 2016.

Breaking the Cycles of Pain: Soul Secrets especially acknowledges all victims and survivors of any type of sexual abuse. Years of education, counseling and spiritual cultivation helped me to remove past the resultant self-shame, self-pain and self-blame of the soul-biting experience. The book speaks out for and gives voice to the unspoken and unheard. Some information and a referral number are provided in the back of the book for all seeking guidance, reporting, healing and love. As my mama used to say. "There is a bright side ahead, if you don't despair."

Introduction

In Breaking the Cycles of Pain: Soul Secrets, Doris Love, who longed to escape her molesting father, the racist South and male rule, had broken the 12:00 curfew. On a rainy summer night, Doris tried to slip in the locked house. From the back porch, she had climbed up on the oil drum and pushed the window open. The window screen fell onto the kitchen counter with a dull bounce. Reverend Love's raging voice greeted her as she stepped through the kitchen window into the sink, "Go back where you come from!"

The kitchen blazed with light. The clock on the stove indicated that it was 3:05 a.m. Well past the assigned hour. Her hair, clothes and shoes were leaking water in the sink. Like someone had turned the spigot on her. Doris didn't answer Reverend Love. She looked outside to see if the car was still there. Her reply was to turn around and to step slowly out the same way she had come in.

Wiping tears and chopping rain from her bowed head, Doris resignedly slumped back to the waiting car. "He told me to go back where I came from."

Jimmy said, "Get back in the car." After a long silence, the honorable Marine decided, "You can come to live at my family house in Winston-Salem. It's about 185 miles away. Only about three hours. It'll be fine. Things will resolve themselves."

This was the incident that would catapult Doris's life into the direction she had been envisioning. Unforeseen events sped up the process. The curfew violation threw her out of the house and straight into the arms of her departing hero and her awaiting destiny. She knew instinctively that it was a crossroad situation. Her life had always been a series of turning points and forks in the road.

QUEEN SHAMALA BESSIE DAVIS SMITH

The throw-out by her lecherous, hypocritical minister father didn't break Doris. Even though the mind-bending child abuse made her feel alone and unprotected, it didn't swallow her up. Instead, she moved to California and continued to use her love of education and her burning desire to write to heal from the childhood abuse and faulty cultural programming. Counseling, journaling, and journeying back in her life enabled the protagonist in the memoir to retrieve life's experiences and lessons. She would eventually realize that challenges are disguised opportunities for growth and development. It took Doris many years of devotion to wholeness before the valence of the atrocity lessened.

Like Doris, when I was a child, I became interested in using writing to express my deep anger and emotions. Growing up, I was full of rage about the family's incest secret, the practice of silencing females and the low status of 'Colored' people in the world. Children are often not aware of the many historical, social, and political circumstances that program their lives. After years of writing, I know now that writing allows us to re-visit our lives as an adult, re-write the old story and re-right our life as we create a new story and a new life. Life writing allows you to analyze, dissect, and evaluate your own life's experiences, by using social, cultural and historical references. Your new perspective becomes more balanced because you now have your own personal worldview of life.

If you have picked up *Breaking the Cycles of Pain: Soul Secrets*, you have probably experienced similar instances of abuse, loss or pervasive programming in your own life. Reading the struggles and triumphs of Doris will give hope to those who have been trapped in the seeming setups, setbacks and set downs of life. Also, *Soul Secrets* is guaranteed to improve your understanding of the dynamics of sexual abuse in the family. The controlling father, the silenced mother and the molested children represent a 'trilogy of shame, pain and deceit'. The book also illustrates how segregation formed the backdrop for 'Colored' life in the South during the 40's, 50's and 60's. Sexual abuse, patriarchy and racism continue to plague homes, churches and workplaces today in 2020.

BREAKING THE CYCLES OF PAIN: SOUL SECRETS

How do you put all the re-miniscing, re-calling and re-membering together to write a coherent story about your life? As a high school English teacher and a counselor, I had acquired adequate tools for composing. The burning desire to write was evident, but something was missing. I came across *Your Life as Story* by Tristine Rainer during the late 90's in a Barnes and Nobles bookstore. Tristine Rainer, Ph.D., is a pioneer and expert in journal writing and narrative autobiography. The purpose of her book on page 2 states: "To give you the tools to see story in your life, and then, if you chose, to give it shape in writing so it can be shared." (1.) Coming across the idea of life as story was an intriguing and thought-provoking perspective that helped me to structure and organize the telling of my story. Seeing my life as story empowered me to write past my inhibitions. The book that I had been writing finally had some focus.

Reading Zora Neale Hurston, a folklorist and anthropologist, validated that autobiographical writing is an effective technique to end the sense of self-exile, powerlessness and voicelessness of unrequited writers. Hurston states in *Dust Tracks on My Road*, "Anyway, the force from somewhere in Space which commands you to write in the first place, gives you no choice. You take up the pen when you are told and write what is commanded. There is no agony like bearing an untold story within you." (2.).

Even after I had structure, I still lacked my own individual sense of voice. Voice refers to each person's unique style, an opinion, or the right to state that opinion. This quality had been hidden away in my secret childhood sorrows about not being loved, not good enough and fear of exposing a family secret. A limiting voice inside had whispered, "This is too dangerous, too controversial and too embarrassing to be put on paper." My desire to understand life far outweighed the constant fear, low self-esteem and 'my secrets.'

In 2008, I attended a writing class in the Pasadena City Library, facilitated by my secret muse, Dr. Tristine Rainer. She spoke on the importance of writing memoir and its healing aspects. After she signed my prior purchased book, I read what she had written. "for Shamala, Please write the stories only you can tell. Tristine Rainer 10/1/08. I went forth with that dictate.

In 2010, I attended an intensive weekend seminar, "Discovering Your Power Voice," at the Los Angeles Sheraton Hotel hosted by Les Brown, a renowned motivational speaker. Brown is an avid advocate of speaking and writing from your power voice. During his presentation, Les Brown convinced me that the mind and heart of the conscious speaker/writer touch the mind and heart of the sincere hearer/reader.

After the conference, Les Brown offered a special scholarship for a series of empowerment classes to local participants who attended the conference. The classes were conducted at KRST Unity Center of AfRaKan Spiritual Science in Los Angeles.

One of the first assignments was to find a subject that we felt passionate about and write on it. Life had chosen the topic for me. My voice came through and I wrote like I had good sense. The essay started with: *While Doris couldn't remember when she began to write down her experiences, she did remember her first secret. This is a secret that Doris never told anyone: the night her oldest sister had a premature baby in the bed that she shared with her two older sisters.*

Right away, after I read my paper in class, Les Brown exclaimed, "You got to finish this and get it published! You must name it: *Breaking the Cycles of Pain: Soul Secrets.*"

Finding my own voice was the thread that stitched the tattered pieces of my life back together. As I wrote, I realized that my family (a torn quilt) was broken (tattered) long before I showed up in it. Using my sassy and rebellious nature gave me freedom to write (to re-right) my life (tattered pieces) in my own way (my voice). To set my voice free, my distinct use of words and my imagination unconsciously set my heart free. I discovered that my voice is myself in the telling of the story. This is the powerful writing voice which is the writer's gift to the reader.

As the essay morphed into a memoir, I discovered creative nonfiction which deals with writings based upon researched facts, opinions or conjectures. Creative nonfiction is a recent genre that also allows the use of literary styles and techniques, usually found in novels and movies. (3.) Character development, dialogue exchange, changing scenes and elaborate descriptions are used to write about actual events in life. This writing includes the personal essay, memoir, biography, autobiography and history. I realized that I was already using these features as I wrote the memoir.

Re-reading Maya Angelo, James Baldwin, Toni Morrison, Ralph Ellison and Alice Walker reinforced the idea that the child abuse and the incest story had already found voice and public acceptance through autobiographical writing. The awareness tossed my lingering angst in the trash basket and I wrote from my own voice, full of power and confidence. These powerful speakers and writers in my adult life helped to galvanize my writer, and caused me to declare, "*I am a writer. I choose to write every day. I am the expert of my life. I give meaning and intent to my experiences. I am the voice of soul.*"

Initially, part of Les Brown's suggestion was used as a working title—*Soul Secrets*. As I wrote about the first twenty years of the protagonist's life, more defining issues unfolded. The mother's escalating depression, the practice of 'secret ancestral arts' (mislabeled hoodoo) and the mystical local riverbank interpenetrated the tale. Growing up in the South had also framed most of my life. It became apparent that Doris's search would deal with healing these mounting issues. In the end, the sketch from the power voice class is included as a foundational writing in Chapter 2 of this full-length memoir. As Les Brown urged, I named the finished book, *Breaking the Cycles of Pain: Soul Secrets*. I also proceeded with Les Brown's vehement exhortation and published the book that you are reading right now. Discovering my power voice helped me to write from my heart.

Another change occurred as I switched from the third person to the first person 'I'. The autographic 'I', which acknowledges the feeling and emotional nature of the storyteller, wanted to narrate the adventures. I wanted the courageous story and my awakened voice to make direct connections to the creative mind, soul and spirit of the reader. Thus, pseudonymous names were given to all characters to provide voice to the author, allow anonymity and to honor and protect the innocent. Names in the Dedication and Acknowledgement are unchanged. Dates, locations, and information are unchanged and as true as I could confirm.

Breaking the Cycles of Pain: Soul Secrets is the re-membered story of Doris's life, which began as childhood notes archived in raggedy journals and hidden diaries. Years later, Doris's writing impulses used biographical essays to explore life's experiences. Over time, writing classes and the creative nonfiction genre added techniques of dialogue, history and setting to her life writing.

The book, a creative nonfiction memoir, is divided into 5 parts. Part I focuses on Doris's early memories of childhood innocence, discovering she is 'Colored' and the family's secrets. When Doris is five years old, she answers the call to understand her family and life. Her mission soon reveals itself as a call of soul and spirit.

In Part II, Doris began a secret investigation of her parents by snooping in their business and questioning adults to unravel life's mysteries.

Part III introduces other factors that influence Doris and her coming of age story. Racism, education, puberty, and television cause Doris to realize that her search in life was about identity, racial pride and healing.

Part IV deals with the Love family's escape places of safety and asylums. Doris finds solace by adopting a family who lives down the street.

In Part V, Doris meets her first love who confronts the lascivious minister. After graduation, Doris becomes a mother, leaves home and begins the journey.

As I finished with *Breaking the Cycles of Pain*, I realized that this creative nonfiction memoir is like the classic hero's journey of Joseph Campbell. This is the tale of the man who goes out into the world to slay dragons and victoriously returns home. Doris Love's early decision to understand life and her abrupt separation from her family propel her out West on a circuitous shero's search for identity, love and truth. This concludes the memoir, but not the quest.

The second part of her journey continues in my next memoir. In *The Journey Let Us Cheer the Weary Traveler,* Doris confronts the larger story of sex, gender and racism as she creates herself in her own image.

Prologue

August 1988
Reverend Love,

Shakespeare wrote, "A coward dies a thousand times before his death, but the valiant tastes of death but once." This letter was written over and over before today. I wrote you a letter when I first left home, but I watched it disappear in the tides when I hurled it into the Santa Monica Bay. At a women's healing ceremony, I completed another letter to you and burned it. When hiking in the woods, I put your letter in a jar and buried it. None of these cleansing rituals freed me of my shame. Nor you of your guilt. Our family secrets rattled around in my head for years.

These bitter memories resurfaced three months ago after I had a consultation with my gynecologist. This led to a turning point in my life. Dr. Stiff Butcher's stiffly starched white jacket, her stern face and her downtrodden eyes cast more murkiness around the vomit green examination room and me. Her hard exterior remained cold, distant and closed. To get through dead encounters and to soften life's blows, my habit of giving secret names to match strange personalities showed up for the stiff doctor. I guess I did get my name changing from Nora, your stepdaughter, my sister.

After a hasty pelvic examination, the doctor declared, without thought, feeling, or looking at me, "The fibroid continues to grow, invading your uterus. We must remove the tumor."

I suggested, "What about the myomectomy that you mentioned before? At least, it leaves the uterus intact."

But Dr. 'Few Words Stiff' Butcher frowned. "The tumor has probably done too much damage. You don't want any more children at your age, do you?"

I screamed! "You take the tumor! Do the myomectomy! I want to keep my uterus 'cause it's mine!" I was disappointed. Three years of treatment had not improved the tumor nor her poor bedside manner.

"What caused the problem?" I asked.

The gynecologist's first answered, "Estrogen. Age. Higher African American women rates." Then she struggled to say, "Rape. Molestation. Abortions. Battery. The question you can ask yourself is: 'What has troubled my womb?'"

She ended the brief exchange by saying, "See the nurse to set the date for your partial hysterectomy." The mechanical doctor turned her rigid back and slipped the cold steel duck mouth pelvic device into a vat of disinfectant.

Dr. 'Love Few Words Robotic Stiff' Butcher scoured her contaminated hands. "We'll take your uterus, but you keep your ovaries." Reaching the door, Dr. Gone 'No Love Few Words Robotic Stiff' Butcher slung her warning words over her left shoulder, "You already know what troubles the womb troubles your life. You decide your healing." The door slammed on my hopes and my healing.

By the time I got home, this milestone question caught me up in an acute panic attack. A whirlwind of thoughts about my troubled womb trailed me from the car to the sofa. When I quieted my racing mind, the voice whispered, *Reverend Abraham Jacob Love*. It was then I decided to address my life-troubling situation in this final letter to you.

Three months later, I took the advice of the doctor. I went on a medical leave from work, packed my bags, my notebook/pens and signed in for surgery at Ross Loos hospital. My weepy troubled womb was cut out in the summer of 1988, three months before my forty-fourth birthday.

Reverend Love, this letter flings the secret wide open. This is the core issue that loomed as a backdrop for my childhood. Some of the anger and resentment from the past have dissolved as I write this letter. The surgery opened a door that will not be shut during the healing season. I've reached a place where I am ready to confront you. Today, I am tired of being a coward.

You were like the David from the Bible. Handsome, called of God, a champion who slew the giant Goliath. You fought the giant of racism, poverty and segregation of Southern life. You and David were both driven by passion and power. Both of you sought what belonged to others. And like David, you can't build the temple to God on blood. This letter marks the end of your reign in my life!

You scarred my innocence and broke my early childhood trust. I was robbed of my 'daddyness' and my childhood. As a little girl, I loved Mama, but I idolized you. Your flamboyant dress, lofty words, the community respect, and your being a minister elevated you to a Jesus-like status. You were my hero.

This letter notifies you that I am breaking my promise to my sister, Nora, to my Mama and to you. I cast the "seemingly fine-covered-up-pretend-nothing-has-happened-just-live-in-that-world-of-silence story" in the trash! I will no longer be quiet! Members of alcoholics anonymous say, "You are only as sick as your secrets." I am going to be well! I am going to re-right my life and write me a new story!

Unlike the other letters that never reached their destination, I am bringing this one to you when I come for the family reunion. Then, we can have our face-to-face encounter. Beginning today, with the troubled womb gone and some of the hurt explored, I move forward in my life!

Just before I fell asleep, out of the darkness, the familiar voice of God said, *Don't forget to breathe. Your voice can heal and free you. Follow your first passion. Write your life out.*

Today, I begin to use my voice.

Doris Love,
a Rising Phoenix

Contents

PART I.
BEGINNINGS

Chapter 1: Growing Up 'Colored' 2
Chapter 2: Soul Secrets 12
Chapter 3: November 16, 1949 Dear Diary: I am Only Five 19
Chapter 4: November 26, 1949: Before and After......................26
Chapter 5: November 30, 1949 Answering the Call..................39

PART II.
LIFE LIVED BACKWARD

Chapter 6: Swimming Upstream..45
Chapter 7: Am I Adopted?..57
Chapter 8: Abraham Jacob Love, My Daddy..............................61
Chapter 9: Emma Lee Love, My Mama 71
Chapter 10: I, Doris Anne Love, Am Born 78

PART III.
LIFE MOVING FORWARD

Chapter 11: Stages of Child-Tending 90
Chapter 12: My Kindergarten...94
Chapter 13: Late to School 105
Chapter 14: Coming Home to School 109
Chapter 15: The High Cost of 'Colored' Television 116

PART IV.
ASYLUMS

Chapter 16: Clotheshorses Create Money Problems.................123
Chapter 17: Losing My Mama and Other Turning Points at 12...136
Chapter 18: Finding a Safe Place...149
Chapter 19: Secret Arts: Herbal Medicine...................................160
Chapter 20: Getting Religion: Jesus Medicine............................166

PART V.
BREAKING THE CYCLES OF SECRETS

Chapter 21: Finding Voice at 14 180
Chapter 22: Launching Out into the Deep 191
Chapter 23: Only Sixteen 206
Chapter 24: Senior Year 222
Chapter 25: Go Back Where You Come From! 240

PART I.
BEGINNINGS

Chapter 1

Growing Up 'Colored'

June 1949
Kinston, North Carolina

"Cut out that racket or everybody stays inside today! It's as hot as hell in here. I show don't want to be stuck in here all day with y'all blabbermouths." Mama's stern frown and wrinkled forehead meant that she and Daddy had another argument. But her eyes were soft and clear. She wasn't mad with us. I was learning to watch her changing moods.

Our excitement about school finally being out filled the small faded gray shotgun house. I had asked, "Mama, why do they call the houses in the alley 'shotgun houses? Aunt Naomi always call us, 'My poor relatives who live in a 'shotgun house'."

"Child, you ask questions that no other child think about. Anyway. the shotgun houses have small rooms set up one behind the other. And doors at each end of the house. Look at our house. The livin' room, bedroom and kitchen all in a row. If you stand in the front room, you can look through the bedroom. And then see the kitchen. It's got somethin' to do with the barrel of a gun. But your dad' can speak on this. He knows about such things."

Even though Willie Earl, my youngest brother, and I had not started school, everybody was loudly planning for the first day of the summer vacation. The thought of having to spend the day inside this small hot shotgun house shut all mouths. The house got quiet! No one would dare say anything after the warning. Mama took pride in keeping her word. For a long time, the only sound heard was the tick, tick, tick of the old kitchen clock and the drip, drip, drip of the rusty spigot. Paul, the oldest boy and bravest, finally broke the silence and mumbled, "I'm goin' down to Miss Vick's house to shoo' marbles with Pete." He had told Mama a story as he slipped out the door.

Reba, my sister, who was two years older than me, said lightly, to no one in particular, "I will see y'all in the back."

She was gone. Willie Earl had already disappeared. He was at the meeting place.

I quickly slipped in, "I wanna play with my friend, Penny."

Mama quickly decided, "You ain't going nowhere. My mama, Emma Love, usually kind-hearted and soft-spoken, shot me a warning look. "I tol' you about playin' with that girl!"

Was Mama mad with me, too? This was a surprise. I missed the clues this time.

"But, Mama, all the Colored children and the White children play together in the back. I only play with her during the holidays and when school is out. Or on Saddy."

This didn't matter with Mama. "I don't care what other people let their children do. Keep your ass away from those White children. They're trouble."

I didn't wanna argue with Mama, but I wanted her to see it my way. I continued, "What's wrong with me playin' with Penny? Is it 'cause she's White? She's my friend."

"You talk too much for your age. Gettin' a little too mouthy, Doris. Besides, I ain't got no time for your foolish chat."

Mama turned her work-worn back and stormed outside to the backyard. I followed her to the smoked-covered iron wash pot that sat on two separate rows of red clay house bricks. A wood fire blazed on the bottom of the pot as the white sheets churled and burped. The boiling bed clothes looked and sounded like the hog chitlings that Mama cooked in the wash pot sometimes. Looking down into the boiling wash, she intently stirred the dirty sheets with her wash stick.

On any given day, Mama read messages from designs in water, clouds and dreams. She was looking for a sign for the day.

"Doris, are you going to the jungle today with us?"

Penny shouted across a large sprawling bush that hid the opening to our playground. Penny's white house sat behind the big field that separated the White and Colored neighborhood. And my small faded, gray shotgun house was located at the end of the Colored alley. Our house was the daily meeting place for the Colored children before we went to play in the field behind my house.

Penny's commanding voice startled me. *Did she have to talk so loud?*

I glanced quickly toward her, hoping Mama didn't see the joy in my eyes. At the same time, I could see the restlessness in Penny. She was stretching her arms and legs and swirling around on her toes. The first time I saw her dancing like this, I had asked, "Penny, what are you doing?"

When Penny finished her spin, she flashed a smile. "I am a ballerina. I have a ballet class at the swimming pool. Ask your mother if you could come with me on Saturdays."

"What's balay?"

"Ballet is a dance that rich people in France do."

Penny always practiced her balay steps when she was nervous. Her shrill voice let me know how she felt. "We are waiting for you!"

Mama had stopped stirring the boiling clothes and was watching me, "Doris, I've warned y'all not to go in those White folks' yards."

After telling the truth didn't work, I boldly told Mama, "I am going to play in the back."

I ran off before she could answer. I knew I would have to face her when I got home, but the fun of summer was calling.

The neighborhood school crew in Downing Alley was happy to be free of heavy books, grumpy teachers, dull homework and second-hand shoes. We looked like the characters from the *Our Gang* television program. The show was about a mixed crew of poor Colored and poor White children who played together.

Our favorite spot for playing was in the overgrown field. The 'jungle' was a forest of tall magnolia trees that reached up to the sky.

Their blossoms filled the hot air with its smells of warm toast and apple butter. A ground cover of thick plants, wildflowers and knotted vines made walking easier. Barefooted, on the scorching ground, we had to skip, hop or run. We climbed the giant trees. Girls caught bumblebees in old mayonnaise jars. The boys trapped green garden snakes in large corn liquor bottles. My older brother Paul and his friend Pete hunted rabbits and squirrels. Our family sometimes ate fried rabbit or squirrel stew for dinner.

This wild area was a place where you forgot your problems and grown folks' situations. A worrier like Mama, I still wondered, *Why is Mama troubled that playing with White children causes trouble.* We were careful to find adventure, but we never went in their yards.

In the childhood play and fantasy, we forgot the warning about playing with White children. Holding a talent show under the big shady mulberry tree in the middle of the field was our favorite activity. We played characters that we sometimes saw on television in neighborhood stores or my mama's friends' houses. Reba, the emcee, announced, "Let us welcome Gene Autry, the singing cowboy and Dale Evans, the singing cowgirl." The singing pair were opposites. Paul, the cowboy-tall, skinny and Colored-had a high cracking voice. His partner, Bonnie, the cowgirl, was short, fat and White. She spoke with a stutter.

They sang "Frosty, the Snowman" and "Happy Trails" as duets. Dale Evans Bonnie mixed up the words. Gene Autry Paul dragged the words, so he wouldn't go ahead of Dale Evans Bonnie's stutter. They were so out of tune it sounds like a toothpick stuck in a whirling fan. We laughed at them so hard that the dueling duo stopped before the second song was over. One of the older boys criticized the act, "Roy Rogers would shoot you if he heard you mess up his song like that."

Penny, very outgoing and quick-witted, moved to the stage area. She got everyone's attention by saying, "You have to guess who I am." Penny quickly moved her arms and body until the air around her was a field of motion.

Jonathan, Penny's seven-year-old cousin visiting from someplace he called the 'Midwest', hollered out, "A big bird?"

Penny shook and nodded her head, "Yes. No."

Reba wondered, "A helicopter?"

Again, Penny shook and nodded her head. "Yes. No."

Pete, Paul's best friend, called out, "I got it! It is a plane! She's the White girl from the television show *Sky King*, who knows how to fly a plane. This's my fav'rite television show. Ev'ry week Penny, her cousin and uncle solve a crime. Many times, Penny flew the plane by herself 'cause her uncle was wounded, kidnapped or blinded by the crooks. Her name is Penny, just like your name."

Others played the Long Ranger and Billy the Kid. The roles for girls were limited.

Willie Earl offered, "I can be Tarzan and you can be Jane."

"No! Jane is White! I rather be a Colored person."

I protested. I knew I had to come up with something. I took my bow and arrows that I had made yesterday from a fallen limb and some dried sticks. I put an arrow in my bow and drew it back. In Indian language, I said, "Me Tonto's sister. My name is 'Alope'".

The problem with this selection was that all the gang had a common enemy—the Indians. Before I got attacked, I switched. I picked up my books that I had placed near the tree to play school later. I proudly walked up to the front and waved my books. After a long silence, I said, I am a teacher." They looked at each other and laughed.

The more they thought about my choice, some of them fell to the ground, laughing and teasing, "A teacher! Who wants to be a teacher! Besides, there ain't no Colored teacher on television!" They all agreed, "You're odd!"

Around midday, Penny would say, "We have to get lunch." We, meaning the White children. They came back with sandwiches.

Occasionally, my oldest sister, Nora, would call out the kitchen window, "Y'all better come get a sandwich. Mr. Abraham bought some bologna home."

The other Colored children left the field and came back with slices of watermelon, cookies, cold biscuits with jelly or even a popsicle or candy. The White ham sandwiches always had lettuce and tomatoes with mayonnaise on them. When we did have sandwiches, the Colored bologna sandwiches had sandwich spread and mustard on them. Sometimes, we didn't have meat in our sandwiches. We had sugar, sliced bananas, or pickles as a filling. Whatever the group had, we would share. I described this as, "They liked our food; we liked their sandwiches."

In the afternoon, my brother, Paul, announced, "Let's go to across the cemetery to pick plums in the wild orchard. We can get some bags at my house."

One by one, each White playmate mumbled, "I can't go."

The White children seemed to disappear when it was time to move past the overgrown field play. Mama had told us not to go in the White children's yard. I guess the White children's mamas had told them the same thing. *Was this part of the trouble?*

At the end of the plum-picking trip, some of the gang came in the back to share the luscious, mouth-watering plums. Our group was smaller now. The older girls told us, "We have to help fix supper."

Peggy Ann added, "I have to babysit."

The older boys had gone swimming, White boys in a White pool in a White neighborhood and Colored boys in a small river behind the Colored high school. Only Willie Earl, Jonathan, Bonnie, Penny and I remained. The boys ran into the jungle, chasing a scared squirrel. Bonnie picked up her grass doll and stuttered, "Let's play 'Ma-ma' with our dolls."

I answered, "No. Me and Penny have already decided that we're playin' school. I am the teacher. You have to call me Miss Love."

I held up one of my books up that I had placed under the magnolia tree. Having the book would show that I was in charge.

"You and Penny are the students. Any questions?"

Bonnie knew she would have to play Mama with her doll at home.

I returned to my teaching. "Each student will find a picture in the book and make up a short story to match the picture."

The book was an old gardening book that I had found in the trashcan next door. I gave them five minutes to think of a name for their story.

In a few minutes, Penny raised her hand, "Miss Love, I thought of a name for my story, *Penny's Peonies.*"

That was why I liked my friend! She was as quick and as smart as me!

Soon Penny's mother yelled, "Penny, it's time for you and Jonathan to come in for supper!"

Penny waved goodbye. "I promise I will finish my story tomorrow."

She disappeared into the jungle, looking for her cousin Jonathan.

Bonnie, undecided about which picture to write about, dropped her doll that she was hugging. She stuttered, "We can't play with niggers anymore."

Her collapsed face was a puddle of fear and anger.

"What is a 'nigger'?"

Bonnie, the fat, nervous girl with long, stringy blond hair, shrugged her shoulders and struggled, "I don't know. That's what I heard my grandma and Penny's mother say at lunch today. They called the people who live in the alley, "lazy niggers".

"I ain't stud'ing you!"

The news filled me with a new kind of sadness. I tried to control my tears by sniffing the snot back up my nose. Then I picked up my books from under the tree. When the tears dried up, I left the deserted field, the backyard pretense and gentle rebellion.

An unnamed fear hung over me as I ran back to the safety of the alley. I never saw my play buddies anymore. I lost my first friend, Penny and never got to 'balay' with her at the White dance class. We liked books, playing school and creating our own stories together. The reality of Mama's signs and warnings hit me boldly in my heart. I could see that being a Colored 'nigger' would be a problem.

* * *

That evening when I was sitting on the sofa coloring, Mama came up to me, dressed up in matching clothes, like she was going somewhere. Mama's restless eyes showed that she was in a hurry. "Put your colorin' book up and put on this clean dress. You're goin' with me to meet your Aunt Naomi at the Grayhound Bus Station. She's comin' back from New York."

"You mean the long brick building with the big blue busses with the big dog on it?"

I changed into the clean dress in a split second. I liked the excitement of traveling, coming and going. *Maybe one day it would be my turn to go.*

As we walked to the bus station, I asked, "Mama, what is a nigger?" She didn't answer and looked like she had things on her mind. I was trying hard to read her moods. I decided to hush my talking mouth and wait.

Inside the shiny, bright bus station, Mama mumbled, "I am goin' to find Naomi. You stay here near the back door." She disappeared into the moving crowd. But I was thirsty. I wandered over to a clean sparkling water fountain near the front door.

Before I finished drinking the sweet, cold water, a bus station worker snatched me by my front plait and yelled in my face, "Gal, can't ya read?"

I screamed, "Mama!"

Mama and Aunt Naomi rushed over and rescued me from the mean man with a face the color of a burnt tomato. "I told you that messin' around with White people can lead to trouble!"

This time I knew for sure that Mama was mad at me.

I greeted my aunt, "Hey, Aunt Naomi." I shifted my eyes to Mama. "What did I do?"

"I see you're still getting in trouble," answered Aunt Naomi. Tall, golden orange skin, moon-faced. Her hair was mixed like her blood—curly, straight, nappy and plaited into two long Indian braids. She wore a long flowery dress like the Mexican woman at the fish market. Five jingling, bracelets-red, yellow, blue, green and purple, clashed on her arms, Which were as long as broom sticks. Her flashing red nails were the brooms' straws. Not given to smiling, she swallowed me in a soft hug. I liked my daddy's sister, his only family member I knew.

Aunt Naomi pulled Mama to the side and gave her a large stuffed shopping bag. They whispered together for a few minutes. It was none of my business and I knew I had better not ask.

As they walked toward me, Aunt Naomi said, "I'm glad you picked up your supplies. Start practicing your work," and to me, "Doris, you be good." Another hug, but not as long and I could feel a smile.

"Thanks for bringin' the supplies, Naomi. I'll be coming by for a class."

A class? But I said not a mumbling word.

My aunt became the crowd of travelers. But it took a while for her magical scent of dried flowers and spring rain to disappear.

On the way home, Mama taught me how to recognize and read Colored and White signs. "Look, Doris, 'White Entrance' and the 'Colored Entrance' in the bus station." A block away, we passed the White hospital with the 'Colored Entrance' sign on a side door. As we passed Woolworth's 'White Counter/Colored Line' sign, Mama told me, "You can order food inside, but you can't sit down and eat at the counter. Seg'gation is practiced all over Kinston."

I began to get the idea when we came to two movies on the same street. The new White Paramount Theater with a 'No Colored Allowed' sign was uptown in a White neighbor. Not surprised by now, the old 'Colored theater' was in a poor section of the town, our Colored neighborhood.

"Mama, what is the curved mark in front and behind the sign 'Colored Entrance'?" I made a curve with my finger. Then I pointed to the sign.

"There's no curved marks around nothin'. You must be seein' things."

"But Mama, I do see them." *I'd better leave that alone before I get slapped.*

"Like I was saying, the signs indicate White people's way of emphasizin' their special cat'gories for us. Child, there is so much to know about this craz' system we live in."

I could hear a little irritation in Mama's voice as she spoke. Not at me but at the craz', separated system we live in.

I made my point. "Mama, from now on, I will always point out that 'Colored' is their words, not ours. When I learn to write I will use those marks."

Mama didn't say anything to my idea because she didn't see any marks. *Maybe the marks were just for me to see.*

Then I asked, "Mama, what happened to us? Why do they hate us so much?"

From looking at Mama's apricot-colored face, which had darkened into a gloomy unreadable mask, I knew she was getting tired of my questions for her sad eyes had turned stony. I was old enough to know that children were not included in these kinds of talks. And, old enough to know when I was pushing Mama to her limits. Mama's frequent bouts of silence and gloom created a distance between us that was hard for me to break through or understand.

I waited, but only for a moment. Then I flooded my Mama with my stored-up questions. I could feel a fire burning deep in my chest. "Mama, who decided to call us 'Colored'?

My voice got louder with each question.

"How did 'Colored' people get in this condition?"

Fear made my voice sound hallow, like an empty bucket in the rain.

"Why don't 'Colored' people do something about the way we are treated?"

These nagging questions, circling around my head, followed us down the street. Mama and I together, but as separated as our town.

Reaching home, we stood outside the front door to our shotgun house at the end of Downing Alley. My mama watched the fading sun sink slowly behind the skyline. I followed her lead.

Daddy's cranky truck ended the quietness of the early evening as he parked. Mama broke her own silence by saying, "Your questions will lead you to the answers. I have to heat Abraham's supper."

The curtains of her eyes came down. She disappeared behind their mist and went into the house. I was dismissed.

What a day I had! I had climbed trees, eaten wild mulberries and green plums, decided I wanted to be a teacher, lost my first friend, and learned I was a 'Colored nigger'! And this was only the first day of summer vacation.

Chapter 2

Soul Secrets

Downing Alley was lined with nine identical shotgun houses with rusty tin roofs. Each house had three rooms—living room, bedroom and kitchen. Years ago, the houses had been painted gray and trimmed with white. Seasons of sun, rain, snow and dust had worn away most of the paint. The unpaved alley, either dusky or muddy, was lined on both sides with chinaberry trees, tall hedges and magnolia trees.

All the houses had various family members living in them. Daddies, mamas, sisters, brothers, aunts, uncles, cousins, grandmamas and granddaddies sometimes shared the three-room shotgun house. This depended on the changing situations of family members. They slept on rollaway beds, cribs and sofas and hallways and closets and under sinks and on pallets—wherever there was a floor.

In our shotgun house, my mama and my daddy slept in the living room. Five children shared the bedroom next to the kitchen. On one side of our bedroom, my two brothers shared a lumpy bed. My two sisters and I shared a similar bed in the cramped room. I slept at the foot of the bed in the middle. My complaint every night was, "Nora, get your foot off me!" Or "Reba, give me some cover! You always hog the blanket!"

In the middle of an unforgettable night, the dizzying scent of Lysol woke me up. A few days before, Mama had told me, "I have to go next door and help Miss Annie Mae. She had a baby." As soon as we stepped into her house, I frowned and held my nose.

"What is that stinking smell?"

Mama whispered, "It's Lysol, used to clean the furniture, the bed and the walls and the mama and child too. When a woman has a baby, this keeps the mother and the newborn baby in a germ-free room."

Since Mama seemed open for a question, I chanced, "What's having a baby?" Her dark serious witch eyes had shut me up during the rest of the visit.

On that particular night in our half dark bedroom, from the foot of the bed, I saw my oldest sister, Nora, lying on an arrangement of old newspapers and assorted sheets. For some reason, two pillows were stacked between my two sisters. Nora slept in the outside where it is easier to get in and out of the bed, a big sister's privilege. Nora, moaning softly, said to Mama, "It hurts so bad!"

Mama, washing up the room with that stinky Lysol, answered, "You have to bear it." Mama was dressed in a big white dress I had never seen. She looked like the women at church who gave you seats and fans.

I was trying to figure *it* out! *What was* happening to my *sister?* I was five. She was seven years older than me. A ghostly figure dressed in white also, whispered to my mama, "Emma, get the boiling water and the torn sheets ready."

I could hear my mama in the kitchen, turning on the spigot for water. Pots and pans rattled slightly as she found the large one she needed. As soon as she lit the gas stove, the smell of rat pee and the leaky gas floated throughout the house. The stove—the rats' home which smelled of pee— the mixed smell of the Lysol, and leaking gas made me gag.

Slowly, I recognized the voice of the woman in white. It belonged to Miss Ellen. She was sent for when a woman was about to have a baby. Whatever that meant. My mama and her friends called her a 'midwife'. The midwife assured my sister, "Try to relax. It will be over soon."

Mama came back into our small bedroom and sat a pot of boiling water on a rickety makeshift dresser. Shadowy figures danced across the wall from the flickering light of the kerosene lamp. Then I asked, "Mama, what's the matter?"

"Go back to sleep and mind your own business."

The midwife said, "Emma, I need your help. Hold her legs." Squinting my eyes in the dim light, I saw the midwife rubbing Nora's stomach. It looked like the watermelon was still in it.

I thought about the secret Reba had told me. I had asked Reba, "What is the matter with Nora's stomach? She didn't go back to school when it started."

Reba said, "Nora swallowed a watermelon seed. Make sure you look out for the seeds when you eat watermelon." From then on, I lost my appetite for all melons.

Mama took one of Nora's hands and began to say lightly, "Lord, take away the pain and remove her sorrow."

She always prayed when something was the matter. *What was wrong?*

Turning my face toward the window, I clasped both of my hands together as in prayer and rolled on my side. My body became a stiff board wrapped in wrinkled bed covers. I closed my scared eyes and pretended to sleep.

As I lay in the darkness, I was terrified by not knowing what was going on. The hushed whispers of the women sent a deep shiver of quiet fear through me. The silence echoed throughout the house. Miss Ellen said softly to Mama, "Midwives have always provided physical, emotional and even financial support for the married and unmarried pregnant woman. In traditional Africa, the midwife knew about the personal life of the whole community."

"I guess they knew ev'rybod's business, huh? Like counsel'rs?"

"Yes. The midlife and her secret group were the mysterious secret bearers."

After a short space in time, Mama asked, "How did they treat a woman who had a baby without a husband?"

"Sometimes, when it disturbed the community peace, the unmarried woman could be run out of town. Because of secret arrangements of the midwife's society, few children were considered illegitimate. This community of women became the unmarried woman's protection. Fathers who disappeared to avoid parental responsibilities were considered outcasts."

In the silence of faked sleep, I, 'the great pretender', heard many stories about women love, "in the family way" (pregnancy), boyfriends, miscarriage, death. I was too young to understand most of it, but I knew I was connected to the talk in some kind of way.

There was a long pause. I lay limp, sad and waiting.

Miss Ellen changed to another story. "Emma, who has done such a terrible thing to this child? She is only a baby herself. She is only twelve."

I strained to still my loud pumping heart so I could hear. Mama answered, in a muzzled, cracking voice, "I think it may have been Abraham."

"You have two other girls. Reba is seven and Doris is five. You have to protect your girls. Emma, you know they are subject to men's appetites."

In the dark, I remembered my mama had warned me, "Doris, you're so nosy. Always snooping around trying to figure out what is going on. One day you'll come across something that you don't want to hear or see."

This was one of those times. Hearing this shocking news threw me into some strange fear. *But what was the terrible thing?*

Again, the scents of rat pee, stinking Lysol, leaking gas and Nora's sorrow made me sick to my stomach. Warm, bitter vomit rose from my stomach and traveled up my throat. I shifted my stiff body and bent my head down on my chest and swallowed. I didn't want the vomit to strangle me. I burped, ever so slightly. I still wasn't sure what the baby talk was about. But a bottomless pit of loss and some cold fear filled me.

Mama shook my shoulder and asked anxiously, "Are you awake?"

I went back into my play-dead position. I remained as motionless as a possum and as silent as the night. My little life was falling apart!

Nora began to whimper and thrash about on the bed. My other sister, Reba, woke up and asked, "What is going on?"

She was told almost the same thing: "Go back to sleep. This don't concern you."

Reba, a heavy sleepwalker, fell back into her deep slumber. The only thing I heard from my two brothers on the other side of the room was their loud, roaring snores. We all slept in the same room. I hoped that someone else would wake up and share the horror with me.

"Emma, it is coming! Put this towel in her mouth! Nora, push down! Act like you're having a bowel movement."

What's coming?

Nora made a few grunts and moans. I joined her in her pain as I struggled to keep my grunts and moans to myself. I still didn't know what was happening, but I wanted to help her out. She pushed so hard that she kicked me in my butt. I loved her so much that I was not mad about the butt kick. The last strong push completed whatever she was trying to do.

I could feel Nora falling back on her pillow. Panting loud like she had run a race. The midwife reported, "Your water broke as soon as I got here. I have only been here twenty minutes! Nora, you behaved well for someone your age."

For a while, the midwife was busy with Nora. I waited for some sound in the darkness. With a slight tremor in her voice, Miss Ellen whispered, "Emma, there is no heartbeat, nor breathing. The baby is blue and quite undeveloped. Nora was only seven months, anyway. Maybe, the fact it's stillborn is good for her. It's a boy. Emma, burn it tomorrow when you wash."

Mama added, "You know stillbirths run in my family'. Your mama delivered five of my eight children. When Doris was born, another unexpected one was expelled as she began to clean me up. Your mama first thought it was the afterbirth. The large clot of blood was a small unbreathin' baby."

I didn't hear all what Miss Ellen said for I was thrown in a cloud of confusion and wonder! *I was a twin? And it seemed like Nora had a baby!* Then it came to me! *The same stinking Lysol was used when*

Miss Annie Mae had a baby! The only thing that I remembered after that was Miss Ellen and my mama removing the newspapers and old sheets from under Nora. Crying softly and weakly, Nora didn't ask about the dead baby. In a scratchy voice, she begged, "Can I have some water now?"

I drifted into a nightmarish dream, searching for my twin.

In the morning I played school in the yard, scratching out numbers in the ashes around the wash pot. The washing stick that had been used by my mama to stir dirty clothes now became a drawing stick. I pushed my new writing tool under the pot and touched a hard, half-burned object. As I scooped the *thing* out, I was thinking to myself, *this is the burned baby from last night. It is about the size of my brother's fist when he threw a baseball.* My screams stuck in my throat. I eased the partly burned baby back into the ashes under the wash pot, ran under the house and hid for hours. This picture burned into the deepest part of my mind.

The dark crawl space under the shotgun house was very cool in the sweating summer and warm during the freezing winter. The house rested on four rugged stilts made of bricks. The stilts protected the house from the flooding rains in the summer and the hard-flowing hurricanes in the fall. It was my favorite spot for hiding out or playing school. I leaned against the base of the stones which extended up to the cast iron stove in the living room and ended with the chimney on top of the shotgun house. Plaiting my grass doll's hair, I wondered, *How could a twelve-year-old girl swallow a watermelon seed and have a baby?*

I remembered the dreamy state from the night before. Slowly, I was able to re-create it. I slowed my breathing and began to cry. Mama had told me, "When you have a problem, take it to the Lord in prayer."

I prayed, *"God, please help my family. I am scared and sad. Can you help Nora feel better? Drive the devil away from our house. Thank you. Amen."*

I fell asleep and spent most of my birthday, hiding under our shotgun house, on the back side of the chimney so no one could find me. After then, every time I saw a wash pot, I remembered my nephew. I wondered, *Is there a burned baby under it?*

This incident marked the end of my childhood. The night in the dark with the women introduced me to a sense of sisterhood, full of power, secrets and fear.

Chapter 3

November 16, 1949 Dear Diary: I am Only Five

The day of my fifth birthday, November 15, 1949, was the day my nephew died. It was also the day my early childhood ended. I didn't want my birthday to be connected with a death day, but it was.

I remembered before I went to sleep on November 14, my mama came into the bedroom. "Doris, tomorrow is your birthday. Tonight, I'm gonna make you your own cake, a three-layer yellow batter, pineapple coconut, white icin', lemon-flavored cake."

Mama liked to tease me about how much I loved my favorite cake. Just the thought of the ingredients made my mouth water.

When the lights went out, I closed my eyes to tell my birthday wish to the moon. More excited than ever before, I couldn't sleep. Soon, in the darkness, I became a silent witness to my twelve-year-old sister, Nora, giving birth to a dead baby in a bed we shared. Being 'nosy' as my mama always called me, I had heard the midwife asked, "Emma, who would do such a terrible thing?"

I had held my breath as my mama answered, with great sadness, "I think it was Abraham."

Abraham! I had moaned softly within. *That's my daddy's name!*

* * *

The day after my birthday, I woke up with a broken heart. I no longer felt safe, loved or protected. Instead, I felt lost and scared. Even my favorite birthday cake had not erased the quiet screams of Nora from my troubled mind nor the faint smell of Lysol from my darkened world.

With these things on my mind, I wandered up to Mama's and Daddy's bedroom door. I stood outside the closed door and strained to listen. At first, my heart was thumping so loud I couldn't hear. When it calmed down, I heard my mama's troubled voice say, "I gotta do sumthin. She don't wanna live here anymore. Maybe we can send her away to live with her dad'." Then, out of her grief and helplessness, I heard a soft bitter scream, "When I find out for sho' you had anythang to do with this, I'm winna have your ass fixed! I'm gonna see the root worker today!"

It felt good to hear the meanness in Mama's voice. But I was a little disappointed that she didn't get the shotgun out of the closet and shoot him through his rotten heart. I wanted to scream, *"You told Miss Ellen that Daddy was the one who had hurt Nora! Why are you acting like you don't know?"*

I was glad 'the cat held my tongue.' Mama's mama, Grandmama Quintilla, used to ask me, "Do the cat have your tongue?" when she asked me a question that I had refused to answer. To make sure I still had a tongue, I would say something, usually answering her question and freeing my voice from the cat. It was good the cat kept my mouth closed so I could finish listening.

Before Mama said anything else, Daddy began to defend himself. When he spoke, I thought I was hearing the wicked voice of the devil. "That's fine by me!" he roared. "But don't blame me. I told you that Nora was too fast for her own good."

What really threw me off was the sharpness and hardness of Daddy's voice. I knew for sure that love was leaving the Loves and that my mama lived in a world of pretending not to see the truth. My daddy also was living in a world of not admitting his evil deeds. He added, "I tried to remind Nora that the devil punish sinful adults and disobedient children. They show nuff going to hell! Nora got real sassy with me and told me, 'Go to hell!' As much as I do for that girl!"

"I noticed months ago how you were always naggin' Nora and tryin' to keep her home. 'Cause Nora was always not comin' home. She seemed liked she was runnin' from somethin'. I now believe it was you."

I decided I had heard enough. I knocked on the door. "Mama, can I come in? I want to get my notebook that Miss Doris gave me on my birthday."

Mama and Daddy stopped talking. When Mama opened the door, I felt awkward as I stepped into their private talk. None of us was dressed for the day yet. I had on my bedclothes, an old, faded, too-short dress. Mama, wearing a plain-looking housedress, surprised me with a long hug. Hugs were only given at special times, like birthdays and graduations. Mama had already given me my birthday hug yesterday.

Daddy, in a tee shirt and some dress pants, acted like I never came in the room. He treated me like I was invisible. His favorite family greeting, "How's we be doing?" was never spoken. He didn't look my way. Daddy turned his back from Mama and me, put on a white, starched Sunday shirt and sat on the bed to put on his shoes. Daddy's shadowed face didn't hide his troubled feelings. I was a face reader.

I was slow about getting my notebook. Taking my time would give me a clue to what happened to Nora. Mama came over and tapped me softly on my shoulder. Her eyes, swollen from crying, looked at me from the far place she had traveled. She barely parted her dry, sad lips as she whispered to me, "We need to finish some business before Abraham go to church. Take the whole bag."

Shortly after I left with my bag of gifts, my daddy left for church and I went back into the bedroom/living room. *Now I was wondering why we didn't go to church.* But I let the thought slide by as I watched Mama make the bed. When she looked up, I asked, "Mama, where is hell?"

In a dead voice, she spoke, "This is not the day to bother me with questions."

I believed her and joined in her no-talk world. Both of us were captured by the silence. She continued making the bed and I continued not to talk. The only sound was Daddy's car struggling to start. After several backfires, it coughed and choked until the engine caught and it limped down the alley. I knew a trail of white smoke and grayish water was following the tired '39 Dodge.

Mama's face was brewing a storm. Her cloudy eyes and tight lips threatened the usual Sunday morning calm. She grabbed Daddy's rumpled sleep clothes and threw them out in the hallway. Her slender hands broke the silence as she thrashed the pillows about on the bed. She beat on the pillows like she was fighting an enemy. I knew Mama was fed up with my questions about family life and my snooping into hers. But she was mad about other things that I didn't even know about.

Her disgust about both things forced her to spit out, "I will tell you this. Hell is a place of pain and punishment. When you get there, you burn forever. Hell is where you are going if you don't stop worration with this nonsense. Get the hell out of here and stop wastin' my time! Go play with your paper dolls!"

I left the room and decided to follow her advice this time. The voice of hopelessness and sorrow in my mama followed me to the gloomy death bedroom. Yesterday, I had just witnessed my sister having, what my mama called a 'stillbirth'. Later, I saw the charred unborn baby under the wash pot. Today, fear and confusion kept a flood fire burning in my heart. I didn't know what Nora had done to suffer. But it sounded like Miss Ellen, the midwife, had agreed with Mama that it was Daddy who had hurt Nora. *Was he on his way to hell, too?*

As I sat on the bed, I looked in my bookbag of writing tools and I took out a new dictionary, my note writing pad and a sharpened pencil. The soft voice spoke inside of me.

I dropped my study tools and curled up on the bed. The voice got my scared attention. I listened to my inner spirit as it spoke, *Don't be afraid of life. Go to the river. Many people go there to clear their mind. You will find healing.*

The rest of the day I balled up on the deathbed like a snail in its shell. My thoughts bumped into each other in a world of betwixt and between. Aunt Naomi had explained to me, "Little Doris, being in a world of betwixt and between is a place or situation when you ain't sure whether you're comin' or goin'. Hot or cold. Lovin' or hatin'. Heaven or hell."

Trying to understand, I asked her, "How do you decide which place you want to be in?"

I spent hours sorting through feelings of hatred, anger, love, forgiveness or punishment for my daddy. I knew I needed the healing waters of the river, so death would leave our house.

Before the afternoon was over, my mama yelled into the room, "Come out or I will send your daddy in there!"

She didn't know the word "daddy" fanned the flames of anger. The anger nibbled at my peace and led me out of the safety of my sad bed. A voice begins to whisper, *Burn him*. It followed me and lingered, egging me on. Fear and sorrow burned inside of my head for a long time, a fire of anger. Out of control but contained for a moment.

When Daddy came home from church, we ate a sad, silent supper. Mama's eyes were no longer watery. But I had heard her crying for hours in the bedroom. After Daddy finished his plate, he stood up and said, "Your mama, who's in one of her 'not talking moods', and I are going to visit Miss Doris."

* * *

The next day my sister, Reba, found me crying under our house. Even though it was cold outside, the underground part of the chimney had heated up my secret play space. A faded worn blanket spread across cardboard boxes was my furniture. Reba sat next to me on my pallet and put her arms around me. "Wipe your face."

No toilet paper around. I used the bottom of my play coat sleeve to wipe the tears, snot and slobber from my face. She said, "Don't be sad. I feel bad, too. Nora went to stay with her daddy out in the country."

We sat there for a long time, both of us missing our oldest sister. But not comforted by the thought that we still had each other, I continued to cry.

Then Reba remembered, "My mama said to tell you to come get a biscuit and some watermelon preserve."

My stomach swirled like my spinning top that Santa Claus left me for Christmas when I was three. *Watermelon!* I screamed inside. *It was watermelon that caused Nora's problem! I'm not going to never eat watermelon again!*

I didn't say this to Reba. In fact, for a while I said nothing. The good quiet voice was speaking. It was under this house, sitting on the same spot, when the quiet voice spoke to me on my birthday. A soft breeze came under the house. I could feel the hair on my neck fan. The soft familiar voice whispered, *Calm yourself down like you did in the dark.* I practiced 'not to think', but 'to feel'.

The voice had taught me to ignore many scary thoughts that came from my head. I practiced listening to my heart. This slowed my racing heartbeat down right away. I didn't understand why it worked, but it calmed me. My thoughts disappeared, and my stomach stopped spinning. I felt the deep pain, shame and secrecy of what had happened to my sister. At that moment, I knew the brokenness didn't just happened to Nora, or Reba or me. It had happened to everybody in the family.

Completely calmed, I asked, "What is going to happen to us?"

Reba was only seven and a half. *How in the world would she know?* Both of us tried to follow the pattern that was taught in our family. "Children are to be seen and not heard."

Reba didn't tell me, "I stayed awake, and I know what had happened to Nora in the dark." Reba also didn't tell me that my mama had told her, "'Don't ask your daddy if you can ride in the truck with him to the store.'"

I didn't tell Reba how I really felt about my daddy. After Reba left, I was so mad with my daddy. A lingering voice inside of my head spoke harshly. *I'm mad as hell.* This voice was different from the calm pleasant Love Voice. I threw what my mama would call a 'hizzy fit'. I kicked the hot chimney. The heat from the hot bricks traveled through my high-top brown brogan shoes. "Ouch!" I jumped back. I looked around at my pitiful hiding place. Angry, I turned around and tore up my cardboard furniture.

Again, the strange mean voice cussed in my head, *Damn my daddy!* My out-of-control behavior ripped up the raggedy blanket. *Burn it down! It ain't real anyway.* By now, I knew it was the voice of the devil, as Daddy and Mama called it. The sound was loud and dark.

And I didn't care. This was how I felt. I took a long wooden match from my secret box and struck it against the brick chimney. The match burst into a hot ball of red, purple, and yellow flames when the small fire touched the strips of old blanket. The blaze ate the pretend paper furniture quickly. Amazed, I moved away from the fire and watched the dancing flames. *Was this like the fires of hell destroying everything in its path?*

The flames crumbled my playhouse furniture the same way the hot wood stove melted my White doll that I hid in it last Christmas. I had told my mama, "I didn't want the White plastic doll with the moving eyes."

She said, "Take it or leave it."

I left it in the stove. The wire that made the sky-blue eyes move was the only solid part remaining.

The ashes also reminded me of what the midwife had told mama about Nora's baby. *Burn it when you wash tomorrow.* Mama never mentioned the burned doll nor the burned baby. The day that Nora lost her baby, I also lost my hiding place and my family.

Most definitely I wouldn't never, ever tell Reba about my fascination with fire. This would be my secret only. Calmed again but still sad, mad, and scared, I slumped toward the house and ate my tasteless snack. A cold biscuit with butter. No watermelon preserves for me!

Chapter 4

November 26, 1949: Before and After

After the birth incident, the way I saw the world changed. From then on, memories of my early life were split into two parts. Before and after. Before the night in the dark. And after Nora had a baby. Before the birth of my nephew. And after the death of my childhood.

Before my sister was hurt, I spent my time in carefree daydreaming, counting the clouds for hours, chasing my shadow, talking to the moon and daydreaming to create other worlds. We children in our neighborhood played cowboys and Indians, caught June bugs, butterflies and bumble bees, ate wild fruit and climbed trees in the big, deserted field behind our house. Life in Downing Alley had contained daily fun and safe experiences for growing up.

After my sister was hurt, I used most of my time eavesdropping and snooping into grown folks' business. Nobody would talk to me about what had happened. They thought I was too young; life didn't think so. At five years old, raw life robbed me of my innocence. I did not have the right words nor enough experience to understand what had happened to my sister.

I decided to use my inspiration, my imagination, and my small voice to remember the good parts of my early life. I did not like the feeling of lost and emptiness that I had suffered on my fifth birthday. I needed to go back to the beginning where there were some happy family times before Nora was hurt.

From my earliest memory of anything, I had always thought that only Mama was raising me. She answered my basic needs with a soothing song and her quick softness. Me and my friend-my shadow-followed her as much as I could all day long. I first noticed my daddy early in the morning. The house seemed to be centered on him. When he woke up, the house woke up. When I looked outside, the sun was up. Everything was up, but my mama.

Mama did her early morning duties with school age children from the bed. Every night, she laid out clothes for all children. She explained, "It saves time. Keeps the house organized in the morning."

After the school children got dressed, Nora, Paul and Reba marched in the living room/bedroom.

Willie Earl and I had dressed in our laid-out play clothes. Both of us eased quietly into the room and sat on the couch. We were not invited, and we didn't want to get thrown out. I had taught Willie Earl to disappear like Mama do it. "Don't move a muscle, blink an eye or say a word!"

I whispered to Willie Earl, "This is training for us when we go to school. Gotta keep quiet and still."

We loved this early morning play and did not want to miss it.

Mama set high on her three soft pillows and looked each child over-up, down and around. She inspected hair, socks and shoes. The daily look-over was to make sure that the clothes worn were the ones she had selected. Mama said, smiling a little, "Let's see who's bein' stubborn today."

Paul passed that day; He wore what my mama had set out. Mama nodded her head, "Okay."

Reba was quiet this morning when she stood in front of my mama. She was tired of fighting my mama every morning about clothes. Reba had done what was needed to get Mama's "Yes".

Nora didn't care about Mama's "Yeses". She was going to wear what she wanted. As Nora eased into the room, Mama's hands flew to her mouth. "You know that dern skirt is too short. It's almost up to your behind! Go change right now!"

Nora stormed out of the room. We could hear mumbled fussing in the other bedroom. When Nora came back to Mama, the changed skirt met Mama's approval. "Much better, don't you think?"

"I think it makes me look like an old lady."

When Nora slammed out the kitchen door, I knew that she had stuffed the short skirt in her book bag. My fashion-loving sister would change when she stopped next door at her friend Velma's house. They walked to school together every day.

Willie Earl and I raced back to the kitchen to get a good seat at the kitchen table, near Daddy. We knew he would be leaving soon 'to go to make a living', as Mama called it. Right away, we smelled the leaky gas and the rat pee. The stove had been turned on and the rats ran from the warming stove and they settled down in the walls. Willie Earl said, "After we eat, they'll come back and have their breakfast!" He laughed, and I turned my thoughts to my daddy.

As my brother and I waited to eat, I noticed that my daddy was the one who cooked in the morning. I saw that he was part of the child-tending in the family. As small as the kitchen was, he whirled around in the little area like he was on roller skates. Quickly from the icebox to the stove, around the table to the sink. I plainly saw that my giant of a daddy was clowning around for us. My fun daddy turned to us with a big grin, "Can you guess what we're having for breakfast today?"

"Rice and gravy!" Willie Earl's guess.

"No. Try something else."

"Tatoes and fried onions!" Willie again.

"No."

"Bacon and eggs? Egg san'wich?" I loved eggs.

"No. No."

"Biscuits and molasses."

Willie loved sweets. My daddy made biscuits better than my mama, but I would never let tell Mama this.

"No."

We named everything we could think of and Daddy still said, "No! No! No!"

Daddy went in the icebox and pulled out a box that was about the size of a baby shoebox. The picture on the front of the box looked like my godmama Miss Doris. The lady on the box was dark-skinned and fat with a head rag on her head. Sometimes Miss Doris covered her head when she was cleaning or cooking. I asked, "Daddy, is that Miss Doris?" I wanted to know.

"No. The lady's name is Aunt Jemina. This is a box of pancake mix. It has everything in it." Daddy poured the mix into a bowl sitting on the table and added some buttermilk. "Buttermilk will make it fluffy and flaky."

As he stirred the mix and milk in the bowl together, he told us, "Emma didn't want me to buy this box mix. She said she can make pancakes so much cheaper. I wanted to surprise y'all with this."

My daddy clearly enjoyed being with us as much as we enjoyed being with him. I liked my daddy for this because he took time with us. For me, the rest of the day was spent following Mama, having fun and knowing that my daddy would be coming home before it got dark. With his tricks and jokes.

Before the death of Nora's baby, Daddy had showed interest in our family. He came home from work in the evenings and made up many creative fun activities. Even though Daddy could be fun, he didn't waste time on small talk, 'chitchatting', he called it. My mama called his way of speaking "making grand announcements". When he spoke to you, things had already been decided.

Last year on a Friday evening during supper, my daddy made one of those surprising announcements. "Every Friday evening, we'll have a family meeting to plan the next week's menu. From now on, everyone gets a favorite dish once a week."

Everybody was speechless, but happy.

"Each meal will include someone's favorite meat. Some type of vegetable. Always rice and bread. Biscuits or cornbread. It doesn't matter."

We planned our menu for the next week as Mama and Nora cleaned the kitchen. The original plan was something like this: Monday-Pork Chops-Nora, Tuesday-Stewed Beef-Reba, Wednesday-Meat Loaf-Paul, Thursday-Stewed Chicken & Dumplings-Mama,

Friday-Fried Fish-Doris, Saturday-Chef Boyardee Spaghetti and Meat Balls-Willie Earl, Sunday-Fried Chicken-Daddy.

The weekly planned menu did not always match my daddy's money. I didn't care that we would have neck bones, rice and gravy for supper many days. Other times, we had fried gizzards, smothered potatoes with onions. Sometimes, there was only butterbeans with fried fatback and rice. Many times, turkey neck soup or fried chicken necks took the place of the beef stew or the pork chops.

Food was an activity that drew us together as a family. Both Mama and Daddy enjoyed cooking. Their tasty flavors spoiled our tongues, and we were glad to eat whatever they fixed—almost everything, except, fried hog kidneys and something Daddy called 'Rocky Mountain oysters'. This was his favorite treat. He had said, "'This is a delicacy.'"

To help us accept the 'delicacy', Mama explained, "I've removed all the veins and membranes in the kidneys and the oysters to clean them and make them tender. I soaked the kidneys in vinegar all day to remove the smell."

Sometimes it's better not to know. Mama's expert preparation and cooking of tender, flavorful kidneys still couldn't hide the pee smell.

One night at supper, Paul waited until I bit into a piece of the meatball. He wore a twisted grin on his face when he asked, "Did you know that the *meatball* Rocky Mountain oysters you're eating is the hog's private parts?"

I gagged and ate string beans and rice for supper. Even when it looked like we were poor, I was happy to have a daddy helping to take care of us.

* * *

A good family activity had occurred a few months before my crushed life. I was sitting on the front porch steps, watching the faces in the clouds. I liked to watch the sky, the moon, the stars, the sun and the clouds for hidden messages and soon coming storms. Aunt Naomi said there is a sign before something happens. Being outside and watching the world were easy ways to be in the world. I was about to go inside when I heard voices. I sat back down and began my favorite activity-listening to grown folks talk.

Miss Harriet, a next-door neighbor, and my mama were both outside, hanging clothes on the clothesline. Mama had some white sheets boiling in the black wash pot in the yard. I heard my mama tell Miss Harriet, "When Clyde gets home from work, come on over for supper and listen to the Joe Louis fight. There's a pot of pig feet on the stove. Nora will help me clean a mess of collards and turnip greens when school is out. Other neighbors are coming with sweet potato pies and some bread puddin'. My sister-in-law's bringin' some fried okra."

Goodhearted Miss Harriet accepted the come over. Mr. Clyde and Miss Harriet didn't have children, but she and my mama got along well together. Miss Harriet offered, "I'll bring a big bowl of 'tato salad. Everyone loves my 'tato salad with my secret 'gredient." I was glad about the 'tato salad, but okra! Umph! When they started to whisper, I went out in the back field to climb trees with any child who wasn't in school that day.

After Nora came home from school, she and my mama cleaned the collards and turnip greens in the kitchen. I heard Nora and my mama talking low so no one could hear. *Why are people always whispering around me?*

When I came into the kitchen, Nora quickly changed subjects and asked, "Please, Mama, let me make the corn bread."

Nora thought she could cook as good as my mama. I crossed my heart, my fingers, and my eyes, hoping my mama would say, "No." Mama said, "Okay."

After we had the family meeting, all the neighbors crowded into our shotgun house to eat the potluck supper. The sticky vinegary pig feet, hot peppery collards mixed with the bitter, sugar-sweetened turnip greens and secret ingredient 'tato salad were eaten with sounds of neighborly talk and appreciation. The Love house was filled with happy noises that people make when they eat, like 'Wow!' 'Yummy!' 'Uh, Good!' "Can I have another piece?'"

The potlucks brought our neighbors together. After these fun activities, we would listen to the Gillette Friday night boxing fights on the radio. These Friday night parties brought the world together in our little crowded house. Daddy and the neighborhood men became brothers. My daddy shouted, "Knock 'em out, Man!"

This victory brought pride to all the 'Colored' people who were treated mean by White people.

At the next Joe Louis fight, Mr. Clyde had screamed, "Abraham! Did you hear that! Ezzard Charles knocked out Joe Louis."

My daddy had a good sense of humor that made us children roll on the floor and laugh until our sides hurt. Mama would say, "He is a born storyteller and a natural liar."

I begged him for my favorite joke. Daddy grinned, showing his even white teeth that looked like two perfect rows of white corn on a cob. He knew the one I was talking about and I was pleased. He remembered. "One day in church, the preacher was saying, God is everywhere. He's in the house, he's in the field, he's in the car. A little boy sitting on the front row whispered to his friend, 'I hope God ain't in my pocket eating my peanuts!'"

Even though we had heard it many times, I still jumped up and down with rediscovered joy! The jokes and stories Daddy told brought us together as a happy family. My daddy was always home in the evenings, especially on Friday for our family meetings. I felt family love and connection during those times. We were a normal family-Daddy, Mama, sisters and brothers.

*　*　*

When I thought deeply on my early childhood, I remembered that my life had started to change months before my twelve-year-old sister Nora had a baby. At the end of the summer of 1949, I discovered what being 'Colored' meant. White and 'Colored' people lived in the same neighborhood separated by a wild field of mulberry and magnolia trees. Over the years, neighborhood children had turned the deserted field into our favorite backyard playground. When I was five, the White parents decided that the White children couldn't play with us anymore because we were *'Niggers'*. At the same time, I had lost my first best friend who was White—although my Mama had been telling me that White people were dangerous. I also learned that summer that White people didn't like 'Colored' people.

Now, the field sat silent, waiting for the boys to 'clop-clop' on their stick horses around the cleared edges. No longer did the girls search for old, beautiful glasses bottles in the 'jungle' to make ice-string bottle dolls. We never got to have another talent show under the mulberry tree in the back.

With these shocking changes, early fun childhood activities lost their importance in my life. Sometimes my fear and hurt were so great it almost erased all memories of good. I used to catch rain with my tongue when it fell. I didn't care how the rain tasted anymore. The birds used to sing sweet, happy songs. Now, the red birds and the blue birds tweeted sad songs as they flew away from me. The yellow birds dropped poo all over our front steps. After the death, the robins changed the direction they were flying when they saw me. A crow sat on a limb of the magnolia tree in our yard and cried for days. Another black bird fell dead in front of me when I was playing jack rocks by myself in the front yard. My good life seemed to be fading away.

My Aunt Naomi wanted us to live somewhere else. I had heard her tell my daddy, "Abraham, why don't you move your family out of this alley? People say a shotgun house looks like shame, poverty and hopelessness. I heard some people say living in them brings bad luck. Why do you think they call it shotgun?"

Now, I realized that I was born into the 'shotgun house of secrets and bad luck', not the 'House of Love'. Even our family name 'Love' was a lie.

***

Before Nora left to live with her daddy, she was the one in charge of the house when my mama and daddy left the house together. Nora and Paul had always told us stories about heroes rescuing women and cities. Most of the stories excited me so much that I wanted to write my own stories. The first night that Nora left, Paul told us a story called, *The Bogey Man's in Town*.

"Who is the 'bogey man'?" I asked my brother.

According to Paul, "The bogey man puts children in sacks and eat them for being bad or those who didn't go to sleep."

Reba, a little older, who knew more than me, said, "Paul is just saying this so we will go to sleep right away. Then he can go outside and tell nasty jokes with his friends before my mama and daddy come home."

I was a good girl, but it was hard for me go to sleep. I hoped the bogey man wouldn't eat me for not going to sleep right after I went to bed. When I got in bed, my big thoughts released themselves fully. Just before sleep, they became most alive. Visions of people, rambling adventures and other lives made me so excited that sleep ran from me. I was chasing sleep and then the bogey man began to chase me. The bogey man was my first scary tale. I hoped it that would be my last.

The bogey man story was not like the fairy tales that Nora had told us. Nora called one of her stories, *The Little Lost Princess*. It went:

> *The handsome Prince Lawrence, the hero, helped the beautiful Princess Margaret out of many troubles. One day the princess and her handmaiden ran through the woods to cross the other side of the river to escape from the evil King Evoler. Prince Lawrence followed them.*
>
> *The prince turned himself into a log and floated right up to the bank of the river. The log spoke, "'You can cross the river on my back, I will take you to safety.'"*
>
> *Just as Princess Margaret and her handmaiden crossed the other side of the river, King Evoler came to the river. The log floated up to the bank and the king said to himself, "'What a perfect log to take me across the river. The princess is resting on the other side.'"*

> *When King Evoler stepped on the log, Prince Lawrence turned back into himself, a warrior who was the rightful heir to the throne. The mean king drowned, and his body was turned into a statute of a smiling, beautiful fish. Around the fish's neck hung a sign, 'Beware: Logs in this water are not strong enough for crossing.'*
>
> *Then Princes Lawrence took Princess Margaret and her handmaiden to live in his castle. They lived happily ever after as King Lawrence and Queen Margaret. The king's personal servant and the queen's handmaiden fell in love and got married. And they lived happily ever after also."*

These are the kind of stories Nora told all the time. She always told us fairytales about pretty girls and princesses in trouble. She used her tales to show us that help comes in many ways. Nora had secrets and troubles in her life. *Did she need to be rescued also? Did she have a friend that she shared her sadness with?* I had Nora. *Who did she have?*

After Nora left, I begged Paul, "I don't want to hear bogey man stories."

He told them anyway for he enjoyed teasing others. I stuck my fingers in my ears and put the pillow over my hands to block out the ugly stories Paul continued to tell.

After the event in the dark, the ugly bogey man, 'Shadow Man' with bloody hands, followed me. The monster Shadow hid in every corner, grabbing at me, calling me, *Doris, Doris, Doris, come to me.* He was in the closet, waiting for me when I got my coat. I felt his creepy, blood-dripping eyes, peeping around corners and looking through cracks. A feeling of unspoken, dark terror filled the whole house. Secrets and the Shadow Man were everywhere.

The Shadow Man was in my dreams, trying to remove the bed cover from me. In the dream, after I could not find the bogey man, I asked, "Where do you hide?'

A voice, answered, *In the darkness, in the fear and in the love.* This soft voice was different from the angry voice of Shadow Man and the evil devil who had told me to burn my playhouse. This voice was saying some things I didn't understand. *What do all this mean?* I thought I was screaming to myself in my dream when Reba pinched me tightly. I woke up and realized I was dreaming out loud.

My fear of being hurt, feeling unloved and unsafe drove me to the edge of insanity. I didn't know then, but Mama walked the dark edges, too. I waited for my knight in shining armor to save me. None came during the year I was five. Both Nora and I needed a Prince Lawrence to get the evil King Evolver out of our house.

* * *

After Nora had the baby, family living became full of fear, constant lying and forced silences. One day Daddy was in a dark mood when he came into the kitchen. No wide smiles, no funny jokes and no special treats. My daddy talked even less; his announcement was all he offered. Now, his word was the final law. "Paul, you are next to Nora in age. When we're not here, you are in charge. Make toast. I have to leave earlier. Lou Dawson needs a ride to work."

I didn't care. Nora was gone and I was in a sour mood, too.

From that day forward, Daddy started coming home later. Or he stayed out all night. The fun breakfasts and family evenings ended. Then Daddy began to go out every Friday night. This is when the arguing started. Soon, he was out five out of seven nights a week. I marked his going out in my small notebook. It seems like overnight my daddy became mean and selfish. He was bossy and strict. Everyone in the household began to fear him when he was home. Daddy didn't know it but my love and respect for him disappeared in the smoke that followed his car.

Along with my mother, everybody in the family, at one time or another, secretly wanted to ask my daddy, *Do you have to be out every night?* We had watched my daddy enough to know when he was going out. If he worked on his car in the yard after work, he was not going. If he took a bath as soon as he got home from work, supper was not going to be happy.

I remember one night all of us sort of ganged up on Daddy. My Mama started it. "I'm just about sick and tired of you going out all the time."

Daddy had come in the kitchen, all dressed up, with matching suit, necktie and shoes. The stinking trail of Daddy's too sweet-smelling cologne flooded the whole shotgun house.

"What're you talking about, woman? I didn't go out the past two nights."

Paul, who always told me to stay out of Mama and Daddy's business, said, "Daddy, you did go out last night. I told my mama this morning, 'I want some of the cologne that Daddy wore last night when I grow up.'"

Usually, Paul agreed with anything that my daddy did, said or thought. Mama always said Daddy smelled like a 'hoe's house.' I didn't know how a 'hoe house' smelled, but I knew his cologne always made my nose burn. I sneezed in his presence.

I knew my daddy was going out when he had called me in the bedroom and said, "Rabbit, bring me a clean towel from the kitchen and put it in my top drawer. Don't let your mama see it."

My daddy called me 'Rabbit' when he wanted something done quickly without any fuss. He and my mama knew that I was always extra good at snooping and keeping secrets.

At the table, I simply said, "Daddy, you always take a bath before you go out at night."

I was relieved. I said what I wanted to say.

Daddy finally looked up from his food, surprised that we were watching him. We were even more surprised that he didn't say, "Stay out of my business."

Seeing it was okay to talk into grown up stuff, Reba threw in, "Yeah, Daddy. Mama cries when you leave."

The youngest child in the house, Willie Earl, who was only four, said, with tears in his voice, "Daddy, you used to play catch with me. Please stay home with us."

If Nora had been there, I was sure she would roll her eyes and whisper to herself loud enough for all to hear, "I wished you'd drop dead or jump off the top of the world."

A bit of my anger and disgust left after I expressed my true feelings about my daddy by burning down my playhouse. Some of my mama's anger and sadness seemed to go behind a curtain for a while. When she heard her children speak out their feelings about the new change in Daddy, she seemed pleased. Before my daddy left for his nightly outing, Mama told my daddy, "Don't you realize that your nightly business is making ev'rybod' unhapp'? Your habits have created problems for all of us."

Mama was right. Daddy's hurting my sister had introduced me to the fires of hell. I had discovered a way to release some of my pain. I knew my mama was looking for her own way.

Chapter 5

November 30, 1949 Answering the Call

Lying on the bed this morning, all these changes came to my mind. When Daddy changed, everything changed. Paul was doing the breakfast now. What a mess! Since Daddy left for work earlier, we only had burnt cheese toast or half-done fried salty potatoes. Mama continued to stay in bed, but she stopped checking what the school children wore to school. Reba was glad.

Mama had tuned off from us, too. Willie Earl still got up early for his messy breakfast and I had gotten tired of it. I stayed in bed so I could think away from Willie Earl. I was trying to figure out the right way to talk to my mama. Had some things on my mind.

I walked through the tiny matchbox of a house, looking for my mama. Everything looked smaller and mattered less now as my heart burned with the loss of something. The adults knew a lot about what was happening in life, but they lived pretend lives. Nora's baby and her absence went unexplained; and they were teaching us to be makers and keepers of lies and secrets.

I found Mama in the kitchen, washing dishes. Just seeing my mama in the kitchen made me feel a little better. Also, in the kitchen Mama seemed to be a little more forgiving of my questions. Today, she was glowing.

Mama wore a pale blue dress that matched the color of the day sky and the kitchen curtains. Something inside of my mama was turned on. It didn't matter why she was so happy. I was so glad to see her sunshine. When Mama smiled, her lips formed a half moon, and her eyes became flashing stars. Laughter spread the full moon across her face.

She asked, "Do you want this last piece of your cake? I saved it in the icebox for you. It's almost gone."

My mama had re-arranged the last bites of my favorite three-layer yellow batter, pineapple coconut, white icing, lemon-flavored fifth year birthday cake. The re-designed ring of cake flowers sat on a small saucer 'for compan' onl' dessert. My mama's creative magic left me speechless. Mama stared at my hurt and sadness until I held my head up and looked past the dancing stars in her eyes—deep into her own ache and sorrow. Finally, she said, "It'll get betta."

Mama offered the remains of my birthday cake to me. It felt like an apology.

When I first came into the kitchen, I was still mad with my mama and daddy. I also felt that only the crumbs of my life remained. But I didn't know how to explain it, but the two things seemed to be connected. When I saw the ring of flowers that Mama had turned the crumbs of my cake into, I smiled. The new re-arranged 'cake' spoke for my mama—who, like my daddy never spoke empty words-chitchat.

I began to breathe. Normal words, like "Thank you, Mama,"; "It's so pretty"; and "How did you think of that?" found their way from my heart and then to my lips.

Some anger faded. I forgave her a little.

I was not really mad with Mama. She had helped my sister. I was angry with Daddy. He was the one who had hurt Nora and the family. Yet, I still felt that Mama should explain things to us.

I had been looking for Mama to talk about the 'voice'. I really wanted to talk about Nora, but I knew this was way past the limits my mama would allow. Right then, she was in a good mood. I thought this was a safe time and topic.

"Ma, how do God and the devil talk to you?"

Mama looked at me a long time before she spoke.

Fidgeting with the dishrag, my mama finally answered.

"Both of them can talk 'rectly to you. Or they can speak through a rock, a tree or even a child, sometimes. God wants you to do good. The devil talks to you when he is tryin' to trick you. Why do you want to know? Is the devil tellin' you some stuff?"

"No. When Aunt Naomi came over this mornin', she and my daddy were talkin' in the livin'room. I was playin' outside, near the window. I heard her tell my daddy. "'There is only good and bad in the world. We can choose which road we want to walk down.'"

"What did your daddy say?"

He said, "'Sometimes the devil can show you somethin' that looks good too.'"

But I didn't tell Mama that Aunt Naomi had lost patience with my daddy when he said those words. Aunt Naomi had told him sharply, "'That's been your problem all along! You let your eyes fool you.'"

Just as I was about to tell my mama exactly how my daddy had answered, she scolded me. "I told you about listenin' to grown folks talkin'. This's a way the devil uses you. By keepin' you in other folk business!"

I was surprised by what my mama had said! She wanted to hear the conversation, but she didn't want to hear it from me. Yet she was always asking me stuff because she knew I was a born snooper. Sometimes she talked to me like I was a grownup. Without saying it out loud, we both knew that she used me to collect information. This was one of our secrets. Asking me about my daddy and Aunt Naomi's talk was a perfect example.

After a long pause, Mama asked me, "Did they said anythin' about Nora?"

I nodded my head "Yes," but said nothing else.

"What did they say?" she demanded. Mama flung the wet rag across the kitchen table. "What are you waitin' for? You know exactl' what they said."

"But, Mama, you told me to stay out of other folks' business."

"Forget what I said in the past. Damn it! I'm talkin' about right now."

"Aunt Naomi wanted to know why Nora left. Daddy told her that Nora wanted to go to school in the country."

"What else?"

"That's all I heard. After that you called me to take them the lemonade."

Mama seemed satisfied with my story. I couldn't say 'lie' because 'lie' was a cuss word. And it was a story 'cause I didn't tell mama the full truth. I was really lying, but if I said 'lying' it would be cussing. *I thought lying was worse than cussing, but who was asking me my opinion?* I didn't tell Mama that Aunt Naomi said to Daddy, "'Something is telling me that you were involved in this.'"

Also, I didn't tell my daddy's answer to Aunt Naomi, "'I swear on a stack of Bibles, I won't touch that girl anymore!'"

I was not able to tell Mama about the strange voices that were always whispering ideas to me. The voice was as real as the 'Holy Ghost' my mama and my daddy talked about or the devil that they said used people. It had told me to burn things. *Had I been used by the bad voice?* The good voice even seemed like the 'Spirit' that Aunt Naomi called God. I decided to call the good voice, the 'Voice of Love' or 'Love Voice' since Emma Love wouldn't talk to me. The voices, and the fire fascinated me, but the fire would have to be my own secret.

I left my mama in the kitchen, staring out the narrow window.

* * *

Not knowing the real truth about life didn't seem to bother the rest of my sisters and brothers. They seemed to live with no care nor worry about things that bothered me. Four-year-old Willie Earl was pretend-flying his folded paper airplane on the porch. I asked him, "Do a voice ever speak inside your head to you?" I pointed to my head with my fingers.

He shrugged his small shoulders and said, "All the time. Which one?"

When Reba came home from school, I asked her, "Do you ever hear a voice talking inside of you?"

Reba rolled her eyes, her lips and her neck. Then she sneered, "What're you talking about? You've been around Aunt Naomi too much." Neither of my sisters liked Aunt Naomi.

When I asked my big bother Paul the same question, he quickly snapped, "If you're hearing voices, you've got a problem! You need to talk to my mama about it."

I went outside and cried to be like everyone else.

That day, I decided to get a better understanding of my family and my life so that life would stop surprising me! These young eyes had seen so much of life too soon. Knowing more I could understand more. First, I needed to find someone who would help me. I quickly remembered the 'Love Voice' had comforted me before. *Maybe it would be the one?* Then maybe I could help my crazy family who was as twisted as a ball of yarn. I kept on questioning life because it was the only way to deal with my feelings of secrecy, shame and silence.

Making this decision eased my unanswered questions, although Mama was constantly telling me, "Stop listenin' in on grown folk talk, eavesdropping' and snoopin' in adult business." But every time I did, some of my questions about life, my family and my path in life were answered. If Mama had known the extent that I went to understand the family interactions, she would have simply said, "Mind your own business."

Later, Nora helped me to use my dictionary as a word guide and speller. When I could write well enough at eight years old, I put the story about the fifth year of my life on paper. Through the years I rewrote and transferred the story from my raggedy writing pad to many diaries, writing journals and notebooks. This is my final written story of the fifth year.

PART II.
LIFE LIVED BACKWARD

Chapter 6

Swimming Upstream

We children of the Abraham and Emma Love family had the habit of each child saying, 'my mama', 'my daddy' to each other. Examples of this strange way of talking were: "Doris, tell Paul I said for him to turn off the radio."

"Paul, my mama said for you to turn off the radio".

Or "Daddy, my mama said she needs some more rice from the store."

Or "Mama, I saw my daddy in the store with Miss Claribel."

Even as I tell my story, it is hard for me not to say, 'My mama'. All of us children talked about how odd it sounded. We had never heard other families use it. We always laughed about it and continued the habit.

Often my mama would say to us, "Give me some breathing room."

I guess we all were a little over possessive of her, especially me. Time with my mama was a special gift that I didn't want to share. It seems that Mama knew how to make each child feel special and chosen.

I felt that I needed love and care from both of my parents, so I was always in their business. If I knew what made them tick, I could understand what caused the pain in their lives. Something had made both sad and secretive. We all lived in the same house, and yet each person seemed to live a separate life. *What was causing this?* The half-truths, unlikely reasons and Southern childcare practices impressed on us didn't go along with the word 'parents'. We had seen too much of their lies to believe and trust their words. It seemed that our 'parents' were bringing trouble into our lives, especially the daddy part. Even though no one else used it in my family, I felt that calling them my 'parents' would make them more responsible for our safety and childhood. *Being 'parents' couldn't be too hard or bad. Could it?*

I thought about the 'my mama', 'my daddy' habit often. I realized that Nora, my oldest sister, didn't say 'my mama' or 'my daddy'.

That was when Nora told me, "We don't have the same daddy, but we have the same mama. That's why I call your daddy 'Mr. Abraham.' Mama divorced my daddy, John Walker, before she married your daddy, Abraham Love. Your daddy's lies, his womanizing and how he treats me as a stepdaughter makes me think of him as 'Mr. Abraham, the hypocrite.' Your daddy is the opposite of God and love. He's the devil hiding in a person."

As it turned out, my oldest sister, Nora, was the person in the family who didn't try to make me stop asking questions. She was at the scene when my memory of life being safe, and loving was almost erased. Then Nora had disappeared. Just like that, without saying "Goodbye," she was gone! I missed her so much!

I was shocked and happy, at the same time, when Nora came back home after three months. Mama didn't say anything about her return. Nora was enrolled back in school right away. The first day back to school she didn't realize that the early morning inspection had stopped. After Nora made a good breakfast of cheese grits and eggs, she went in Mama's room. The Nora that stepped in front of Mama that morning was changing. She was now called "Skinny Nora" by her school friends. Nora stood in front of the bed until Mama remembered what Nora wanted. She studied Nora for a minute and then frowned, "What in the hell do you have on?"

"I remade a dress from an old one and the new dress that I bought when I worked in the tobacco factory."

I wanted to laugh out loud, but I had to pretend I wasn't watching from the door.

My mama was not talking. So, Nora continued. "I cut off the tops of two dresses. Took the top of the new dress and sewed it to the bottom of the old dress. Look, Mama. You can see it is a little longer." She pointed to the hemline. I knew Mama was not pleased, but she was not releasing her hard "No."

Nora finished, "I will admit it is tighter than most dresses or skirts. But I like it tight. "When they call me "Skinny Nora," I know they can see me and my creativity."

My mama nodded, "Okay. Let's do it like this. Wear the new dress that we're savin' for Sund'. When you come home from school, I'll help you sew those two dresses together better. I know you don't want the bottom to fall off your top, do you?" She paused. "When I see Miss Doris I will ask her to teach you how to sew too." Mama was not mad. I thought she was trying to make up for Nora's hard times. I was surprised and happy for Nora.

Nora was really excited now. "You mean you will help me with the sewing?" Nora was smiling the shiny smile that made her look like my mama's twin. She said, "I show don't want to be embarrassed like that!" Skinny Nora ran to change into the fancy Sunday dress that would show attract attention that day.

Other than Nora's being back home, life continued to be sad and silent. One cold February Friday afternoon when Nora came home from school, Mama told Nora, "Go to the fish market and get two pounds of fish heads. I want to make some fish stew. Tell Mr. Brown that I don't want buffalo. The heads have too many bones. Also, I don't want catfish 'cause of the tough skin on them. I rather have sea mullets or croakers."

Nora nodded her head.

Mama quietly said, "Reba is over Miss Harriet's. Take Doris with you. She's been followin' me around all day. Sayin' how bored she is. You can buy yourself and Doris a dill pickle. Mr. Brown's market got the best ones in town. You get a free peppermint jawbreaker when you buy a pickle."

I was sitting in a rocking chair, near the cast iron stove. The stove made it warm and cozy inside, but outside it was windy and cold. My mama turned to me. "Doris, make sure you wear your good coat and your gloves that Miss Doris gave you for Christmas. The ground hog saw his shadow again. We're in for six more weeks of cold weather."

What do a ground hog seeing its shadow have to do with it being cold? I wanted to ask. But I didn't want Mama to say, "'Just for that, you're not going.'"

I shushed that question. But Mama was right. I was bored. Other than practicing reading and writing my alphabets from my dictionary, I was stuck in the house with my cooing baby brother and Mama who was there, but not there.

I jumped up, found my coat in the crammed spooky closet, and chased after Nora, who was half-way the narrow alley. I forgot the gloves. *Maybe I won't need them.*

As I caught up with my sister, my inner voice spoke to me, *Now is the time.*

Time for what? I knew, but sometimes I feared the truth. *Where do I start?*

"Why did you leave without telling me?" This question slipped out of my mouth before I could decide what to say. "You know you are the only one who talks to me and makes sense. Everyone else tells me, "'Be quiet. You're too young to be asking about that.'"

"Well, Sis, in a way they are right. But I don't want to, but after a thousand questions from you since I came back, I got to tell you something." She slowed her pace so I could keep up with her.

"That's why I am always asking questions. I have to know more so I can understand more." *Was she going to tell me?* I could hardly believe it! The freezing winds drew us closer together and Nora wrapped her arm around me to shelter us from the cold, Carolina winter.

"Sis, that night when I had a baby and it died, I know you were listening and pretending to be sleep. You heard Mama tell Miss Ellen that Mr. Abraham was the daddy. Didn't you? I could tell by the hurt in your eyes the next day. From that moment on, I didn't care about anything. Even though you were too young to know, I knew you wanted to know what happened."

"I was going to ask you about it, but you left before I got a chance. Nora, how did he hurt you?"

"He did it when nobody was home, but Mr. Abraham. He caught me in our bedroom, changing clothes. I only had on my beginner's brassiere and some matching bloomers. He said, 'If you tell, I will send people to take your Mama away 'cause everybody knows she's crazy anyway'. He was talking about how Mama forgets things and won't talk for days."

I didn't want to admit that sometimes my mama did act strange. Now I had to know even more. "So, what did he do after that?"

"He pushed me back on the bed and tore off my bloomers. I fought him and tried to get away. He covered my mouth with his hand and dared me to scream. Then he forced his thing inside of me. You may have heard some boys call it 'dick'. He did it many times when he caught me home by myself. He tried to do it one night, but this time Mama heard him coming into our bedroom."

"I fought him and tried to get away. He covered my mouth with his hand and dared me to scream. Then he forced his thing inside of me. You may have heard some boys call it 'dick'. He did it many times when he caught me home by myself. He tried to do it one night, but this time Mama heard him coming into our bedroom."

For once, I was speechless. Finally, a thought came to me. *You better speak up. Mama show ain't goin' to tell you nothin'!*

"What did my mama say?" Nora stopped walking. I stopped too.

"Mama said, 'Abraham, what were you doin' in there at 2:00 in the morning?'"

"As you know by now, Mr. Abraham was quick with a lie."

"'Nothing. I thought I heard something in the kitchen'."

"'You're lyin'. The only thing in that kitchen is the rats. I've been watchin' you and I know what you're up too. I'm goin' to talk to Miss Doris about this.'"

I was good at watching faces. I studied Nora's. Her dark eyes rolled back, like they could watch her pain. The body tensed up as it remembered the sadness it carried. Nora was back in the bedroom where her stepdaddy—my daddy—had hurt her. Both of us were quiet in our own thoughts and we started toward the store.

Nora broke the silence. "Mama had talked to Miss Doris too late. By then I was going to have a baby, I was pregnant. I had not swallowed a watermelon seed. Reba told you a lie, not a story. I didn't have a hen in the oven. Mama need to tell you some real facts of life, not all that fake shit—like you'll have bad luck if a cat crosses your path. Or you won't be blessed if you don't obey your parents. That's why I don't use the word 'parent'. Hypocrites! These lies get on my nerves."

I could see that Nora was getting madder and more upset as she told me what had happened. My hurt sister closed her eyes and let the air out of her angry mouth, ending with a long, loud cry! Then she screamed, "What he did to me is called "rape"! I didn't know about any of this until Miss Ellen, the midwife, explained the whole thing to me!"

By now we were standing in front of the grocery store/fish market. Nora removed her gloves, took my frozen hands, and rubbed her warm hands around my ten icicles. My hands began to thaw out. *Gee! I'd missed my sister. Nora was so sweet! She never mentioned the forgotten gloves.* We stepped to the side to let people come in or go out of the store. "What did Mama say when she found out you were going to have a baby?"

Out of all my questions, this was the most important one. I wanted to know how my Mama felt about it and what she had done because of it.

"When I told Mama my monthly period hadn't come for three months, her head flew way back and she howled like a wolf. She sounded like the man in *The Wolf Man* movie that we saw at the show. I had been afraid to tell her 'cause I thought she would blame me. And I knew how mad she can get. Mr. Abraham had promised to send her to the crazy house if I told. Mr. Abraham was always saying I was fast. I was always finding ways to get away from him fast."

"What is a 'monthly period'? What do 'fast' mean?"

"See. This is exactly why I didn't want to answer some of your questions. It's not your fault but you're just so young. You haven't lived long enough to know. Talking about stuff in life is hard enough, but trying to explain to a curious five-year-old is wearing me out."

She was right 'cause I didn't quite understand all she said. But at least, we were talking, and I was getting some of my questions answered.

"Nora, I feel so bad about what my daddy did to you, but you still didn't tell me what Mama said to you or to my daddy?"

"Okay, your last question for now. Mama must have known what was going on, she was so mad. She called him a "motherfuckin' pervert". This was a turning point for Mama also. She had a decision to make. Mama went to your witch-crafting Aunt Nellie for some herbs to get rid of it, but nothing happened. Then my friend Velma gave me some pills called quinine tables that start periods, but they didn't work either. Then when I was about seven months pregnant, I had the miscarriage. Miss Ellen called it that, but Mama called it 'stillborn'. I think all those pills and herbs caused the death of the baby."

A picture of my dead half-burned nephew under the wash pot flashed across my mind, I wanted to scream but I was able to control myself.

"After it happened, I did not want to live in the house with your monster daddy. Mama asked Daddy's sister Aunt Minnie to ask Daddy if I could come and lived with him. Two days later, my Aunt Minnie picked me up and took me to Daddy's."

"But why did you come back?" Nora looked at me like she wanted to cuss me. "I promised you. This is it!" I wanted to know what a 'mother fuckin' pervert' was, but my time for questions was running out.

"Okay. No more now! Mama is going to fuss 'cause we're taking too long." Nora was quiet again. I leaned closer to Nora. "Daddy was still the mean-spirit, selfish, greedy man Mama divorced!" The anger that shot out of her mouth scared me.

As Nora continued, this time, with everything so quiet, I could feel her disappointment with her daddy. "When I first got to his house, I was still healing from having a baby. I was so messed up in my mind. It was hard for me to get up and take care of myself. I don't even know if Mama told him what had happened. But he wanted me to cook, clean and work. I had to say, 'I'm sick' before he left me alone. I hardly had strength to eat. I won't 'bout to be cooking."

"Daddy had asked, in a mean irritated voice, 'What's the matter with ya?'"

"I asked him if Mama had told him about my situation."

Not answering my question, he said, 'You got two weeks to recover.'"

"He knew and didn't even care how Mr. Abraham had treated me. He had no real love for me as his daughter. I waited for a few days and then I asked him about my brother, Timothy Earl.

"Daddy yelled, 'Don't be coming up in here asking too many questions. Who you asking for?'

I told him, "I missed Timothy Earl; he's my brother. I wanted to hear about him, and I wanted to see him.

"After a while Daddy said, 'Timothy lives up North with my sister, your Aunt Esther. We're going to Mama's house for Christmas— he may be there then.'

"When Daddy knocked on Granny Gertie's door on Christmas Day, Timothy opened the door. I hadn't seen him in five years and he recognized me instantly. Both of us looked like Mama. He was about ten. He reminds me of you. He reads all the time and loves to hang around grown folks.

"Some lady came over with supper every day. Sometimes she spent the night. Daddy didn't tell me her name and I didn't want to know. Two things I remember about her is she show couldn't cook and she drunk as much stump hole liquor as Daddy. Any time he came in the house and saw me still in bed, he rolled his eyes and started slamming doors. Daddy is the meanest and the most miserable person I have ever seen. That hard-cold look never left his face the three months I stayed there."

I listened, mad and sad for Nora.

"After two weeks, I asked about school. He didn't look at me as he mumbled, 'We need money. You gotta work.' The next week Daddy got me a job in the tobacco factory past downtown, near Happerville. I was a sweeper. It was a dirty dusty job. A Colored sweeper told me to wear a scarf on my head and one on my face to cover my ears, mouth and nose.

"But at least you had some money!"

"Yeah! But Daddy took most of my money every week I got paid. He treated me like a slave. I worked six days a week. In the evenings, I had to cook, wash, iron and clean. I refused to go to church on Sunday. It was my only day off. After a while when Daddy got drunk, which was just about every day, he rested his eyes on me like Mr. Abraham used to do. One night, he stumbled into my room, smelling like a whiskey still. He slurred, "Mooove ooover, gal!"

"What! The same thing?"

I forgot my promise and I didn't care. I had to say something before I exploded.

At that point Nora didn't care that we had been gone long enough to be back home. I didn't explode, but she did. "Yes! The same damn thing that Mr. Abraham had done. I cussed him, 'You nasty mother fuckin' pervert! You are worse than Mr. Abraham. You are my father!' I jumped up and got the iron and raised my hand to hit him. I told him, 'If you touch me, I will bash your twisted head in.'"

I was as quiet as Nora's secret had been.

"Daddy staggered back in the kitchen for another drink. That's when I decided to come back to Mama's. The next morning when he was sober, he shuffled into the kitchen, snatched his sausage sandwich breakfast, and slammed out the door, without looking at me or saying a word. He was in a don't-touch-me-I-will-bite-your-head-off mood and I was too. I walked over to Aunt Minnie's and she brought me back here. At least at Mama's house I can go to school. If Mr. Abraham ties anything, he's in for a surprise! I almost rather be adopted than live with a nasty daddy or a perverted stepdaddy."

Nora didn't sound like the same sister who had been hurt by my daddy.

What is 'adopted'? I wondered. I better not ask right now.

To soften the hard truth, Nora gave me some hope. "I'll tell you this, Sis. Write as best you can 'monthly period', 'sex', 'rape', 'parent', 'pregnant' and 'turning point' on your alphabet practice list.

Add 'miscarriage' and 'stillborn' to your list if you don't know them. When I get a chance, I will tell you how to spell these words. Then we can look up the meanings in your dictionary. Don't put those cuss words in. The less you know about them, the better off you will be. And you know you better not use them around Mama and Mr. Abraham. Don't tell Mama I told you any of this. You promise?"

I didn't agree quickly. I wanted to think about what would happen if I told her before I could find the right words to say. After a moment, we did the pinky finger twist to seal the deal.

Nora pulled me toward the grocery store/fish market door. She stopped me at the door and said, "I just want you to know that your daddy is a 'mother fuckin' pervert'! That's what Mama called him."

I followed her into the store, lost in a world of strange words and sad stories.

As Nora looked around in the grocery store/fish market, the fish trapped in the tanks caught my attention and imagination. I asked Mr. Brown, the owner, who was standing behind the fish counter, "What is the name of the fish swimming at the bottom of the tank?"

Nora came over and looked at which fish to buy. Mr. Brown talked to me about the fish in the tank. "That's the catfish which lives at the bottom of the river. The catfish and the salmon can teach us something about life." He pointed to the pinkish orange fish in the showcase. "It costs more than the rest of the fish, live or dead."

Mr. Brown looked toward Nora. "I will be with you in a moment. How's your mama doing?" He knew our family well. Everybody in our neighborhood shopped in the 'Colored' combined grocery store and fish market. Mr. Brown was a tall, brown man with a hint of sadness in his intelligent eyes.

Turning his attention back to me, Mr. Brown went on with his lesson. "Now there is basically nothing wrong with being a catfish. A catfish is not valued because it lives in muddy water and eats dead stuff at the bottom of the river. He never rises from his condition and travels upstream. Do you understand, Doris?"

Nora disappeared for a moment and came back with three small brown paper bags. Each one contained a large dill pickle and two free peppermint jawbreakers. "Here is yours. Got one for Reba too." She looked at Mr. Brown, the fish market owner, and said, "I am ready. I see what Mama wants."

Mr. Brown answered in a friendly manner. "I will be with you in a moment. How's your daddy doing?"

Nora kicked my leg and mouthed to me, "Stop asking questions. We got to go!"

Turning to me again, Mr. Brown continued, "The point I was making is be more like salmons. Salmon lay its eggs in freshwater. Then they journey out to the ocean where they feed and grow. After three years, when they are grown, they return to the fresh waters to lay their eggs and have baby salmons. Nature always has something to teach us."

I dared not ask another question. I wanted to ask, *What is nature? Is it connected to the voice?* I was still learning when to ask these types of questions. Something was telling me it was time to stop. Just asking Mr. Brown about the fish had taught me something that I had never known.

As Mr. Brown gave us the bags of fish, he said, "I sent your mama three pounds of croakers, six whole spots and a large, Atlantic salmon. Threw in a mess of winter peas. I have so many I got to get rid of them before they go bad." *How did he know my mama liked the spot fish that had a black dot between its eyes? Winter peas! My mama's favorite.* I wondered.

On the way home, Nora reminded me, "Sis, don't go trying to figure out how Mr. Brown knows what kind of fish Mama likes. Mama will be in trouble with Mr. Abraham if he knew that Mr. Brown gave her anything free. I could barely understand what Mr. Brown was talking about myself—rivers, muddy waters and salmon. I am sure you didn't get it either. Did you?"

On that cold February afternoon, I admitted to myself, *Nora was right. I knew it was none of my business how Mr. Brown knew my mama liked spot fish and winter peas. I hardly talked to my daddy anymore, now that I knew what he had done to Nora. As much I could, I would not be around him. And I didn't understand most of what Mr. Brown had explained to me about the fish.*

But I was right when I thought Nora was listening to Mr. Brown's talk about the fish. She also knew how to be somewhere and act like she was not there. Just like Mama. But none of that mattered anyway. Now, Nora was back home. And she had called me, 'Sis', a word that sounded liked she loved me and would look out for me.

We were quiet on the way back home. My sister had finally told me what happened to her. I had to know what happened to Nora so the same thing wouldn't happen to me. After the talk, I felt like I had reached another 'turning point' as Nora had called it. I had spent almost every minute since the death in fear and anger. Now, I was just plumb tired of being sad. Being sad was boring.

By the time we got home, my feeling of sadness turned to hope and curiosity. I saw that continuing to ask questions would lead to more answers. On this small wave of hope, I decided that I would use as much as I could of Mr. Brown's advice, "Swim upstream like the salmon and live a full adult life."

My life had started out living in an alley, being poor, 'Colored' and in a troubled family. But now I was on my way up.

Chapter 7

Am I Adopted?

After the school children left for school the next day, I stayed in bed and stared out the foggy window. It was so cold outside that the sky-pointed tree branches were frozen and icicles hung off the downward magnolia limbs. It had grown colder, and I was glad we had gone to the store yesterday. After our talk, Nora was clear about her feelings about my daddy and his ways. I still was not satisfied. *How in the heck did I get into such a family? Maybe, 'Mr. Abraham' wasn't my daddy either.* Oops! we were not supposed to say 'heck'. It's a soft cuss word for 'hell'.

Mama came into our bedroom to make the beds. She was surprised to find me still under the covers. I had stopped jumping up early for breakfast. "You feeling poorly?"

Before I could answer, Mama said, "Oh, I remember, 'I am 'bored'." She said it in a little girl's voice, mocking me.

Then she became serious. "A little girl started living next door, you can play with her. Her name is Carolyn. Miss Harriet and Clyde adopted her."

I thought, *now this is perfect timing! This is what Nora was always telling me about.*

Nora had said, "The perfect time to ask a question is when the other person is talking about what you want to know about. Not the other way around. Try not to bring up a subject, totally out of the blue."

"Mama, what's 'adopted'?"

"Can't I just tell you something without you asking a question? Other people become your mama and daddy; you become their child."

"Was that what happened to our brother, Timothy Earl?"

"How do you know about Timothy Earl?"

"Nora told me."

"There you go. Butting into grownups' business! I must admit you're the most 'telligent child I have ever seen. You're what your Grandmama Quintilla called, 'an old soul'. Must have been here before 'cause you ain't been here long enough to know what you ask about. So interested in ever'thang around. You're always asking what this means, what is this and why this happened. You are way smarter than your age."

"Mama," I dared to say, "Last week, I followed you in the bedroom. I saw you looking at a picture of a baby boy leaning against the rails of the crib. Reaching out to whoever was taking the picture. Isn't that the crib from the living room? You kissed the picture and hugged it to yourself real tight. Was that Timothy Earl?"

My brokenhearted mama had put the picture in the bottom drawer of the dresser. When she turned around, she was crying. My confession didn't bring out the cuss I had expected.

"Yes, the picture's Timothy Earl. He lives with his daddy's sister. He was not adopted, and I didn't give him away. My first husband took him from me when I ran away from that mean man. Your sister Nora got away. I begged for Timothy. The next day when Mama came back for Timothy Earl, no one was there. Mama grabbed the crib and put it in the car. It was special—carved with hopping rabbits and twirling butterflies."

"Mama, what happened to the crib?"

"Mama took it to Miss Doris's house for Mr. Eugene to fix it. Nora's daddy had kicked it in. Made by a runaway slave who was a carpenter from some country in Africa where the whole village carved beautiful objects out of wood. I went to school with his grandson." Her voice sounded shaky and nervous. "You don't need to know all of this."

"He didn't want Timothy Earl. He don't even like chillum. I guess that's why Nora came back so soon."

I said to myself, *That's part of the reason.* It felt good knowing the truth about something, but I wanted to know more about the carved crib.

"He gave Timothy Earl to his sister to hurt me. I look at this picture every day. I love him so much. The thought of him not bein' with me makes me sick. And Doris, would you stop followin' me and eavesdroppin' on my life!"

The crib story ended.

"Mama, I promise you I will." A promise I knew I would not keep. For one time she had answered my question with the plain truth. My mama's usual refusal to answer my questions did not silence me. I had always felt that I was on a different path. I simply wandered away from her and found others who might answer some questions for me.

The inner voice was just beginning to tell me where to go to get information. It had led me to search for scissors in Mama's room, the day I saw Mama with Timothy Earl's picture. If children could be taken from their own family and be placed in a strange home, I wanted to make sure I was in the right family. I knew the question didn't make sense because everyone said, "You look like your daddy spit you out!"

The next day, when Mama and Daddy went to make groceries, I slipped in the front room and closed the door. I inspected the mirror, trimmed in shiny old gold, hanging on the door. It was breathtaking! The story was that Mama's mama, Grandmama Quintilla, gave it to my mama when she and Daddy got married and they 'set up housekeeping', as my mama called it. The mirror had been my first secret friend for a long time.

I had seen many things in the mirror. I wanted to see if I could see me in my parents. Yet, I was afraid to look in it. *What would I see? Whose child would I be?* When I dared to stand in front of it, my eyes investigated my reflection. I saw a combination of Mama and Daddy. Brown skin, lanky legs and thick hair. A mix of Daddy's wavy hair and Mama's long curly straight hair. 'Colored' hair, nappy hair was scattered throughout my good hair, around the edges and in the kitchen (the back hair up from the neck). 'Colored' hair won out when Mama washed my hair. She said, "This is a tangle' jungle of all ya' peoples."

My daddy's curious eyes stared at my snooping nose and moon-shaped lips. My snooping nose belonged to my daddy. The moon-shaped lips were my mama's.

I was relieved! That question was answered. Both were in me. As I stood in front of the beautiful mirror again, I looked at the room through the mirror. My brother's crib, his play pen and bed, sat in the dark corner, behind my right-hand side. Carved rabbits and butterflies soaring through the sky, freely. That was the crib! *Who was the carver's grandson?* I had too many questions for a little girl!

After the inspection in the antique mirror and seeing Timothy Earl's carved crib, I felt that I was in the right family. I knew listening to the Love Voice would help me understand my family. After the mirror inspection, I became more determined to find out more about the family I had been born into. I wanted to understand the kind of people who were my parents.

Chapter 8

Abraham Jacob Love, My Daddy

My mama and daddy could have gotten help with their problem from Miss Doris Barnes, my godmama, I thought. And they had many—Daddy being with other women, jealous of my mama and hurting Nora. But I knew my mama was too closed mouth and secretive to be honest with Miss Doris about our dark family secrets.

Mostly what I knew about my daddy's childhood came from Miss Doris. My name Doris also came from Miss Doris. All 'Colored' women were called "Miss," whether they were married or not. My godmama was a giant of a woman. She was very dark, tall and important looking. Everything about Miss Doris was big—her head, her hands, her heart. She was the closest thing to a giant queen I had ever heard of. Daddy said she was 'handsome' because she had a lot of strength like a man.

Miss Doris was a mother, housewife and a seamstress. Mr. Eugene, her husband, a carpenter, had built their house, a small mansion with many rooms, giant chairs, huge tables and a gigantic bed—all for her comfort. Our family agreed, "It makes our shotgun house look like a doll playhouse." Mr. Eugene had brought one of the special-made chairs to our house for her visits. When Miss Doris visited us, my daddy took her chair out of the old storage shed outside. Whenever I saw Miss Doris's chair, I knew we would have a meal fit for a king's family. And a good family visit with her the rest of the day. Also, Miss Doris always left me a package. Best of all, Daddy would be home that night.

Every evening there would be an argument. As my daddy got ready for his night out, my mama would scream, "You can't keep your tail home one night!"

My daddy wouldn't come in the kitchen and fuss. That didn't matter to Mama. She followed him from the small bathroom into the living room/bedroom and slammed the door. "I know you're on your way to see that Claribel again!"

The paper-thin walls of the shotgun house allowed any talk that was not a low whisper to be heard.

Nightly, we heard about my daddy's 'Claribel', his constant going out, my mama being jealous and Mama spending all his money. All these things came up when they were fussing. Supper would continue as the Love children avoided looking at each other. Sometimes I got a nervous stomach and ran outside to puke. The rest of my supper was eaten by the person who grabbed it first.

During one wild argument, as we sat waiting for Mama to put the food on the table, Nora said to us nervous children, "I do know that Mr. Abraham is as jealous of Mama as can be! Your daddy even thinks Mama have a boyfriend. 'Cause he's a woman chaser. When I went shopping with them last week, men gave her winks and smiles. Mr. Abraham got mad with Mama and blamed her. He fussed at her and said, 'It's your fault. always trying to be so fine.' Mama likes to dress nice, and Mr. Abraham insists that she is dressed up whenever they go anywhere. It's not Mama's fault that she is light skinned with good hair. Your daddy and most 'Colored' men around here love light skin. And y'all know that Mr. Love loves a lot of light skin women!"

I wanted to tell my godmama what was going on, but I was still waiting for the 'Love Voice' to show me how.

My chance finally came. One day on her way downtown, my mama left me and Willie Earl at Miss Doris's house. As soon as Mama left, Willie Earl ran outside to shoot marbles with the little boys next door. My smile began to melt when I didn't smell or see any signs of food, but I was still glad to talk with Miss Doris who was sewing in a wide sunny room. She called it a 'den'. "Doris, get your practice handkerchief and work on making the one-inch hem. Remember? One section of your finger is an inch. Be careful with the needle."

The only sound in the room was the soft purring of the well-oiled Singer sewing machine. As I carefully measured the hem, I asked, "How long hav'ya be'n knowin' my daddy?"

My godmama jerked her heavy body toward me and almost screamed. Something she had never done to me. "Knowin' him? Pronounce your words fully." She waited.

"How long have you been knowing him?" I asked. *Clearly and slowly-no more lazy 'Colored' talking.* "When I do talk right, my family says, 'You trying to talk proper, like White people. Speak regular words.'"

Miss Doris didn't deal with excuse-making. She ignored my attempt and began. "Your daddy left home and came to Kinston when he was about nine years old from Oak City, about 40 miles from here."

"I don't even know his mama and daddy's name." This time I remembered. No lazy, 'Colored' talking.

"Tayanita and Henry Love. Abraham had a rough time finding himself during these times. It was hard for all 'Colored' people in the 30's and 40's in Kinston. He lived in liquor houses and sometimes behind the bus station. When Eugene found him sleeping under the train trestle, he convinced the bus station manager to let Abraham be a porter. He was only twelve. He rented a room from us."

"Did he work while he went to school or just go to school?"

"No. He was busy trying to make a living. When he was a teenager, he played for some of the 'Colored' baseball teams here in Kinston, North Carolina. Most of these ballplayers earned very little from baseball but it still offered 'Colored' baseball teams a means of extra income for players as young as fourteen. They made a living through other jobs."

"Which team did he play on?"

"Baby, I don't know. Mr. Eugene can help you on the name. He played ball in small towns in North Carolina and around Kinston like Greenville, Rocky Mount, New Bern and Elizabeth City which claimed many 'Colored' teams. Your daddy traveled with different teams that played in rural areas. They called it 'barnstorming'."

"What's that?"

"They played out in the country near barns, located on big open fields. Abraham could hit the ball out of sight in any field or stadium. I guess he never felt the support that he needed to go all the way with baseball."

"What kind of work did he do?"

"He worked on various jobs at the same time. Abraham carried more money in his pocket than most 'Colored' people of the time. Some said he transported white lightning for old man Jones from Greenville. Abraham also loaned people money."

"White lightning? What is that?"

Miss Doris ignored me for she had told me what she wanted me to know.

Miss Doris went on to explain, "After he lived with us for a while, I could see that Abraham was, like Abraham in the Bible, inspired by the Lord. He left his family and the hard times behind. Came to Kinston and has prospered ever since. I could see that order and responsibility had been established in him. Despite him leaving home early, he was careful about the way he lived. In the evenings sometimes, he practiced reading and writing. Took great pride in speaking his words correctly. Guess he's fixing up his words to be a preacher."

"Is a preacher like a teacher?"

"Yes. a preacher is a man called by God to teach the word of God and to help people. You know he reads the Bible a lot. A teacher reads other kinds of books that help people."

"I wondered why he studied every Saturday morning."

But I had something else I wanted to understand. I decided this was a good time to ask, "Miss Doris, What is a godmama? How did you get to be my godmother?"

"Emma said you were full of questions, but I don't mind. When your mama was expecting you, your daddy told me, 'Emma and I want this baby named in your honor. You and Mr. Eugene were good to me when I came to Kinston. Our first child Paul was a boy and we named him after my granddaddy. Next Reba's named after Emma's sister Roberta. If this one is a girl, I want to give her your name. Emma said she'd better hurry up 'cause she won't be having too many more children.'"

This was when Daddy loved his children, I thought.

To Miss Doris I said, "I am the only one in our family who seems to have a godmama. I'm sort of special. I get a chance to be around you."

"Your daddy wanted to show his thanks to me and Eugene for helping him. Your daddy has a good heart. I know sometimes he gets a little rough, but I love him like a son. That's why I always buy you clothes and shoes and send bags of groceries over. I want to help ease the load."

After a while I was bored with stitching the hem crooked and having to take it out and do it again. Then my stomach started to growl. Miss Doris asked me what she usually asked when I first got to her house, "Are you hungry?"

When I nodded my head "Yes," she demanded, in a soft voice, "Use your words. It is important for a girl to learn to voice her opinion. What you say matters! I know adults are always telling children 'to be quiet.' But when an important question is asked, speak up. Loud and clear. Are you hungry?"

Corrected, loud and clear, I answered, "Yes. I am hungry."

"Come in the kitchen with me and watch me as I start supper. I'll do my biscuits first."

Miss Doris slowly raised her giant body out of her giant chair, took her special-made walking cane and inched her way down the wide hallway to the large kitchen. She rolled another special-made monstrous chair out from the extra wide table. She plopped down.

Miss Doris told me, "Doris, I decided to let you make your own sandwich. The chops and the bread are in the oven. Get a dish off the sink. Put a fried pork chop and two biscuits on it. Get a spoon out of the drawer and spread jelly on one side of both biscuits. Put the pork chop between the bread. There is a Nehi orange soda in the icebox. Sit here and eat. Don't forget to say your grace."

I was careful to do exactly as I was told. Then, I bowed my head and said, "Thank you, God, for the food. Thank you, God, for giving Miss Doris the food. Thank you, God, for Miss Doris being my godmama. Amen, God."

I still had not figured out the thing about God. I used to see a lot of God in my daddy. That had changed. I still saw God a lot in my mama. Now I could see the same good in Miss Doris which I called God.

The prayer was a little short because I didn't want God to eat on my pork chop when I closed my eyes. Daddy always told us that God was everywhere.

Miss Doris had watched me as I ate. "I can see you were hungry. Are you full? When your brother gets tired of playing, you can make him one."

Mama taught us to refuse seconds. I told a story. "Yes, I got enough." Yes, I was full. But I would never get enough of those delicious pork chops, strawberry preserve and brown cloud biscuits.

I stood on my tiptoes and ran some water over the plate. I wanted to lick it, but I was learning there are some things you can't say or do in front of grown folks. I left the plate in the sink and turned to Miss Doris. I could tell by her shift in the chair that it was time for a lesson.

She said, "Roll the supply cart next to the table. Get the buttermilk from the icebox. Dip a cup of lard and 4 cups of flour into this metal bowl. Be careful and take your time."

The cup was in the mixing bowl that sat on the table. The flour and lard were located near Miss Doris's large chair. I paid careful attention to her directions. After Miss Doris gathered the supplies, she mixed the flour, lard, and buttermilk together in the mixing bowl with a huge mixing spoon. As she rolled the dough with the rolling pin on the floured table, she said, "I knew your mama and daddy before they got married."

She had gone on to a different story.

"Your father was your mother's second husband. By the time you arrived on earth, your mother had married and divorced Nora's father, John Walker. Together they had two children. He was as mean as a snake and as slimy as one."

As she talked, the dough was being formed in small biscuit-sized pieces. I lost interest in biscuit making that day–too messy and sticky.

I was glad that Miss Doris could tell me about Mama when she was younger. But I was so happy that Mama had left Mr. Walker. Still, on the inside, I felt so bad for my mama. She now had a husband who was hurting her new family. I wanted better for Mama.

This information about Mama's other husband made my heart sag. I began to feel that Mama was right. She had told me many times to stay out of grown folks' business. *Was not knowing better than knowing?*

Waiting for Mama to pick us up, Miss Doris said. "Let me sum up your daddy. Abraham Love created a lifestyle with his own strong imagination. When your daddy puts on his colorful suits and matching ties and shoes, everyone sees Abraham Love as their 'Colored' knight in shining armor. He affects everybody's imagination when he entered a room. Abraham may be a 'Colored' man in the eyes of the White people. But in his own imagination, in his house and in the neighborhood, he is king."

Mama rushed in, flinging doors open and breaking the afternoon calm. "Sorry Miss Doris. It took longer than I thought. Come on Little Doris! Where's Willie Earl? Gotta beat Abraham home and get supper started."

Snatching us away so quickly had interrupted my question, *Do everybody have an imagination?*

As we trudged through the evening traffic, I thought, *Daddy and I both have a strong imagination. Our strong imagination gets both of us in trouble with Mama.*

Willie Earl was crying and resisting as Mama pulled him along. "But Mama, Miss Doris said we could stay for supper. I didn't get a chance to eat."

My hungry brother had refused to stop playing so he could come in and eat.

Rushing us across the street, Mama fussed, "You should've ate your sandwich when Doris ate hers. Hush your mouth, you ain't starving!"

From her nervous voice, I could easily see that my mama had her own imaginations of Daddy also. The king had to be fed on time.

Mama was under the influence of Daddy. Nora said that Daddy was under the influence of the devil when he hurt her. The thought came to me. *I was under the influence of the devil when I burned the playhouse.*

I ignored the thought which left as quickly and as silently as it came.

I was learning about my shortcomings, but I knew Aunt Naomi had excused Daddy's behavior this way: "After all, our generation is only few generations from the slavery of our people. Maybe our family came from royal blood, where the kings had many wives, families and relationships. From what I've read and seen about Africa in the picture show, having more than one wife was a common practice in many African villages."

I think Aunt Naomi had used her imagination to excuse her brother's bad behavior. Adults were good at using truth to tell lies. *Could fire be a way to burn to the truth?* Or *was my devilish imagination using fire to punish?*

* * *

My godmama knew that my daddy wanted to be a man of God. I needed to talk to him about the things Mr. Brown had told me about nature, the seed and God because Daddy studied about such things. But Daddy had always made me a little nervous, especially after I knew Nora's secret.

That evening after supper, when I was going out on the porch, I saw Daddy in the living room, putting his Bible on the shelf. When I saw that he was finished with his studying, I stopped in the hallway and I asked him, "Daddy, what makes a tree grow?"

Mama came out of the kitchen to see what we were talking about. She nodded her head to both of us and went back to her chores. I was surprised that Daddy had time for me. Loving to use Bible talk to answer questions, he took his King James Bible off the shelf and pointed for me to sit on the couch with him. I went in the living room and sat next to him. Daddy thought for a moment and answered by reading from the Bible, "Psalms 1:3 says "He shall be like a tree planted by the rivers of the water that bringeth forth fruit in his season. His leaf shall not wither, and whatsoever he doeth shall prosper."

Those big words sounded like a poem.

"To grow a tree, you need a seed. The seed for an oak tree is an acorn, like Willie Earl and his friends throw at each other. It must be planted in the ground to grow a tree. The oak tree in Clyde's yard next door won't grow without water."

"What are you saying, Daddy?"

"Give me time. I am going to show you how the law of God is found in nature and in us. You see me studying the Bible a lot, right?"

"I was wondering why."

"Nature is a tree, a seed, God or the ground. We are part of nature. Our heart is the ground where the word of God is planted." As he spoke, Daddy's voice began to get louder, he shouted, "I am a preacher in training! Not an ordained minister yet, but people call me 'Reverend Love.' I study the Bible because it is the word of God. I want the word of God planted in me." He pointed to his heart and looked up, then he turned back to the Bible which was clutched in his right hand. "The word is the seed, just like an acorn that produces a big tree."

"Daddy, does that mean that something will grow from whatever we say."

Again, pointing to his heart, and with his voice full of some emotion that sounded like sadness, he taught me. "Yes, our heart grows when we water it with dedication and love."

Looking at something in the distance, Daddy stopped talking. When he started back talking, his voice cracked. "The heart shrinks when we tell lies." *I thought he was going to cry.*

"Good words produce good fruit. Good fruit is truth, rightness and peace. Do you get the idea?"

I got it, but that was the first time I had ever known that Daddy could be sad. "I get it when you talk like that."

What I am wondering is why you don't get it! Of course, I didn't dare say this to my daddy. I was a child, to be seen and not heard. Daddy had explained nature, seeds and God in a clear way. Daddy was a good teacher but not a good daddy nor a good husband and show nuff not a good man of God! This is the reason Nora always said, "He's a fake and a hypocrite!"

Chapter 9

Emma Lee Love, My Mama

The next day, I told Nora what Miss Doris had said about my mama's first husband. Then she told me even more about Mr. Walker. "Mama divorced Daddy because he was extremely selfish, suspicious, cruel and jealous. He'd sweep the yard lightly with a broom so he could find any new tracks in the yard. Sometimes Daddy would climb up into the oak tree, high above the house. He wanted a good view as he watched to see who came to the house when he was away."

"He was that jealous?"

"Yeah. the mail man was the only acceptable man visitor on his property when he was at work." Nora continued, "Daddy had such an enormous appetite. At supper, sometimes, he would eat the whole dinner and leave just scraps for us. Mama would fix us a snack, later, after he went out to the juke joint."

Nora repeatedly told me this family legend:

> "When Mama dared to leave, she attempted to slip away while Daddy was at work during the day. Our Grandmama Quintilla drove out in the country to help her. Daddy came home two hours early. Mama was still packing. When Mama saw him, she grabbed for my little brother Timothy Earl.

He was a knee baby. Just beginning to walk. Daddy snatched the baby from Mama.

"The same crib that Willie Earl sleeps in now?"

"Sho nuff is."

Mama had shouted to me, "'Git in the car!'" I scrambled out of the house, stumbling, screaming and waving! Grandmama Quintilla eased out of her old gray Ford sedan. Grandmama was a big, tall woman who would fight a man or a bull. Daddy and Mama came out on the porch, Daddy twisting Mama's arm. Mama was hysterically crying, over and over "He won't let me have Timothy Earl!"

Grandmama screamed to Mama, "'Emma, git your ass in the car! We'll come back and git him!'"

Grandmama Quintilla went to the back seat of her car and came out with a double barrel, sawed-off shotgun and pointed it to Daddy. "'Take your fuckin' hands off my daughter! If you touch her again, I will blo' your goddam head off!'"

My mad grandmama started the car and Mama jumped in. The door to the back seat was locked! I jumped on the running board and held on to the car rack as Grandmama flew down the road. A trail of smoke and dust choked me.

The next day Grandmama Quintilla and one of her sons went to get Timothy Earl from Daddy. No one was there. Uncle Bill kicked the door in. She took Mama's clothes, some pictures and the antique crib. It was made by some family friend a long time ago.

Mama told me later, "One of your daddy's sister is raising Timothy Earl up North."

The talk helped me to understand where Mama may have gotten her cussing from. *But why didn't I get to sleep in the special family crib?* Our family secrets were like a torn quilt. Patched together, with missing parts, blindly stitched back together. The family story was as crooked as my hems that I made when I practiced sewing.

* * *

Unlike the small information about my father's family background, my mama's family was better known. Being around my mama's family members, a family history book, a living family historian, and a tradition of family reunions made me more familiar with Mama's side.

I thought some family history would clear the mystery on my mama's side. Cousin Babs Moses Tyler, the family historian, was the perfect person in the family to ask. "Cut'n Babs," as my mama explained her to me once, "was smart in school. By the eighth grade she was teachin' at the elemen'ry school. The 'Colored' head principal had begged, 'Please, Mr. Moses, let Babs go to college. The 'Colored' School Board will pay her tuition, books and travel expenses.' After much talk, Uncle Moses finally agreed."

One afternoon, Cousin Babs' husband, Mr. Tyler, dropped her off at our house. Mama was outside hanging clothes on the lines. Cousin Babs came into the kitchen to wait for my mama. Dressed in the best, Mama's cousin was medium height, honey brown with a proud, strong walk. She didn't have any children, but she was a teacher who loved talking to us children to make us know the history of our family and our people. Her words were well chosen and often larger than my understanding.

I wanted to tell my mama's first cousin about Mama and Daddy's arguing but her demand for perfect speech sometimes messed my thoughts up. Also, Cousin Babs's strange symbols and use of words left me confused with more questions. Before I could decide what to say, Mama finished at the clothesline and came into the kitchen. The chance to talk was over. I went outside, as Mama would say, "to play with people my own age."

After Mama and her cousin had their private time, we ate supper without my daddy. He was 'out in the streets.' Later, before Cousin

Babs left in the evening, she sat on the couch in the living room and told this story. Everybody at home gathered around her.

"This is as far back as I can go. Pap Wilbert, as he was called, was born in slavery, around 1854 and migrated from Bluefield, Virginia. My grandmama Beulah (Grand Mu as she was affectionately called) was born after slavery around 1874. After slavery, Grand Mu came from the Edgecombe County area to Kinston. Her grandmama was half Indian. Pap Wilbert's grandmama on his father's side, Alfred Dillon, was full Indian. Any questions?"

What was slavery? I wanted to ask but when I looked around, Nora, Paul, Reba, Willie Earl and even my Mama were satisfied with just listening. I joined them as Cousin Bab continued, "Your great grandmama's parents," pointing to us children, "Wilbert and Beulah Green, met and married in Lenoir County. They had ten children. They all grew up in and around Kinston, North Carolina and they were tenant farmers. Pap Wilbert worked the land until his death. Grand Mu Beulah was the 'Colored' midwife who delivered many babies around Lenoir County."

Cousin Babs paused for a moment and then added, "Grand Mu Beulah spent many of her last days, sitting in her rocking chair, sewing quilts. She lived with Grandmama Quintilla after Pap Willie died. Grand Mu Beulah died in 1953. Pap Wallace had died years earlier."

By now, Cousin Babs was fully into her favorite subject. She kicked off her expensive red New York shoes and stood up. "In fact, all our ancestors toiled the land which they referred to as the 'Tar Hills,' from birth to death. Some were farmers, teachers, nurses, musicians, midwives, masons, attendants, cooks, soldiers, janitors, housewives, housekeepers and maids. All were called 'Colored'."

After wiping her upper lip and her forehead, Cousin Babs went on. "Your Mama's mama, Quintilla, was their oldest girl. She married Hamm Moses. They had seven children and they were tenant farmers also. Emma's mother and my daddy are sister and brother. We're cousins."

She answered my question about how she got in our family.

BREAKING THE CYCLES OF PAIN: SOUL SECRETS

The family history glued us to our seats. The annoying blare of Cousin Babs's husband car horn jarred us from the story. Cousin Babs had to stop the family history. Everybody hugged Cousin Babs goodbye and went outside to speak to Cousin Harold. My mama disappeared in the kitchen. I stayed with Cousin Babs while she put her brown leather coat back on and straightened her beige leather hat. She reached into her red pocketbook, took out a small silver box and gave it to me. She said, "This locket is for you. Happy late birthday."

"Thank you, Cousin Babs."

Mr. Tyler honked the blaring car horn again and Cousin Babs was gone. Before I went to the kitchen, I opened the box. Inside was a small, thin shiny necklace with a hanging piece of metal. Engraved with 'DAL' and a girl reading a book. *How interesting!* I wanted time with my gift before I told Mama about it. *Reba will be mad.* The thought came to me as I hid the locket under the bed. I went to the kitchen.

* * *

The kitchen was the one place where I got to know Mama better. It was the smallest room in our shotgun house. Mama had explained, "Even though our house is small, we use the kitchen for many things. Cooking, eating, bathing. Home beauty parlor for washing, straightening, curling and plaiting hair. Also, for sewing, ironing clothes and having company. We do so much in our kitchen that it must be kept clean and organized."

And a home for rats, I said to myself. Mama had just turned on the leaky gas stove. I could hear the rats scrambling to leave the heat. They would return home when the stove cooled. The baking turkey aromas and the herbs and spices from Miss Doris's garden evaporated the lingering rat pee. The gas odor was barely noticed. Mama was cooking a special dinner for tomorrow. My giant of a godmama Miss Doris was coming for Thanksgiving. Cousin Babs was thanksgiving with her husband's family.

According to Mama, "Cut'n Harold won't allow himself to darken the door or eat in any shotgun house. Even if it's his wife's cousin's house."

I felt this was a good time to ask my mama about her school years. The family history talk seemed to open Mama up. Her face was soft and glowing. The 'Colored' 'lazy speech' had disappeared. Her words, clear and exact, surprised me.

"Mama, how far did you go in school?"

She thought out loud. "I was the oldest. I had to leave school after the eighth grade to help with the harvesting. If it was a good crop, our family would get a bigger share of food and seeds for the coming year."

Mama got quiet for a while. Then she spoke again. "I loved school. I didn't want to stop learning. After I married your daddy, I continued to learn away from school. I had the *Kinston Free Press* and the *Raleigh Daily Observer* newspapers delivered to the house. Picked up *Ebony* and *Jet* magazines from the barber shop where they were sold. I guess that's why you like books and words. Reading helped me to relax and clear my head. My mama used to shush my thousands of questions. I was just like you when I was your age."

In the kitchen, Mama shared with me many ideas about the importance of living my dreams. "If you want to be a teacher, you've got to go to school and learn so you can teach. If you want to be a writer, write something every day. I'm a mama. I mama every day."

She burst out in a happy laugh. I was glad to see Mama being fun. Again, serious, she said, "Don't let boys interfere with your goals. I believe you can do it. Of all my children, you have the ability to do well in life."

Out of the blue, Mama said. "Marry someone who loves you more than you love them."

Did Mama love Daddy more than he love her? Or was Daddy in love with someone else? I didn't know anything about love, but the questions danced around in my head often.

Mama allowed me to sift the flour. "Sifting the flour helps to remove all stuff in the flour. Like rocks, rat balls and sometimes dead flies and roaches."

"Roaches?"

"Yes. Roaches. We have almost as many roaches as we have rats in this old shotgun house. That's why your daddy is always fussing about the lids being left off the flour, the cornmeal and lard buckets under the sink."

Miss Doris had introduced me to biscuit making, but I was so busy questioning her about Mama and Daddy that I didn't really get it. As Mama blended the lard and buttermilk, she explained, "Lard mixes better at room temperature."

She put a small pan of water in the oven as they baked.

"What is the water for?'

"The water will keep your baking from falling." *Falling? What's that?* I thought. *But I really don't have to know.*

Mama explained how cooking is related to life. "The ingredients are your experiences and tests. And the seeds of life that produce life. The rising agent is the spirit—the God that makes things happen. And the cake is you. You are the final product that comes through the furnace of life. It is our nature to be tried. But still, we are beautiful, beloved and bold."

Now, Mama is sounding like Daddy and Cousin Babs with what Nora called 'symbolic talking'. The only thing to do was allow these things to simmer in my mind. Soon my imagination would open me to their meanings.

I left the kitchen, having a better understanding of Mama and her family. I was glad that she had talked to me without fussing—this time just like we were equals.

The visit with Cousin Babs, who was so honest about her life, seemed to relax Mama a little. I didn't understand all that Cousin Babs nor Mama had said, but at least she got Mama talking more. And it sounded good. Being around Cousin Babs seemed to make my mama feel smarter and better about herself. After Cousin Babs's visit, my mama and I tried hard not to use the 'lazy 'Colored' alley talk'. Sometimes we slipped. But we never strayed too far. Except when we got mad and cussed. Or when we became, what Mama called, 'emotional'.

Chapter 10

I, Doris Anne Love, Am Born

How in the hell, I mean heck, did I come to this family? According to Aunt Naomi, "Your strong desire to know the truth about life was placed in you from birth." She had told me, "When you are born, your destiny is placed in your heart. You chose this family."

She never told me that the search for this meant a long, fearful, going-in-circles, crossroads, turning points journey.

I argued with her. "No way would I chose a lunatic family like this. I did not choose this path. I just followed footsteps that led me here."

To find out I went to my mother, the one who knew the most about me, but who was not quick to tell me anything. To find meaning in my life, I had to use snooping, eavesdropping and my imagination to pencil it together. My life seemed to be one long trail of incidents and mysteries.

Even my coming into the world was a strange family matter. The story was told many times in different ways. This is the version I heard in the middle of the night:

> *I woke up and my sister, Nora, was having a baby. She was twelve and I was five. The only light in the dark bedroom was the flickering light of the kerosene lamp. I had asked, "Mama, what's the matter?"*

Mama snapped, "Mind your own business! Go back to sleep!" I pretended to be asleep. But I listened as my mama and the midwife shared secrets. My mama had told the midwife, *"After I had Reba, I didn't want to have any more childr'n. After each child I would swear to myself, 'This is it! No more!' I declared to myself, 'Reba is the last one.' And I had meant it.*

When I was still nursing Reba, I woke up early one morning before Abraham went to work. Nauseous, dizzy and sweating. As I threw up in the chamber pot, Abraham asked me, '"What we going to do?"'

Both of us knew what morning sickness looked like.

I told Abraham, "I'm at the breaking point. Another child seems almost too much. Besides, where would another child sleep?"

Dizzy, I continued to throw up and sweat for most of the day. When Abraham came home, I told him, "I am going to visit Naomi. You know that your sister assist women with female troubles. This's a real female problem!"

I burst out in tears.

Before I could carry out my plans to visit Naomi, I felt the quickening of the new life inside me. I felt renewed. My herb and roots plan evaporated as the baby leaped in my womb. Remember in the Bible how the baby leaped in Mary's cousin's 'Lizabeth's womb when Mary went to visit 'Lizabeth?

Miss Levira, at first, I didn't tell Abraham 'cause I didn't want him to change my mind. I didn't want to hear him say, '"What about how tired you always say you are? What about we don't have enough room already? What about my small income? And so on and so on and on."'

So, I didn't bring it up. I confessed. "Yes. I'm still pregnant."

"And you think I don't know?"

Also, I didn't want to admit to Abraham that this pregnancy was more than I had imagined. For it was the most trying ever. The developing baby seemed to be restless and I was always hungry. Mama had said, '"You eat like you're feeding three, instead of two."'

When Little Doris was born, a second child came out a few minutes later. Another stillborn. I had one more live birth before the baby-making machine shut down.

I'm not sure I didn't really want more children. It's just that the sorrow that comes when you lose a child is so haunting. I never forgot those children. The midwife agreed, "Something happens to the spirit of women who have lost a baby during birth. It can cause deep depression and sadness."

Sometimes, I think Little Doris's still connected to her twin that died when she was born. She is a strange child, determined and old beyond her years."

I was shocked, but I made Little Doris remain silent and still in the dark. As silent and as unmoving, as my dead twin.

Hearing this made me want to know even more about my beginning. Earlier when I had snooped in the dresser drawer and saw Timothy Earl's picture, a stack of birth certificates fell out of a large envelope. I could read well enough to recognize my name 'Doris Anne Love' on one of the certificates. It showed that I was born in Kinston, North Carolina on November 15, 1944 at 204 Love Street. A midwife, Miss Levira, had signed her name for the home birth. She didn't write down the time of my birth. The exact time of my birth was left blank. *Why?*

After seeing my birth certificate and knowing I was almost not born, I wanted to know more about the mystery of me. I was willing to suffer Mama's sharp tongue. Liked my sister Reba had said, "If you get what you want, the pain is worth it."

I decided to try Reba's way. Even though I knew Mama had been a little depressed and withdrawn lately, I didn't delay.

* * *

It was a sunny spring school day. A Monday. Mama's wash day. The stay-at-homers spent part of every day in the yard. Like the kitchen, the yard was a school, a meeting place and an escape from troubles. Willie Earl was playing with his slingshot. Mama had taken a break from washing clothes. I was following her around, as usual. She sat on the front porch swing and picked up a book. *Ask her right now. Don't wait* ran through my mind until I blurted out, "Mama, the day I saw Timothy's picture, I also saw all of our birth certificates. Everybody's had the time they were born except mine. Why?"

Mama looked at me and slowly shook her head. "Lordy! Lordy! Lordy! Lord ha' mercy! Where did this child come from?"

As if she was asking God, she raised her head toward the sky and threw her arms upward. Her hands spread out like she would catch the answer when it fell from heaven.

Time was suspended as I waited for my tongue lashing. Which never came. "Anyway, what difference does it make?" Mama gave in. "I just started my break anyway. I will tell you what happened. But under one condition. You cannot interrupt me with any questions.

"I can't even ask one thing?" *This would be a test.*

"Not one. I know some things that I say will be hard for you to understand, but you're always asking hard questions. Nora and I can explain some things later. I know you know about stuff you shouldn't know anyway. You're so interested in everything. Take some weight off your feet and sit down."

I wanted to know, so I agreed. I knew it would be hard not to interrupt. "Okay, Mama, I promise. I won't say a word."

Like my daddy, my mama had a way of telling everything like a story. Mama re-called:

"Shortly after Abraham left for work that morning, I felt a gnawing familiar pain at the bottom of my stomach. Paul, who loved school, had left already. I told Nora, the fashion plate, 'Get out of that mirror! You're going to be late. Knock on Miss Hamm's door and tell her I think it's time. Take Reba to Miss Hamm. She will know what to do.

"As I returned from the toilet, I put more wood in the kitchen stove that had four legs. I had argued with Abraham when I first saw the stove. "You know we can't afford an expensive stove like this."

"'I know it cost a lot, but it heats the whole house,' Abraham had said.

"The cast iron wood stove had room to hold four pots, a reservoir for heating and holding hot water, a large oven and a small food warmer. The grand stove added style to the kitchen. When the stove was loaded with wood, it heated the whole house. I sat down at the kitchen table to wait for Miss Hamm. It seemed like my stomach and the large, expensive wood stove had swallowed up all the space in the midget kitchen. I talked to myself to reassure me. *We already have our plan worked out. I know she will be over in a minute.* The time felt close. I was constantly going to the toilet out on the back porch. The bed chamber pot was too low for me to place my big awkward body on.

"I changed the radio from the early morning spirituals to get the weather forecast. After the static left the radio, the announcer's voice came in. 'The sky above Kinston is birthing a brooding tropical rainstorm from a distant port. From behind dark clouds, cold bitter rain is beginning to pour over the coastal towns and cities. The hard rain reminds us of the 'Great Atlantic hurricane' in September from which the city is still recovering. Stay tuned for a possible hurricane watch or a rainy-day early school dismissal.

"The weather forecast was right. The rain that beat down on our tin rooftop that fall morning sounded like popcorn dropped in hot grease. Lightning whipped across the sky like a match lit in darkness. A rolling thunder bolt rocked the house and my nerves. The howling wind whirled like it would lift the houses and slam them against the train hurrying down Love Street.

"The clock on the front of the radio read '9:05'. I asked myself, *Where are they?* The weather report did not calm me down. I turned back to the spiritual music program, but it had signed off. I decided to turn the radio off. Thunder rocked the small kitchen like the giant foot of God has stepped on it! I turned the radio back on so the music would drown out sounds of the raging storm. I could barely hear the distant radio announcer from Nashville. "Now I will play for our radio audience who is listening out there, "Into Each Life Some Rain Must Fall" by the Inkspots and Ella Fitzgerald.

"'Into each life some rain must fall, But too much is fallin' in mine...'

"I smiled and turned the radio up louder.

I listened to the radio and continued to stare out the window as the rainstorm grew. I realized it was now hailing.

"Instead of the swollen raindrops earlier, the sky was spitting out crystal-clear frozen rain marbles.

"As they hit, they left broken flowers, shredded leaves and crushed grass.

"All of a sudden, I felt an uncontrollable urge to pee. I stood up to get my jacket off the chair, to make my way to the outside toile' again. A bucket of slim', warm water rolled down my legs, into my shoes and across the kitchen floor. My next-door neighbor Miss Hamm, my midwife, Miss Levira and I collided at the back door. They were drenched from the rainstorm. I was wading in pee and pre-childbirth fluids.

"Like Mama would say, 'Seeing Miss Levira and Miss Hamm at this crucial time was a good sight for a sore eye!'

"'What's going on here?'" asked the midwife.

"Just seeing my two helpers who were my friends and neighbors relieved my anxious mind. Miss Hawkins, my midwife for all my previous births, had retired. Miss Hamm had found me a new midwife Miss Levira. Miss Hamm, a half Cherokee Indian, her 'Colored' lumberjack husband and their eight children, lived next door. Miss Levira was a tall pecan tan, middle age nurse, with short cocklebur hair that stuck out from her nursing hat. She had a permit from the County Health Department to deliver babies at home.

"When we first met, Miss Levira had explained her occupation to me. 'Prejudice against women, farm workers, 'Colored' people and poor white people give the work of the midwife a low-class position.

"I told her, 'Catching babies' is an honorable profession. My great-grand mama, my grandmama and my mama were midwives. To heck with what people think.'

"Although Miss Hamm wasn't a midwife, she assisted families in other ways. She would organize the house, cook supper, and manage the children as the women regained their strength from childbirth. Neighborhood women did this for each other as we recovered from childbirth.'

"I said to my rescue team, 'I had to use the toilet. But the baby decided it wants to be part of this stormy Wednesday action.' I knew that the breaking of the water sac that held the baby meant I was in the first stage of labor. Despite the growing pain, I was beaming when I saw the midwife. Little Doris, there are several stages of childbirth."

I did have a question at that point, but I was able to keep it to myself. I could see that Mama was really getting into the telling.

"Miss Hamm and the midwife guided me to the living room which was also our bedroom. I eased down on the sagging couch in the corner as a sharp pain zigzagged up my back. When I saw them turning the sofa bed back into the sleeping bed, I told Miss Levira, 'There's a rubber sheet, clean bed sheets and receiving blankets for the newborn on the small couch in the corner.'

"The midwife helped me to get in bed, gave me a bed bath and placed me in the right beginning position. Legs up and parted. Then she asked, 'Miss Hamm, would you check to make sure that there are two large pots of water on the stove boiling?'

Another scene of boiling water flashed through my mind.

"Miss Levira prepared herself for delivery by putting on a clean white gown, a white hair net, her white nursing cap and a white mask.

"When Miss Hamm came back into the room, she was now wearing her clean white assistant clothes. Miss Levira and her assistant began a complete cleaning process to reduce infection in me and the newborn. She told her assistant, 'I use Lysol, alcohol and vinegar to clean all wood and glass surfaces. After a full wipe down, they scrubbed their hands and arms and put on some white rubber gloves. The midwife opened her deliver' bag and laid her supplies and tools on the sanitized bureau dresser top.

Mama mentioning the Lysol brought back the night in the dark with Nora. The memory of the smothering fumes from the Lysol made it difficult for me to follow the story. At least I knew what having a baby meant.

"Then Miss Levira reminded me, 'When a pain comes, Emma, breathe through the pain. That's why it's called labor.'

"After I caught my breath from a hard spasm, I moaned.

"Miss Levira said, 'Giving birth works the baby, and the mama and the midwife. A midwife is the person who works between God, nature and women to bring forth life.

"'Midwives provide one of the most important services in the world. I come from a line of midwives and birth assistants. My daughter Ellen is a registered nurse in the Women Army Corps. When she comes out of the service, she is going to midwifery school. It's hard to say that word. Ellen wants to be a licensed midwife.'"

'Midwifey school?' I had to remind myself. No interruptions. No questions.

Miss Levira got quiet. At the same time, both of us checked the large wall clock that was hanging over the bed. It showed 9:15. *Wrong time.* The midwife closed her eyes. After a while, the midwife asked in the silent bedroom, "'Are you okay?'"

"There'd been no contractions for a while. I relaxed in the empty space, where the pain left me weak and worn-out. "I'm okay."

"'Midwives provided important pregnancy care that the while segregated medical system begrudged the 'Colored' people. The respectful position of the midwife goes back to African traditions. Our ancestors brought the African knowledge of herbs and how to bring forth children with them from Africa.' The midwife had finished her story and sat back in her chair.

"Then remembering the stopped clock, Miss Levira spoke out, 'Miss Hamm, please change the music station to the weather station on the radio and set the radio clock. The wall clock isn't working. I want to hear the weather. Let me know what time it's getting to be also.'

"Miss Levira almost jumped out of her chair and her daydream when I screamed, 'I think I feel the head!'

"The second stage had begun! Where's your notebook, Doris? Just playing. No need to answer.

But what is a contraction? I needed Nora who is not here. I listened as Mama went on with the story.

"In the next hour, the hurricane watch closed school at noon. The school children were home before 1:00. Miss Hamm had told the children, 'The time has come for your mama. Change your wet clothes and go next door. Your little sister Reba is already there with my sister. My daughter, Velma, will fix you something to eat.'

"'Praise Jesus! I got here in time! It is 1:30.' Your Grandmama Quintilla announced her arrival just after the school children were ushered next door. She stepped from the tiny porch into the tiny front room/bedroom just as I let out a wail.

"The storm came howling in with her. Trays, bottles and the chamber pot rattled around, but everything remained it its upright position.

"Your grandmama was fully prepared for the rain. Her rain gear included a long purple and green raincoat with a matching rain hat, purple galoshes, and a purple and green umbrella that the wind had turned inside out. Mama was a Baptist pastor's wife, a missionary, the mother of seven children, a retired midwife and recently a prophetess and an astrologist.

Um. Two more words I had never heard.

"Mama answered. 'You can't have your cake and eat it too.' Then she began to quote her favorite scripture in a loud, high missionary voice. 'To everything there is a season, and a time to every purpose under the heaven. A time to be born, and a time to die; A time to plant, and a time to pluck up that which is planted.' Her message calmed me.

"Although Mama was soaked, nothing could rain on her life. Rambling though her overnight bag, she found her birthing clothes, changed into them and then turned to me. 'How's we be doing?'

"To make me laugh and forget the increasing discomfort, your grandmama mixed her role of prophetess and astrologist. Mama had told me earlier; a prophetess tells the future, and an astrologist tells the present by using the past and the future. They use signs from nature and God to help people. She believes many things that your Aunt Naomi teaches. Then Mama said something crazy like, 'The devil is beating his wife, there is a rainbow in the cloudy sky, and the Adkin River its flooding its bank. Everything in creation has lined up to support this birth.'

"'Doris, that meant a divine event was taking place in the Love household.'

"The midwife told me, 'Push!' I pushed and I groaned. I groaned and I pushed.

"Mama joined the midwife. 'Emma, push again! There is no power in hell that can stop a baby who is ready to be born!'

"Doris, a contraction is a pain which jumps on you and beats you up. It leaves you when it gets tired. They followed each other, like chicks in a row, following their mama. Like all y'all needing something at the same time from me.

"Then, Miss Levira said, 'This's it. Don't push!' I held my breath as the midwife caught the baby, who popped out from my private part. You were gooey. Sticky and bloody.

"On the alert for any problem, your Grandmama Quintilla whispered, 'There is a thin piece of skin covering her face.'

"The midwife looked shocked! She squinted her eyes, quickly snipped two small holes for the nose and one for the mouth so you could breathe. Then she slowly peeled the thin film from your face to avoid any damage. Screaming a loud protest, you started to breathe. As you cried, Miss Levira held you upside down to drain mucus from your mouth and nose. You, the newborn baby, squirmed and squealed! The midwife told the baby, 'Good lungs.' She added some drops in your eyes to prevent infection.

"Miss Levira explained that doctors call the skin that was on your face a *caul,* but your grandmama called it a *veil.* Mama thinks it is a sign of good luck. Soon another unbreathing baby came out of my privates. All of us were shocked!

I was not. Knowing about the dead baby had led me to this point. But this was when I wanted to forget my promise. But I decided to stay quiet so I could hear it to the end.

"Abraham came home in the evening, supper was ready and an eight pounds, three ounces girl, you, Doris Anne Love had been added to the family. When your daddy asked what time were you born, the midwife told him, 'The storm turned off the radio and the wall clock. About 10:30.'

"This telling is as close as I can remember. It didn't matter that I had given birth many times. Your birth, Little Doris, was just as painful as the first. The baby was not easy and usual. The child continues to be strange."

Mama looked at me and laughed. I laughed too.

I knew when the story was over. I stood up and stretched my arms and legs. Mama was tired of talking and was about to go into her silence. Before Mama left to finish washing the colored clothes, she touched me on my arm. For some reason, Mama never touched us. "Nora can help explain some things you didn't quite get. But, Doris, you did a good job in not interrupting me. I didn't think you could do it."

I didn't either. Sitting in the silence and keeping my mouth shut was a hard thing to do. But when I saw Mama lose herself in the telling of it, I made myself be quiet. Yet, when Mama went outside to finish her washing, my mind wondered about my nameless, dead twin.

PART III.
LIFE MOVING FORWARD

Chapter 11

Stages of Child-Tending

My clearest memory from my childhood took place sometime when I was two years old. One afternoon Mama fed me a small snack and put me down for a nap. Each day when Paul came home from school, Mama made him study his ABC's and numbers. I soon woke from the nap that I hadn't wanted to take. I could hear my brother studying his schoolwork. Over and over, counting numbers and saying his ABC's. To stay awake, I started to practice counting from one to ten and then started over. I also created words with the letters without knowing the spelling rules.

I played these games to occupy my time when I was bored and to delay sleep. One day when I still a little awake, I held my eyes open with my fingers, and I looked into the mirror in the corner. I was floating in a pool of warm, cloudy water. A strange, but a family-feeling form surfaced and floated next to me. The eyeless unmouthed form said, "Can I go with you and be your friend?"

I said, "Yes. Please come." Then I asked the floating form, "What's your name?"

The strange form echoed, "Rabbit."

"Rabbit! That's a name my daddy calls me! Who're you? Where you from?"

Rabbit mouthed, "I am your twin that was with you in the beginning. I never got a chance to live. I can help you. Can I live through you?"

The mirror allowed for all things. I said, "Yes."

My hands became numb and fell to my side. And my eyes blurred as I fought to stay awake and look in the door mirror. Then, my eyes closed. I fell into a deep, dreamless sleep. When I woke up, I was surprised and pleased that I could count forward and backward to ten! Most of all I wanted to know the twin I had met in the mirror.

* * *

One day around the time when I was three, I was playing on the couch with my corncob doll. I heard Mama say, "Miss Doris, the old folks used to say, 'When a woman is going to have a baby, the first nine months, the baby's in the 'nest'. After the child is born, it's in the 'nursing stage' for one to two years. Then, it becomes a 'lap' baby. Doris is a 'lap' baby right now. I guess Willie Earl's birth will throw Doris out of 'my lap!'"

Mama and the big mama form laughed.

I got quiet so I could hear better. "Little Doris is going to be assigned to Nora. The new baby have been sleepin' in the top dresser drawer of the bureau in the corner. He barel' cries. Just whimpers when he is wet or hungr'. I was goin' to brin' him to the bed with me sometimes. Now that Mr. Eugene final' got Timothy Earl's old carved crib out of the shed and fixed it. Abraham said, 'No more babies in the bed. It's his time to be the baby!'"

They both laughed again.

A new baby! When did a new baby come? I was shock! I knew the word 'baby'. Mama had told me I was 'the baby'. I didn't understand all the talk, but my ears were alert to the word 'Doris'. I knew it referred to me. Now Mama was calling this lady 'Miss Doris'. The lady always told me, "Little Doris, I love you so much."

I was glad to know that Mama's friend Miss Big Doris was connected to me, Little Doris.

Miss Big Doris asked, "Do you think this may affect Little Doris? I love my godchild and I'm concerned about her. She's already a little different from most other children. She'll only allow you to feed her or change her clothing, without crying. Her colic shows her temperamental nature. It may bother her, not having more personal time with you."

"I know, but the midwife told me that Willie Earl is so small and fragile, he needs extra attention."

I began to understand later that night when my mama took me to the bed where my two sisters slept.

"Nora, I need for you to help me a little more with Doris. You can watch out for her when you come home from school and on the weekends. But Willie Earl needs a lot of my attention and care."

That night Nora put me in the middle between her and Reba. I started my worrisome cry. Nora called out to Mama, "Doris keeps on scooting done to the foot of the bed. Plus, she won't stop crying."

Mama came in and took me from under the covers that were smothering me. She asked me, "What do you want?" Over and over again. I finally pointed to the small, cracked mirror on the little table next to the end of the bed. Mama understood. She lifted the covers and tucked me in, at the foot of the bed, in the middle between my sisters' feet. "Doris likes to look in mirrors. This way she can see Abraham's old shaving mirror that he cracked."

Just before Mama turned the light off, Nora said, "A broken mirror means bad luck."

I was now okay. Rabbit was sleeping at the bottom of the bed with me. In the dark, Rabbit gurgled in a strange language. For some unknown reason, I understood the odd, mixed up sounds. "A broken mirror. Bad luck." Nora had said the same thing.

I asked my twin, "How can I get good luck?" *How did I know to ask this?* The same way I knew not to mention Rabbit to my mama. The same way I understood the conversation with a mouthless strange form. Some things I just knew.

In the same unusual language, Rabbit answered, "Go to the river."

Grandmama had always said going to the river would wash your troubles away.

The next morning, I wrapped the cracked mirror in an old raggedy towel and put my project in the back of the closet. To wait for more words, understanding and direction. I spent most days in the front room, sitting on the couch, staring into Mama's mirror. I prayed for a mirror of my own. Then I noticed Willie Earl's new bed, the crib with the carved butterflies and hopping rabbits. The antique mirror on the door and now the antique carved crib near the window added a little specialness to our shotgun house.

Sometimes I felt a sharp aloneness as I continued to cling to my mama's skirt tail. I was barely four and was not quite up to my mama's knees. But I still entered the 'knee baby' period, ages 3-4 before I was ready. This was my next stage after I was thrown off the 'lap'. I had not spent enough time in her lap or at her breast. I felt like I had been abandoned, again. But remembering that my twin Rabbit was around somewhere eased the lap need.

During my early childhood, I did not have the words to express all these things, feelings and thoughts. But my eyes and ears were quick to see and hear. As a young child I thought these voices were just part of my mind. By the time I had begun to talk and gather more words, a lot of those shadows, sounds and daydreams took on faces and events. I hid all these experiences away in my memory and was able to dig them up, at any necessary moment. As I grew up, the mirror continued to connect me with my twin, my memory and my lively thinking. Later, I discovered that my lively thinking was another word for 'imagination'.

Chapter 12

My Kindergarten

When I met Rabbit, I realized that I knew this form. We had floated in our mama's stomach together before we came to earth. I was sad for my twin sister. Rabbit had died shortly after being born. 'Rabbit' was the first name the daddy form had called me. I was shocked after I met Rabbit. *Did he hear me talking to Rabbit or calling her name? No one knew but me.* For a long time, I didn't have the words nor the courage to tell Mama about meeting my twin.

One day I was sitting in the corner with Reba's old coloring book, looking at the pictures she had colored. I heard my mama asked my daddy, "Why do you call her that, Abraham?"

"Just like rabbits grow quickly, she is growing up fast as wild grass. She prefers vegetables, likes to be alone and is very quiet and secretive. That child uses full sentences and words that adults use! She's only four, but she acts so much older. One day Little Doris asked me if I was her daddy. I was shocked! Acts like she's been around this way before. Even seen her talking to someone in the mirror. Did you know she watches everything that we do? Plus, she is as quick as lightning, and as smart as a teacher."

"But Rabbit is the name of an animal!"

"But you have to admit she is a strange creature! I also call her Rabbit to remind me I have either fathered a genius or a retard."

He went into a whisper on the word 'retard' when he realized I was sitting in the corner, listening. "See, this is exactly what I mean."

Pointing to me, he said, "She's always around peeping and listening in on our business."

Again, he whispered, "She's so nosy. She even sniffles her nose, just like a rabbit. Besides, you have to admit, she has big front teeth."

Mama, upset about what my daddy was saying about me, threw the sheets on her dirty clothes pile as she changed the bed. "Doris's a pretty child. Got her eyes, nose and teeth from you, Mr. Wolf."

Then she burst out laughing. And Daddy joined her, his big white teeth, shining like new moons. Since they knew by now I was listening, I laughed too. But I was laughing at Daddy.

Being as quick as lightning, I had caught his word. Later, when I found out what 'retarded' meant, I knew I was not a retard. Not only was I his smartest and fastest child, but I had his large brown eyes, his sniffling nose and his large front chopping teeth.

In the first four years in the shotgun house in front of the train tracks, my mama, daddy and family had spoken for me. When I cried, Mama would say, "The baby is hungry." If I let loose a string of poots, my daddy would say, "Doris's diaper needs changing."

Sometimes others speaking for me worked. My diaper was changed and I was fed. When it didn't work, I was fed when I wasn't hungry. My diaper was changed before I had finished boo booing. They tried to talk for me. But often failed.

As I began to talk and discover words, I realized the importance of words. Words helped me to express my ideas and thoughts. Using words made it possible for me to talk to others. Most of all, words gave me a way to speak for myself. Knowing how to talk was good. I remained frustrated because I still couldn't express myself fully. I wanted to be picked up and hugged more, but I wanted my mama to know these things. She was supposed to know. She was the mama. Just as I had decided to trust that the world was a safe place, I decided to trust the voice that brought me wisdom and comfort. Also, Rabbit's voice became a trusted guide as I grew up.

* * *

When I turned five, I noticed the coming and going of the day and night, the rising of the sun and the setting of the moon.

I saw that every day my daddy, Paul, Nora, and Reba left the house early in the morning and came back before it got dark. During the day, Mama, the baby Willie Earl and I were left at home. In the morning, it seemed that Mama threw dirty clothes, uncooked food and needy children up in the air. By 12:00, clothes were scrubbed, rinsed and hung out on the clothesline to dry. Food for supper was simmering on the stove. And Mama's no-school children were situated for the long, boring day.

After having tea parties with my imaginary play guests and listening to 'grown folk talk', I wanted to go, also. A feeling of freedom and possibility made me desire a change in my daily life. *Where?* I did not know, but somewhere beyond the shotgun house, my peeing brother and my busy, but always sad-face mama.

On a slow dull Monday morning, while the white clothes were boiling in the washing pot outside and collards greens and ham hocks were simmering on the stove, Mama said to no one, "I'm plum' tired!" She's flopped down in a chair at the kitchen table and picked up some thin sheets of paper. I saw another side of her. I jumped with joy the day I discovered that my mama did other things outside of cooking, cleaning and washing.

I had asked my mama, "What you doing?"

Mama continued to look at a large piece of paper that flapped over until she folded it in half. "I am reading some old copies of the *Kinston Free Press* and the *Baltimore Afro-American* newspaper."

She answered with her head buried in the large, limpy, dull white paper. Looked like two long sheets of rough-dried beige white paper.

"Why do you do this?'

"I want to know what is going on in my town and the world. So, I read to find out.'"

"I want to know too. How do you read?"

"You use the ABC's. I see you are already studying them. I'll ask Nora to help you."

Would reading help me to understand my family better? I didn't dare ask Mama that. By now I had learned this was an area forbidden to children. Family business meant grown folks' business.

"Mama," I begged, "Please read one of the stories out loud."

She agreed and picked up a paper. "The headlines from January 30. 1948 states: Mahatma Ghandi was assassinated by a Hindi fanatic."

When she finished the article, the tossed aside newspaper got my attention. I looked to see if I could find what she had read. When I found it, I asked, "Ma, what does it mean?" I was pointing to the words 'Ghandi' and 'fanatic'.

Mama answered, "It means some crazy man shot the leader of the people in India, a country far away."

My best part of the day was when Nora got home from school. As soon as Nora stepped up on the porch, I met her at the door. "Nora, can we read now?"

"Wait until I get settled. First, I have to see if Mama needs some help in the kitchen."

I had been assigned to my oldest sister and I knew I was getting on her nerves. I followed her around, like a shadow, anytime she was home.

Later, we sat on the front porch to practice my reading. Nora said, "When you turned five and missed school, Mama could have enrolled you in kindergarten."

"What's 'kintargardin'?"

"Kindergarten is a school before the first grade. Four-year-olds can go to a school called a 'nursery'. Five-year-olds can go to a kindergarten. Both schools help preschoolers get ready for school, but they do cost money. I think she didn't because it's not free like public school is."

"Nora, since we don't have money to send me to a nursery or kintargardin, would you help get me ready for school? Like they do in kintargardin?"

"I will read with you one hour every day. But promise you won't tell Mama that I sit with my boyfriend when we go to the movies. Do you have your word list? What is our word for today?"

"Kintargardin."

Slowly, Nora spelled the word for me. "*Kindergarten.*

This is the word. The thing. The form I wished I had a name for earlier. Of course, I knew not to mention kindergarten to Mama. I had received too many scoldings, pinchings and eye-rollings from Mama already for asking too many questions. I just rolled my daddy's big brown eyes and pouted Mama's moon lips. Stomped my feet and walked away to find the answers in my little life. Often unattended and alone, I wandered throughout the house, in the yard and to neighbors' houses. I was determined to see one day what lay beyond the street we lived on. I continued to look-read at anything printed—old church books, a worn, coverless dictionary and used fish market newspaper wrappings for signs and answers.

One day I had heard our neighbor Miss Hill and Mama talking in the backyard. Both were hanging clothes on the clothesline. Miss Hill told Mama, "I clean house for a rich White family who live up the hill. Miss Murray's husband is a principal of a school. They give me books and magazines for my children to read."

After hearing this, I visited the Hills while rambling through the neighborhood. Their woodshed was crowded with old books. After snooping in the woodshed, I knocked on Miss Hill's door. "Can I have some of the books on the ground in the shed?"

"And what you going to do with those old, faded books? My boss's children had already read them, and my children usually are Not interested in them.

"I like to look at the words and pictures. I'm learning how to read."

"Strange. Other than Ronald, my children want to play with dolls, skates, jumping ropes or cowboy guns. And you wanna learn to read. You can have as many as you can carry home."

Adult did this kind of talking out loud to themselves a lot. Since she wasn't talking to me, I didn't say anything.

I turned to go down the steps to the back. Miss Hill called out, "Doris, the next time you ask your Mama if you can come over to my house. You hear me?"

Again, I didn't answer.

BREAKING THE CYCLES OF PAIN: SOUL SECRETS

Even though we couldn't live in their White neighborhood, I was so glad their books could live in ours. I couldn't read, but I often picked a book that had a mysterious picture on the cover. Like the one with a little girl with strange objects, *The Wonderful Wizard of Oz*. Or the book that had a rabbit on the front because 'Rabbit' was my nickname. *The Velveteen Rabbit*. Other titles were *Gulliver's Travels*, *Tom Sawyer*, and *Charlotte's Web*. Nora would read my collected books later with me. After the visit with my neighbor, I discovered my best friends—reading and writing, who became my other secret twins.

Even before I knew how to read well, stories took me on a magic carpet ride. The words magically revealed themselves as keepers of stories and secrets. The characters became alive. I could hear and feel their actions and thoughts. When I read books alone, I rewrote the books in my mind, gave new names, different situations and strange places to the stories. I could rely on books to give me some comfort and temporary escape from the sense of being alone. Spending hours in books eased some of my fears about life. I felt sure that reading would give meaning, order and understanding to my life. *How did I know this?* I just knew.

At the same time, I was reading without rules, I decided I had to write books as well as read them. Before I had written one story, I had already created hundreds. I got caught up in the creative power of writing. Writing got my attention the first time I scratched across a piece of paper. The soothing sounds of the pencil formed calming words, like 'aaooh', 'mucve' and 'xzoesa'. This time, I was writing without rules. What started as a desire to know grew into what Mama called my 'obsessions'. Reading and writing. Aunt Naomi used the word, 'passion'. I wrote both words in my word dictionary for Nora to explain.

* * *

Saturday was my favorite day because this was the day I walked with my Mama and Nora uptown and downtown. Early one hot morning in July, Mama had told me, "I have to go uptown to pay some bills. Do you want to go with me or with Reba? She's going over to Miss Hill's to play with her children until I get back."

Mama was smiling. She already knew the answer.

I was ready in a minute. "Can I carry my schoolbag that Miss Doris gave me for my birthday?"

As soon as we stepped on the sidewalk, I felt like a bird freed from a cage. Cars were rolling down the street, blasting their horns. Older children were roller skating on the sidewalk. People were walking back and forth and passing each other with a polite, "Good morning. How you doing?" There was so much activity, and I was finally a part of it.

I walked behind so I could pick up reading material without being seen. I saw a paper stapled to a telegram pole three houses from our house. "Nora, what is this piece of paper saying?" I whispered because my Mama was always fussing about me bringing junk into the house. Cigarette packs, tin cans and wet things that people threw away were strictly forbidden.

"Dance, date, band." Nora quickly summarized the meaning of the paper. She pointed out the pictures of the dancing people and the band. "This paper's an old flyer. It let people know that a party on Sugar Hill was taking place on June 19. Sugar Hill is downtown where the 'Colored' people run shops and own businesses."

As we passed the 'Colored' barbershop, I slipped a thin, small book which was laying on the steps into my bag. My mama was busy speaking to our neighbors as we walked. "Good morning, Brother James", a barber sweeping the sidewalk. The barbershop was a block from our house. I then picked up a sale paper in front of the neighborhood grocery/fish market store which was two blocks away from our house.

Mr. Brown came out of his store and greeted my Mama, "How you and your family doing, Emma? We got some fine spot fish on sale today."

"Fair to middling. Much obliged. I'll see you on the way back."

For some reason Mama barely looked at him, but this was none of my nosy business. Soon we were uptown where the streets and stores were filled with 'Colored' and White people shopping, looking and buying. My mama went in Rose's Department Store to pay on her layaway. Nora and I sat down on a bench in front of the store. I showed Nora my finds. Pointing to the small book, Nora said, "This is a *Jet* magazine. Mama buys them from the barbershop. We like *Jet* because 'Colored' people's in it."

"Will you read some of it with me while we wait for my mama?"

Nora started to read an article, "'Colored' family run out of town in Arkansas."

"I don't like the sound of that one. Read something else."

"Klu Klux Klans killing Negroes is on the rise."

"What is that? No. Find something not mean."

It seemed like 'Colored' people were not liked anywhere. Nora tried a few more articles and I continued to say, "No." I put the small magazine back in my book bag.

Nora said, "Sis, I am tired. And hungry. My eggs and grits are long gone. Let's go ask Mama if we can have a hot dog. Rose's hotdogs are better than Woolworth's."

That's why I like being with Nora. She knew when it was time to do something else.

We found my Mama in the store, standing in the front of the line with some household stuff she wanted to buy. The clerk's plain face and simple clothes were no match for Mama's noticeable beauty and dignified style. A White lady came up to the front of the line. The mean-faced clerk turned to the second customer and with a big smile, asked her, "May I help you?"

Then it happened again and again. Mama remained silent, but her eyes snapped fire. Nora and I walked up to Mama and each stood on a side. I waited for my mama or Nora to say something. My mama gave us the 'Don't-say- a-word-'eye' and finally said, "Ma'am, I have been waiting for a while. It's my term next."

The determined sound of Mama's high-pitched voice scared the pale unavailable clerk. When she looked in my Mama's flashing eyes, her whole manner changed. "Look, lady. My supervisor reminds us every day to serve the White people first. Regardless of how long the 'Colored' ones' been waiting."

Mama said, "I come to this store a lot. Today I came to pay down on my layaway. I guess I'd better find me somewhere else to shop."

Mama was mad enough to leave, but her organized life didn't allow such 'tomfoolery'. 'Tomfoolery' described what Mama and Daddy called my 'forever questioning and snooping into other people's business. "'Such behavior is a waste of folks' time'", they would say. I knew my mama was not going to allow anger from ignorant White people throw her off her path.

I was so glad when Mama used her words calmly and wisely. Smiles came over Nora's face and mine as our mama demanded her rights. Mama took her money sack out of her big pocketbook and asked the surprised clerk, "How much do I owe you for four baking pans, six large stirring spoons, this coloring book, the jumbo crayon set and the two pair of bobby sox?"

My mama was ready to be served and ready to go. Eyeballing the nervous clerk, Mama paid on her layaway, bought her items and gathered her shopping bags. Then she announced, "Let's go to Woolworth's. Their hotdogs are juicier."

By now all of us were starving. As soon as we got to Woolworth's, I rushed to the beautiful cushiony counter. Mama grabbed my hand and reminded me, "Remember, this is just like the bus station. She pointed to signs everywhere. 'Colored'. 'White Only'. 'White Restroom'. You can't drink, eat, sit or use the restroom in the 'White' sections." The hot dogs may have been juicier, but Mama must have forgotten that 'Colored' people couldn't sit at the counter to eat them.

"Well, where is the 'Colored' section?" Nora and I asked at the same time. We quickly crossed our right little fingers together so our good luck would come quickly. We needed it to fall on us right then.

"There is no 'Colored' counter. So, we have to stand up and eat." Mama kept her head down, looking ashamed like she had done something wrong. The only thing Mama had done wrong was to decide to eat at Woolworth's.

Nora, who was really getting upset, threw out, "The counter can hold fifteen people! There are only five White people sitting down eating. It's not fair and it show don't make sense."

Another White clerk, standing at the end of counter toward the back door, called to my mama, "Ma'am, we serve 'Colored' people down here."

She was pointing to a sign that Nora read out loud for my benefit, 'Colored Service Line'. I had already slipped one of the Woolworth's menus into my bag before Mama had snatched me up from the counter. As for me, I was ready to go too.

Mama snapped. "I have been knowing this all my life! Unfortunately, today I have to explain the same thing to my children. I pray they don't have to say it to theirs!" Disgusted at the practice, Mama shouted at the frightened worker, "To hell with your piss ass hot dogs, anyway."

She turned to us and announced, "Let's go downtown to Sugar Hill and gets some Jack's barbecue. There you can sit down with your family and friends and have barbecue, chicken, fish, hamburgers or real barbecued hot dogs."

Jack's was crowded with Saturday shoppers. This time the 'Coloreds' were sitting at the counters and tables eating. White people were lined up in the front waiting to pick up their 'Colored' food to take to their white houses and eat with their White families. They didn't like us, but they loved our food.

As we ate our dripping, chopped barbecue sandwich, we were as happy, like Daddy would say, "As a pig wallowing in slop." Mama suggested, "Use that napkin to keep the vinegary, peppery sauce from splattering on your clothes."

The napkin had a picture of a pig on a chopping block, standing near a pile of burning wood. But no words. No need to take home. I did as Mama said.

When we got home, I carefully sorted my finds and folded them away in a box behind the clothes in the closet. This was the same place I hid the broken mirror until we moved. Only the rats and I knew this location. I would study my papers more thoroughly with Nora who was helping me read. Reading had replaced my earlier secretive favorite pastimes of sucking my two fingers and looking in the mirror all day.

* * *

I had an uncontrollable desire to go to school. It was an itch that only school could scratch. Sometimes a mean voice would tell me, *God ain't stud'ing about a poor little 'Colored' girl who asks too many questions!* I rubbed on my necklace with the little girl reading that Cousin Babs had given me and whispered, *I don't believe it. Jesus loves me.*

My mama called the fifth stage of child-tending before school starts 'wanderlust' (4-5). My mother's word 'wanderlust' meant just about the same thing as kindergarten. She believed children around this age were curious about life and learning.

My 'wanderlust' stage was prolonged when I didn't go to school. When my mama explained to me about her names for the stages of tending children, she told me, "'When I think of this period of child raising, I think of you. When I left you for Nora to watch, you became a wild weed. Once, you were over at the neighbors' house by yourself. When I went to get you, I asked you, "Where's your sister?"

"You barely looked my way. You mumbled, 'I don't know, and I don't care' and continued looking through a book. I knew you had an early interest in reading and knowing about things. I realized that my baby was growing up. You should have gone to school last year. Or maybe even the year before."

The delayed 'wanderlust stage', the fifth stage of child-tending, my kindergarten period was full of book discovery and invention. I continued to collect and read anything printed-old church song books, my dictionary from Miss Doris, used furniture store ads. During this time, if someone wanted to know what I was doing with the old, wrinkled papers, my reply would be, "I'm studying my alphabets." By the time school started, I had developed a growing word list in my head.

Chapter 13

Late to School

The most earth-shaking thing happened to me when I turned six. I didn't start school in the fall of 1950! The last week of August, a week before school opened, Mama came home, carrying large shopping bags from uptown Kinston. Mama's favorite activity was shopping and putting things in the layaway. Getting items out of the layaway seemed to bring her joy and ease in her life.

The school shopping spree had made Mama especially pretty that Saturday. The usual sadness in her face had disappeared. Her new face was beaming with sparkling eyes that lit up the dark places in the room. Mama's sleeveless yellow dress with the matching sash reminded me of the gigantic sunflowers in the yard next door. Mama was the most beautiful flower that day.

All of us children gathered around Mama in the living room/small bedroom. Without trying to, we lined up according to age. Nora first, then Paul, Reba and me. Willie Earl last. He's the youngest. Mama carefully laid out the new clothing as she looked around the dim, well-organized room. Then she opened the curtains to let in the last light of the day.

Miss Love, a skilled housewife, took pride in her tidy, but sparse shotgun house. She was very creative in making the best of what she had. Watching my mama was a habit that I was becoming good at. I could read her thoughts as she looked at each item. *My bright, shopping bags bring life to the room. I am going to ask Miss Doris to make me some light-colored living room curtains. Abraham needs to get the walls painted. The fading, curling wallpaper looks out of date. I want to replace the old rickety couch, and the lumpy sofa bed. Every husband and wife should have a decent bed. The new bed's already in the layaway. That will be my next project out of layaway. Abraham fixed the 4-legged iron cast woodstove, with a metal crate to replace the fourth missing leg. Did the best he could, but it must be replaced also. The antique mirror hanging on the door is magical. Given to me by Mama. I will always keep it.*

Lost in thought, Mama finished her quick examination of the room. Then she turned her attention to her children and her selection of their school clothes. "Nora Linda, this skirt and vest set's for you. You'll be going to the eighth grade. I also got you three yards of material from the fabric store. You can make an outfit. Just don't make it too short or too tight. Paul Anthony, I bought you two pair of pants and some matching shirts. You're going to the fifth grade. Roberta Lynne, here's the blue and white navy sailor dress you wanted. And the dress that was in the window at Brody's. You'll be in the second grade. Do y'all like them?"

At the end of the display, Mama gave the well-chosen clothes to the proper child. There was total quietness and approval as each child fingered and inspected their garments. I was surprised. I never knew they had middle names. 'Roberta'. I didn't know that was Reba's real name.

Willie Earl had turned four last week. He just watched. I understood why there were no clothes for him. I asked, "But what about me? Where are my new school clothes?"

Mama, surprised by the question, answered as if it didn't matter. "Oh, I thought you knew. Your birthday comes two months after the enrollment age cut-off. You've to wait until the next year for school. Anyway, when I remembered to enroll you, I had missed the deadline!"

In total disbelief, I forgot who I was talking to. I screamed! "How could you forget such an important date? You didn't question the stupid rule! You show didn't mention it to me! You know I am way past read' for school! You spend so much time worryin' about where Daddy is that you forgot about what is important to me."

Desperate, I added, "Did you tell Miss Doris?"

I was beyond mad! Mama had a lot of secrets. I wanted to shock her like she had shocked me. I allowed my special secret to slip out. "Besides, I ready know how to read!"

Mama pitched a fit! "A five-year old can't read! You have never been to school! You lying hussy! Get out my face! I am going to tell Abraham about your mouthy self as soon as he gets home!"

The earlier sweet honey in her voice had turned to cloudy, sour vinegar. Mama's good mood vanished. My shattered dreams about going to school in a few days faded in my useless screams.

By the time my daddy came home the next morning, Mama forgot about me arguing and questioning her. Instead, Mama jumped on my daddy as he was getting ready to go to church, "You lied again. You swore that you would take me over to Miss Doris' last night! You didn't even come home. Were you with your 'woman'? Now you going to church and pretend you follow Jesus!"

Daddy continued to dress. Not a word came out of his mouth. As he opened the bedroom/living room door, all of us children slipped quietly out of the small hallway that separated the two rooms. We backed into our bedroom. He took his car keys from the hook in the hallway, next to the picture of Jesus on the cross. The eyes of Jesus watched him as Daddy opened the partly unhinged screen door. Looking toward the bedroom door, he reminded Mama, "Make sure supper is ready by 2:00. No. I was not with 'some woman'. I went to invite Miss Doris over today so we can talk with her."

"You lie so much I don't believe you!" Daddy ignored Mama and continued to talk.

"On one of my auto parts deliveries, I dropped by to make sure we could still talk with her. Her sons were there from New York. All of us talked so long that Miss Doris and Mr. Eugene invited me to spend the night. You know I sort of grew up with them when I first came to Kinston. I will be glad when I can get a telephone for the house."

We children silently mouthed, "Telephone!" as we eavesdropped behind our partly closed door.

From the time I was five years and ten months old until I turned six years ten months, I stayed mad at Mama. Because she didn't tell me about school. And she didn't tell the school officials that I was ready for school, even though my birth date was past the cutoff date. Mama knew how important books and learning were to me. She didn't see my desire for schooling as a serious matter.

I thought, *Burning up her favorite yellow silk blouse is too much punishment. I don't want to hurt her that much. Still. I need to be on my path and find a more comfortable way to stay in this nutty family!* One day when I was home alone, I decided to burn it anyway. The flames from the burning silk blouse were smothered by the wet towels and soggy bath rags in the dirty clothes basket. The fire scorched the bottom of the tin basket and the wooden floor in the tiny bathroom. By the time I burned the yellow silk blouse, my mama was so withdrawn in her other world that clothes didn't even matter. The act was still soothing for me.

Chapter 14

Coming Home to School

A year later, in August, Mama went shopping for school clothes. Again. This time I was old enough to go to school. When Mama walked into the house, she threw the bags on the new couch, next to the brand-new bed. She didn't notice the newly painted walls or the new upgraded white enamel stove in the corner. There was no parade of new school clothes. No announcement of our full names and the grades we were going to like she had made last year. She simply mumbled, "I'm fixin' to make supper. Nora, separate the clothes."

Mama was changing. She didn't take interest in life like before, but she didn't forget my hair. The night before school started, Mama came into the bedroom after supper. "Doris, let's choose which new dress to wear the first day of school tomorrow. I need to press some of those kinks out of your napp' hair."

"But Mama, ever since Nora burned my ear, I hate getting my hair pressed."

Mama looked at me, her lips tight. Those mean lips reminded me, "We are Christians and Christians aren't supposed to hate anything."

I quickly changed 'hated', a forbidden word to 'dislike'. "Yes. Mama, I mean dislike. If it takes straightened hair to go to school, I will tolerate the pressing, the hot grease burning my scalp, and maybe a burnt ear."

I was joking and being smart-mouth at the same time. My pressed hair was combed into two ponytails and a big fat loose bang that announced me. I had long, thick bushy hair, but Paul called it a 'rooster tail' to mock the short, tight hair of some 'Colored' girls.

Mama had said, "Pay no attention to Paul. He's color struck. He likes light skin girls with long good hair."

I was nervous and scared when I woke up for my first day in school. I begged, "Ma, please let me walk by myself. You don't have to stop your housecleaning."

She refused. I wanted to show her how grown up I was. In two months, I would be seven. I joined the other students in their new clothes, shiny shoes and oily, pressed, greasy, straightened hair. And for the boys, barber shop hair and mammy cuts. With my new orange and green dress making me look like a Halloween pumpkin, I tried to walk like my new penny loafers didn't hurt. My old brogans felt better.

The first graders were assigned to an area marked near the front door of the school. Soon, Principal Davis, tall and kingly looking like my daddy, came to our assigned area and called my name, "Doris Anne Love." My mama gave him the enrollment paper. And he gave her another paper. Mama took me to Room #100A. When I saw it was a regular first grade class, I was so relieved. It wasn't like the dream I had when I was assigned to 100B, the first-grade class for dummies and repeaters. Mama said, "You can go in by yourself. Give Miss Ford this paper."

Full of pride and joy, I presented the paper and extended my right hand and said, "Good morning, Miss Ford. My name is Doris Anne Love."

I had practiced my introduction. I did well for the teacher took my hand, held it for a moment and then shook it. She really meant it when she said, "Welcome to the first grade."

I said, out loud, without thinking, "I been waiting for school all my life."

The tall guy in the back whispered loud enough for the whole class to hear, "What a screwball!"

Everybody laughed at me. I laughed with them.

Miss Ford said, "All right, Billy, don't start this year like last year if you don't want to be in the first grade for a third time."

This time everybody laughed at Billy. I didn't. I thought, *He must have a problem and needs some help. Probably can't read.* Billy, who had slumped down in the last row, was ordered up front. The only front seat available was next to me.

I leaned toward him, patted my bangs, and whispered for his ears only, "I will help you, Billy."

I could hear Mama's voice, "Busybody!"

When Miss Ford had as many students as desks, she started to turn down my friend Carolyn, who had been adopted by Mama's friends, Miss Harriet and Mr. Clyde. But Miss Ford remembered repeater Billy. "Billy, go next door to Room 100B. Carolyn, you can stay. Sit there."

I lost the first student I could have helped, but there would be many more. My best friend was assigned to the empty seat next to me. Carolyn needed some help too.

The teacher turned her attention to the class. "Good morning, my glorious flowers. I am here to attend your growth and development. My name is Miss Ford. I have taught first and second grade here for five years."

After roll call, we were drilled on the class rules, like raising hands before speaking. Getting to school on time. Studying the alphabets at home and lining up for all bells. By lunch, I was bored as a scientist learning how to count. After lunch, we practiced learning the ABC's and writing the letters 'A', 'B', and 'C'. I did learn the difference between capital letters and small letters that day.

I missed my mirror. The big clock on the wall gave me something to imagine into. I saw Rabbit change the hands of the clock and mix up the time. I entertained myself with the swirling clock hands until I felt a tug down below. I knew the rule. 'Use the restroom before recess or lunch is over'. The big hand was on 2, but Rabbit may have mixed the time up. Anyway, I didn't know how to tell time. This didn't matter. I couldn't wait. I raised my hand. "Miss Ford, can I go to the toilet?"

Everybody laughed. We had gone over this rule many times today.

Carolyn whispered, "Say 'restroom'".

The teacher looked up, hesitated, then answered, "Yes. You may go to the Girl's Restroom."

Everyone laughed again. I laughed too. Something must be funny. I didn't want to wait for the first-grade tour tomorrow. Mama always, said. "You are too fast."

But I didn't tell a story. I did have to pee.

As I went on my own tour, I thought, *There is so little to read in our house. This school has books, magazines, pamphlets, folders, maps, charts, encyclopedias, pens, pencils, ink pens, paper, notebooks and crayons everywhere.*

Near the Principal's Office, I saw a large bookcase, leaning on a wall, from the weight of books. I quickly stepped around the bookcase and peeked into a small book room. I looked up. Over the door I saw the word 'LIBRARY', painted in black letters on a piece of brown wood. I knew this word.

The "wee library" was packed with books up to the ceiling, on the tables, against the wall, in the closet and in boxes on the floor. I saw books with titles I had never heard of, but knew I would be reading them. My teacher had already told the class about a library visit for the next day.

Principal Davis came out of his office and followed me into the library. "Are you lost?"

"No, I'm on my way to the toilet. Oops! I meant restroom." I didn't tell him that I had been lost, but school had found me. And I had come home.

After using the restroom, I returned to my class. My first day at J. H. Sampson Elementary School on Tower Hill Road was my dream come true. Life in school and the world of books were more than I had expected. The largest ABC's I had ever seen lined the wall over the wide windows. Students sat in desks, row by row, saying 'Present'. The various teachers' voices, the laughing students and the ringing bells were welcomed sounds.

The constant questioning of students was a game that motivated me to know the answers.

"What is the name of our school?"

"J. H. Sampson Elementary School"

"What is 2 plus 6?"

"8."

"How do you spell 'must'?"

School was a system that supported my growing desire to know and understand the ways of life. At school I received favorable attention for being an interested learner. At home, I was ridiculed for interest in my ragged books and torn magazines.

These soothing tones of school were different from the strained sounds of home life. My parents' continuous arguing and the loud children rivalry were almost forgotten in the ordered rules of school life. The thoughts faded into the shadows as I remembered the comfort that school was bringing into my life.

"Good morning, my glorious flowers. I am here to attend your growth and development." This was Miss Ford's daily greeting. When my teacher spoke, all students were charmed by the warmth in her eyes. Her voice sounded like the calm morning river that cruised around the town. When Miss Ford walked up and down the aisle, her smell of dried roses and toasted cornflakes scented our classroom. The combined lingering smell made me miss my mama. At the same time, I felt safe and cared for.

I admired my teacher so much. I wanted to be a teacher like Miss Ford when I grew up. I would copy her in the way she dressed, talked and walked. As we lined up and filed out for lunch, her eyes glowed as she reminded us, "You can come in here at lunch and read."

Her concern for us made us want to be good students and better citizens.

But Miss Ford didn't have a husband or any children and sometimes seemed unhappy. I wondered if Miss Ford had a secret, too. Sometimes when we're doing our group work, I saw a faraway look in her eyes, just like the look in Mama's eyes after her argument with Daddy. Mama called it a look of 'troubles', meaning troubles from the past still cause problems in the present and the future.

I always finished my work right away. It was too easy for me anyway. My mama had said, "An idle mind is the devil's workshop." I didn't want to be used by the devil, so I made my way up to Miss Ford's desk. I knew I was becoming more of a busybody because there was so many troublems around me. I wondered, *Is Miss Ford troubled?*

"Miss Ford, can I help you out? You looked unhappy a little while ago. When my mama is sad or tired, she starts to sing. Maybe if we could sing some songs, everybody would feel better. Billy don't like school 'cause his daddy's in jail. I'm sorry he left. When Sudie May got home yesterday, their furniture was out on the sidewalk. My sister hates my daddy. A lot of the students in this class have troublems."

"How do you know?"

"My mama says that the world is a troubled place. And that I am such a busybody, worrying about other peoples' problems."

Miss Ford looked surprised that I had noticed when her clouds came and that I confessed my secret. I waited for her to say something about being too nosy or talking too much. Instead, she stood up and made a grand announcement. My daddy's announcements usually came with frowns and rules. Miss. Ford's came with the sun spreading across her smiling face and ours. "Class, put away your books and paper. We are going to start our music class in a few minutes." We quickly obeyed. All her students were glad to get a break from 'rithmetic and writing our names.

"Who knows, "Michael Row the Boat Ashore"?"

All hands went up! We had learned this song during Vacation Bible School.

* * *

I noticed that Miss Ford spent a lot of her time with two types of students. Those who were poor readers and those who were pretty, with light skin and long, straight or wavy hair. They lived in a 'good' neighborhood and had educated parents who had good jobs. In a few days, she asked the class, "Who has been to kindergarten? Please raise your hands." The students who had attended were placed in Group 1. The rest of us were sorted into groups by our last names. I wound up in Group 3.

I knew I would not be allowed in the circle of students who'd been to kindergarten. Also, I was skinny with dark skin and kinky hair, lived in a shotgun house in an alley across the street from the projects. My parents had little book learning and had no money for kindergarten. I didn't let those things bother me too much. At least I had a daddy who had a job and a mama who was pretty. So, I, the "great pretender," tried to act as if I was slow or "retarded," Daddy's word. I laughed to myself as I stumbled with words and mistook "Jane can run" for "Jane can ride."

This way, I would be in the presence of my teacher more. I did this for three weeks until Miss Ford tested the class and put everyone into groups, by ability. Immediately, I became bored with this arrangement and forgot to pretend not knowing how to read. Miss Ford noticed right away and hastily shifted me from Group 3 to Group I. I was not smart enough to hide my truth about reading. Miss Ford asked, "Who taught you how to read and write? I notice that you catch on quickly."

"My sister/mama Nora and me taught me how." To my surprise, I had discovered another group of students that teachers loved to spend time with! I was welcomed into the world of eager readers and learners! Being poor didn't mean you had to be a poor reader!

My early years had focused on my family, especially my mama and the small confines of the railroad street, shotgun houses and alley living. Because of my early inspiration and successful start into the "halls of learning", I was able to break some of my over-dependency on my mama. I shifted my main attention away from the family to the larger world beyond 404 Downing Alley. The next five years merged into magical school days of knowledge and discovery. School became my heaven. And a word I soon learned, my "haven."

Chapter 15

The High Cost of 'Colored' Television

One day coming home from school, my middle sister, Reba, age thirteen, took a shortcut through the White projects. Panting and sweating, my sister ran the rest of the way home. She fell into the front room like she was being chased by a ghost, blabbering something about a lot of money. "When I was coming through the construction site near the White projects, I found a bag full of money, sticking out of a wrinkled brown paper. It was under a big rock. When I lifted the rock, there was another bag stuffed with money."

Reba was glad she had found the money, but she had found it in a forbidden place. She told my mama, "I'm afraid to let my daddy know. 'Cause he's warned us about walking through the White people's neighborhood alone."

Daddy had explained to all of us earlier. "In Kinston, 'Colored' people live in neighborhoods that are clearly marked off: near the river, the downtown Sugar Hill area back of downtown, Lincoln City and the cemetery, across from the railroad tracks and in three public projects."

A while back, Paul had warned my daddy about this. Daddy made his announcement like we didn't know. "To reach the 'Colored' elementary school and the 'Colored' high school, you have to walk through several White areas, pass White schools, White neighborhoods, a White project and mad White people. Don't walk through them by yourself or after dark."

Ray was happy that he and my daddy agreed about this. All of us found this to be true. We never walked in the White areas by ourselves. Reba was rebellious so we weren't surprise at her shortcut. But we were full of excitement and wonder at her discovery.

During childhood play dreaming, we all decided what we would buy with such a find. We agreed that fortune for one meant fortune for all. My oldest sister, Nora, had said, "I will buy many tight dresses and matching-colored high heels to wear on my dates."

We knew that Paul, my older brother, loved fast cars and pretty clothes. He told us, "I'll buy me a new red Chevrolet with shiny, expensive hub caps. And a lot of city clothes to match my car."

Reba, the finder of this fortune, had emphatically stated, "I will wear mink coats and silk dresses and go to the gambling joints."

We laughed when Willie Earl, the youngest of all, said, "I am going to buy me a year's supply of food, candy and clothes."

They understood what 11-year-old me, the bookworm would do. "I will buy books, magazines, crayons, coloring books, pens, pencils and paper. I will use most of mine to go to college. I want to teach, travel and write books."

We waited to hear my mama declare her dream out loud. She knew it was only a game. As usual, she remained silent. Maybe Mama didn't know what she wanted, but her children did. All, except me, determined to save money and go to New York after high school. I wanted to go to college here and move to California.

When Daddy got home that night, Reba wanted our daddy to be part of the good luck. We held our breath as Reba gave him the bags of money. After he counted it, we waited for the sharp fussing, which never came. He never mentioned, "Didn't I tell you of the danger in walking through the White area?" He never reminded her, "I told you how bad things could happen." Instead, he said to her, "You did the right thing." We moaned in silent defeat. Surely, our dreams were gone. Our disappointment turned to sadness as we waited for my daddy to spend the money.

* * *

The next week, my daddy took us uptown and downtown, looking at televisions. We looked at televisions in uptown department stores and we were all stumped at the way they worked and how much they cost. The White owner of the furniture store told us, "If you're just looking, don't be 'just looking' here." He didn't say it, but we knew the Whites could look as long as they wanted to.

When Daddy's anger flared, he was always quick with a reply. "I guess we'll go downtown and buy a 'Colored' television." He laughed in the White owner's surprised face. We moved down the street, to store after store, and we still couldn't find a White owner who didn't mind that we were 'Colored' people, just looking at the most mind-expanding invention of our lives.

The family crammed in my daddy's 1949 Plymouth and rode from North Queen Street uptown to downtown Sugar Hill. South Queen Street was where 'Colored' people owned beauty shops, taxi companies, funeral homes, nightclubs, barbecue joints, juke joints and liquor houses. The best spot to watch televisions was in front of the 'Colored' furniture store, located in the busiest part of the 'Colored' business area. Daddy parked the car in front of the furniture store. When we got out, he said, "I'm going to look at the televisions in the 'Colored' furniture store and see how much the 'Colored' televisions cost."

His laughter mixed with the happy sounds of the 'Colored' shoppers on Sugar Hill.

Mama said, "I am going to get us some food. Today is Saturday. You won't catch me dead in a kitchen on Saturday!"

Mama went in Jack's to get us supper. The teenagers and the younger children watched television from the window and danced to the music from the record store next door. The 'Colored' disc jockey was playing the popular song, "Mama, He Treats Your Daughter Mean," by Ruth Brown, which was not allowed in our house. The teenagers slyly courted and exchanged hungry stares. Nora had that look in her eye when one of her boyfriends was around.

Daddy came out of the store and watched the television in the window as he waited for Mama to finish her Saturday supper shopping. Soon, Mama came with some fried fish, a large tray of chopped barbecue, Cole slaw and hush puppies. When Daddy drove us home, he said to my mama, "Emma, you wouldn't believe how much a television cost. Whether it's a White television or 'Colored' one."

The joke was no longer funny. *Why was he mad? He had the bags of money.*

Mama answered him, her voice, loud and insistent. "All those things cost a lot for our little money. We should only buy from our own people who sell them. That mean man didn't even want us to look at the television from the window. I'm fed up this mess!" I was feeling the same way. I was glad Mama spoke out. *But don't Mama want a television too?* Disappointment and sorrow filled my thoughts when Daddy didn't buy a television.

Maybe, like Mama and Aunt Naomi said, 'He's a tightwad!'

Monday, when we got home from school, a brand-new large RCA square television, with two tall slender wires sticking out the top, sat on a table next to the RCA radio/record player combination. In the living room. Everyone was speaking at the same time, "I can't believe it!", "A television! For real?"

I said, "Daddy loves RCA appliances. I'm not surprised, RCA again." The afternoon light from the window shone through the window and danced circles on the shining brown television. We danced our surprise with fun and loud happy sounds.

I said to myself, out loud, "I dreamed that we were going to have a television soon."

Reba threw a fit! "You think you know everything! Just 'cause Cousin Babs gave you a necklace you think you're special! Now I can buy my own."

Wow! I knew she had something to say about the necklace, but it took a long while. I wanted to say something to defend myself, but I was growing tired of explaining myself to others.

Everyone I knew dreamed of having a television in their own house. Now we had our own. We waited patiently for my daddy to turn on our Christmas-in-May present. We sat down and watched the television like it was already on. The television was inspected the same way we looked at dried leaves and shells in my science class. In both cases, we knew to "look and don't touch."

Mama watched from the doorway, a pleased far-away look in her eyes.

My daddy's tight control on the family became clear with the television. "Tonight, we're watching *The Lone Ranger*." Even though we were glad that he liked *The Lone Ranger*, we didn't care what was selected. Our family was glad to have a television to watch. The bonding, laughter and love we exchanged together as a family occurred while watching television.

Mama had told me when I was five, "Your questions will lead you to the answers." Television gave me a way to question life through the things I saw on television. Most important for me, television made me aware of the differences between 'Colored' people and White people. At first, I felt a little invaded by their White presence in our 'Colored' living space. We could not eat with them, attend their schools, go to their churches nor live in their neighborhoods.

Yet, the television brought the White people right in our front room. They lived rich lives with shiny cars, big houses and happy, smiling families. Our lives were opposite— crowded, shotgun houses and poor, sad separated families. From television, it looked like 'Colored', 'Negro' people got the short end of the stick. I wanted television to include us. *Why were we left out of the society, television and the world?*

I asked my teacher in the third grade, "Why do White people always get to be the people in the stories and movies on television?" In the fifth grade, I asked my teacher, "Why do 'Colored' people play the cooks, butlers and maids on television?' Their answer was the same. "That's the way the things are done. 'Colored' people usually work for White people in life and on television."

As I watched television, I studied the characters, actions, places, words and endings of the shows on television. These were the same parts of the stories that were written in books. I asked my oldest brother Paul, "Do you think I could be a writer who could put these parts together and tell stories about our people?"

BREAKING THE CYCLES OF PAIN: SOUL SECRETS

Paul told me, "I have never thought about who wrote the programs for television. But I know it's probably not a 'Colored' woman. Maybe White men. If you pay close attention, White women and 'Colored' women are given the same roles on television as in life—mothers and homemakers. Just fewer 'Colored' people are on television."

I wanted to argue, but when I watched closer, I saw that the parts given to all women were usually less important than men. My teachers and my brother were right. It seemed to be the same way in life.

Along with the high price of a television set for the poor, television shows like *Amos and Andy* and *The Little Rascals* always made us look like clowns and fools. I even heard 'Colored' people in the neighborhood called each other 'black', 'stupid', 'Nigger', 'strumpet' and 'sissy'. These names didn't make me feel good. Television was influencing the way we saw ourselves. And the way we treated each other. This was a high price to pay for entertainment.

As my journey in school progressed, I realized that the whole system left out positive images of 'Colored' people in school textbooks, newspapers, history books, magazines and movies. I continued to ask my teachers in history and social studies, "Why don't all the books, magazines, encyclopedias show the lives and the achievements of our people?"

When education and television became a part of my life, my imagination began to soar, like a kite in the spring wind. Both opened up worlds of possibility and at the same time, promoted more segregation, negativity and violence for 'Coloreds'. More knowledge about the world increased my fear of being murdered, kidnapped and hung. I realized that education and television were influencing my decisions about life. By the sixth grade, it became clear that my search was about my identity and healing my people. I could see that racial pride and family healing were not going to come from television.

PART IV.
ASYLUMS

Chapter 16

Clotheshorses Create Money Problems

Mama and Daddy seemed to live in a betwixt and between world of constant change. Never settled, normal or plain. Up and down. Love and hate. Money and broke. Smiles and frowns. Order and insanity. Fun and pain. My parents seemed different, and at the same time, so alike. I asked myself, *What do they have in common?* When I narrowed it down, they both loved shiny, pretty clothes. Daddy and Mama were what people in our neighborhood called 'clotheshorses'—men and women who were always well dressed.

Daddy wore a different suit, a laundered, stiffly starched white shirt and necktie every evening he stepped out, which was often. My mama always left home wearing a stylish dress, matching hat, pocketbook and shoes and sometimes, matching gloves. Her long straightened, shining hair, flowing in the wind, joined in with the soft jingling of her swinging earrings. Whenever one of them left the house, the neighbors would peek out of the window and say, "They look like a fashion plate." My friend, Carolyn, told me this.

My daddy had many jobs to support his flair. My mama had my daddy, partly. She was at his mercy when it came to money. I had heard Aunt Naomi tell Mama, "Abraham's stingy spending his money on the house. But he don't spare himself, right? Demand some of that money for yourself!"

She was always telling this to my mama. And Mama did demand! And sometimes it worked; usually by Mama arguing, being playful or cooking Daddy's favorite treats. One day when Mama was acting playful, I heard Mama tell him, "You act like you're king of this shotgun house! I mean castle." Mama seldom played around. That day, Mama burst out laughing as she curtsied, like she was bowing down to the king. "Don't you want your wife to dress like your queen?"

Mama returned from the stove and sat Daddy's supper in front of him—a plate of hot, fluffy buttered rice surrounded by an ocean of plate-licking gravy, with a mess of smothered kidneys, sizzling in the middle. Daddy placed folded money near his saucer as he finished eating his favorite dessert, grated sweet potato pie. It was like Mama's laughter and food had cast a little spell on Daddy. Sometimes Mama's cleverness worked.

When Mama's cunningness didn't work, there was war in the Love household. I remember the day of the big blowout about money. Mama's money situation changed after that.

All of us children were sitting on the new Sears and Roebuck couch, waiting to go uptown with Mama. Mama was nervous as she told us, "Just wait here. I have to get some money from your daddy." Dressed like a fashion model in *Ebony* magazine, Mama paced around the front room, rolled the window shades up higher and looked out the window. She smoothed her dress to herself to prevent wrinkles, then sat down. Picked up the newspaper but stared out the window. All of this before she made her request.

I never heard Mama fret about the rent, utilities or food. Daddy provided the basics and he issued out seasonal money for Easter, Christmas, Thanksgiving and school clothes. But asking for shopping money at other times set the house on edge. We heard our mama announce, "Abraham, I need some money to get out my layaway." Layaways included household items, children's clothes and clothes for herself.

My daddy, relaxing in his new matching rocking chair from Sears, had complained, "Damn it! Emma, every time I get paid you want to put something in layaway or take something out! I just brought all this new furniture. I'm broke. Y'all taking me to the poor house! You think money grow on trees?"

Mama yelled, "Both you and your sister Naomi are as stingy as sin! But you spend money freely on cars, clothes." And under her breath, which we all heard, "On other women."

"I'm broke! Just plain damn broke!" To make a point, he spelled the word. "B-r-o-k-e! Do you get it?"

Mama was tired of having to fight for money. She jumped up from the couch with the unread newspaper. She flung the paper toward Daddy's head. He ducked. This made her even more furious. Mama roared, "What do you mean you don't have no money? You always have a pocketful of money! I see you in the evenings, when you empty your pockets and money sack on the dresser. They are full of dollars, shiny quarters. And dimes. And nickels. Am I lying?"

"But—"

"No 'buts'!" Mama cut him off.

We all waited and watched. Another day in the drama of the Love family about money.

"I know where the green bills are neatly tucked in your wallet. You even have money hidden away in your jacket in the closet. Right?"

"Are you spying on me?"

It looked like she didn't care what he thought. Mama ignored him and kept telling his money secrets.

"When you do give me any money, you turn your back so I can't see your wallet packed with dollars. Just remember, 'All shut eyes ain't sleep and all goodbyes ain't gone!'"

Whatever that 'shut eye goodbye' stuff meant, it made my daddy mad enough to fight, too. I held my breath and waited for the moment to be over. Enraged, he pointed his wiggling finger at Mama and threatened, "Go in my stash when I'm asleep or away, you'll be sorry. If you think I'm tight now, I can really show you tight. A man got to be tight with a woman like you who want to be dressed in finery all the time."

And a woman like Mama wouldn't let this pass. She screamed, "You want me to be the best dressed woman in the room!"

"Still, do you have to leave the lights on all over the house? Y'all have the radio, television and electric fan on at the same time.

Cooking day and night. Running water and eating all day long. You think I'm rich? Y'all are running me ragged!"

As my mama rolled her eyes, she asked, "What about air? Do you charge us for that, too?"

Sarcasm dripped from her words like melting wax. Daddy's eyes were popping red. They stared each other down for a long time. And after a while, their anger passed. Daddy had remained true to his promise: 'I will never hit a woman again'. He had promised this after he slapped some sense in Mama when she threatened to kill all his children. He picked up his keys from the table and said, "I'm going to Naomi." As he walked out the door, he called back over his shoulder, "I'll be back soon."

Together, we all let out a long breath and wondered, *How long?* Daddy and his sister were extremely close. Both Miss Doris and Aunt Naomi gave him advice on money and private matters. Although Aunt Naomi may have been stingy also, she encouraged him to give to his family. I had heard her tell my daddy, "Abraham, Emma's a good woman and you've a fine family. Treat them right."

When my daddy came from Aunt Naomi's, he walked up to Mama and handed her a roll of dollars. "Is this enough?"

* * *

Aunt Naomi, sensitive to the spirits and vibrations—her way to describe her work—came to our house the next day. Looking a lot like her brother with a head of long, black hair, an Indian-looking face and a long slim body. Aunt Naomi seemed to know and understand something about money that my mama didn't. Being a moneymaker and keeper, she opened my mama's eyes. I pushed the rickety door open, and Aunt Naomi stepped in. "Good morning, Morning Glory! What's your latest story? How's my favorite niece? Tell Emma I'm here."

"Mama's in the kitchen cooking fifty pies for the church building fund."

As soon as I said it, I knew I was talking too much. My favorite Aunt was carrying her working bags. She followed me to the kitchen.

"Morning, Naomi."

Mama was sensitive to the spirit too. She watched Aunt Naomi as my aunt sat at the table, but said nothing else.

Just like Daddy, she went straight to the heart of the matter. "Morning, Emma. Why don't you include yourself in the making of this money? Don't give all your money to the church. Tithe them their 10%. Use your secret knowledge and your talents to make you some money for yourself and the children. Abraham got his. Get yours."

Aunt Naomi always saw a need for balance in life.

"I've been thinking about keeping some of the money."

"It's yours. You make it, don't you?"

"You're right. Why don't you stay for a spell?"

"Good. I want to talk to you about making your own money. I have something for Little Doris, too. While I'm here, I want to dress a new mirror I have for her. She's anxious to start using what she's been learning."

I watched as Mama cleared a part of the kitchen table to serve as a work area for the cleansing of the mirror. Before the dedicated spiritual worker moved into action, she said to me, "Little Doris, you're one strange young girl. I am glad Emma allowed you to develop the craft."

Aunt Naomi stood up from the table and presented to me a round package wrapped in many layers of paper. "Open it but be careful. Let us help you."

I gave the box to Mama because I was getting stuck to all the tape that sealed the package. Mama removed the last of the paper and gave me the unwrapped gift. I screamed out, "A Princess mirror! Just like the ones in the children department store uptown!"

The round mirror itself was set in a circle of white pearls. Between each pearl was a tiny silver rose. The handle on the special mirror was made of the same tiny silver roses. When I pointed to that mirror in the department store, Mama said, "That mirror cost $20.00." It was hard for me to imagine paying $5.00 for something.

I had wanted a mirror. Now, my prayer was answered. This special magical mirror would replace the cracked one I hid in the back of the closet.

To continue her work, Aunt Naomi held up a bunch of dried plants. She spoke again. "This is sage. It's related to the sage, which Emma uses to season her turkeys. This sage clears out old energies and negative thoughts. It cleanses the mind so you can hear the voice within. Put the mirror down."

I placed my prized mirror on the large white cloth prepared by Mama.

"To dress a mirror means to cleanse it to remove old negative energies. Emma, get your money bag. I want you to start seeing your business expanding. That way, you can have enough to still give generously, to yourself and others."

Mama left and came back quickly.

"Place it on the clean cloth on the table. Now. Both of you. Speak into the money bag and the mirror what you can imagine and what you want to happen. This is what I call in-spiriting and in-voicing."

I closed my eyes and imagined a new happy life for me. Mama closed her eyes and I hoped, imagined something. Aunt Naomi continued to speak. "Remember. All is spirit first."

I knew this was a lesson and I was in class, paying close attention.

Before Aunt Naomi left that day, she walked around the kitchen. She chanted some unknown words as she tapped some special oil on my mama and me, the mirror, the money bag, the stove, the ice box, the pantry, the table and the sink. I was glad I had on my necklace from Cousin Babs so it could get blessed too. *For protection, privilege and prosperity.* As she picked up my cleansed mirror and Mama's money bag, the kitchen table collapsed. Two crumbling legs snapped and simply caved in. The table had carried the weight of too many activities.

"What the hell is this? Emma, you know you need to use some of that baking money to get a solid table. I'm glad it didn't have those piping, hot pies on it. That table could have fallen on any of us. Remember Emma, the Lord helps them who help themselves."

Turning toward us, Aunt Naomi, a little shaken, straightened her lopsided hat and put on her gloves. The peacock bird on top, sat up straight on her head, its tail a rainbow of changing colors. "Emma, Ecclesiastes 11:1 reminds us, 'Cast your bread upon the waters; for thou shall find it after many days'. We shall talk, in not many days hence."

With that, Aunt Naomi, who spoke in symbols and ancient languages, disappeared from the kitchen. We could hear her rubber-soled black and white Oxford shoes, squeaking on the linoleum floor as she walked through the bedroom and the hallway. In a minute, the front aluminum screen door slammed, as its rusty hinge came to a screeching halt.

Later, Reba helped me to hang the dressed mirror over the wall at the head of the bed. It was the first thing I saw in the morning to imagine my day. At night, I looked in the mirror and imagined a new life until I disappeared among the stars. I fell into the arms of the unknown God, who I prayed, kept watch at night.

* * *

Food was one area that my mama excelled in. Once you ate her delicious food, you wanted more. Soon, Mama put Aunt Naomi's suggestions to work. Emma Lee Love turned her cooking skills into a pie, cake, banana pudding, fish fry and turkey business. Her children Nora, Paul and Reba, Willie Earl became her delivery service. I was her kitchen helper. Soon Mama asked, "Who's not turning in all my money from the pies?" She learned much from their silence. Mama began a record keeping system. Immediately, the money turned in matched the orders taken out.

Mama continued to raise money for the church. Her big seller and moneymaker were fried fish dinners-croakers and spots. Mr. Brown, the fish market owner, always gave Mama free supplies when she had a fish fry. Fish-the main item, potatoes for the potato salad and cabbages for Cole slaw. Mama made a lot of money.

At the end of a busy cooking day, Mama would say, "Little Doris, bring me my pocketbook. It's behind the bed in a white hat box." Mama did the same thing Daddy did with money. She turned her back, counted her money and divided the money in two stacks. She placed one in a church envelope and put the bigger pile in her slender blessed money bag in her pocketbook. "Put it up to keep it away from prying eyes." She winked her eyes. Meaning our secret only.

One Saturday when I was in the kitchen with Mama, I heard her tell Daddy, "I have a life that I want to live. I need money to make it happen." I was surprised to see Mama stand up for herself with Daddy. In the past, Mama had argued, screamed and cussed against my daddy's rules and control. This time it was different. Mama was calm yet demanding. She explained in a relaxed voice her special concerns. "I need to use the gas to cook the food that I sell so we won't have to argue about money. I can't cook in this dim, dark kitchen. I need the lights on." With a playful grin on her face, Mama concluded, "After all, I am the king's wife. I need the full wardrobe and cash to help others."

Mama persisted with her cooking business. It flourished. The extra money helped Mama to express her life through her own personal pursuits. These activities included more layaways, beauty shop appointments and giving to the church and the fatherless. The arguments about money lessened. Mama continued to use the kitchen lights when she cooked, but gradually the lights in Emma Love's head began to dim.

* * *

I grew up in a family where all my mama's children were lovers of clothes and fashion. All children in the household used dressing for expression of beauty, style and personality. Everyone followed the adults' fondness for high fashion. Nora, the oldest, was first of the children influenced by their love of clothes. Nora was a younger version of my mother—pretty, light-skinned, slim and sweet. She set the trend for all the rest. When Nora was a thirteen-year-old junior high school student, clothes began to matter greatly to her. Being very creative, she went to thrift stores and bought skirts and dresses to shorten and to tighten. Nora was probably the first person to wear a mini dress or mini skirt in Kinston, North Carolina. With Skinny Nora's quick fingers, the mini skirt style was introduced to K-town in 1950. That's the nickname Nora and her older friends called our hometown. Nora used her creative imagination to be well-dressed.

The rest of us didn't have jobs and money or the cloth design and talent of sewing to secure fashion. The Love children used the creative moneyless-way—shoplifting. When I was younger, Nora had told me, "Shoplifting is when you take something from the store and not pay for it."

"Are we shoplifting when we take a cookie from the cookie jar in Mr. Brown's store, put it in our pocket and eat it when we get outside?"

Nora nodded her head, "Yes. Even that is shoplifting. Just don't let anyone see you do it."

Part of Mama's emphasis on wearing nice clothes related to the importance of being clean, neat and well-groomed. She used to say, "If you only have one outfit, keep it clean and ironed." We also heard her say, "Tall bodies look good in beautiful clothes."

I think Mama had my daddy in mind when she said this. Her eyes got sort of misty and her voice cracked. She may have believed the 'one clean outfit' in the past. Married to my daddy, she never experienced the 'one clean outfit' again. Abraham Love took pride in high fashion and required that his wife dressed on his level. Getting beautiful clothes for our tall bodies motivated my mama and all the children in the Love household.

The shoplifting started with Paul, the oldest son in the house, a younger version of my Daddy. He had told us one day, "I want to dress like my daddy when I grow up." Paul would cause a problem if they wanted him to go to church in an outgrown suit. "I am not going today." He made up his mind, picked up his *Superman* comic book and went out on the front porch.

Soon, Paul was wearing matching pants and shirts and shiny shoes. Nora told me, "Paul got a job at the fish market. Mama is crazy to believe that he makes enough money to buy all those clothes." According to Nora, "Paul refused to start school without new clothes.

He didn't go to school dances because he wanted to be the sharpest one in the room. As he started shoplifting, his participation and popularity increased at the same time."

One day, after Willie Earl refused to go outside and play in his torn jacket, Daddy came into the kitchen and said, "Put him a coat in layaway and I will get it out in two weeks."

By the time Daddy gave Mama the money for the layaway, Willie Earl already had a new school coat. While Paul was shoplifting, he got a new jacket for Willie Earl. My baby brother always wanted to look sharp. Even when shooting marbles or racing tires in the alley. Everybody spoiled him.

Daddy told Mama, "I am glad you got that boy his coat." I was watching the way she would handle this. As usual, she didn't. Another secret in the house and a sign that something was wrong with our family.

I had been watching Willie Earl. Not only did Willie Earl love to eat food, but he also loved clothes and having money. It started with candy and cookies he stole from the corner store. My baby brother wanted the best right now. Soon Willie Earl came home and slipped pork chops in the icebox. My mama never asked, "Did Abraham go grocery shopping?"

My daddy thanked Mama. "Emma, I am glad you got the pork chops. I had a taste for some."

My youngest brother, Willie Earl, may have introduced the idea to Paul and Reba. Willie Earl was smart enough to know he needed some help from his big brother Paul. Although Willie Earl and I were closer in age, Willie Earl, Paul and Reba were closer in personality. They were companions in crime.

Since my mama had turned me over to Nora, I was dependent upon Nora for my day-to-day living. This excluded me from many of their other secretive activities. I chose to hang around Nora so she could help me read and help me with my sewing. And she needed me to watch my daddy. Together, they agreed, "Nora and Doris are scaredy-cats."

They were right. I was. They were wrong. Nora wasn't. She'd rather create her own clothes designs.

I discovered shoplifting through Reba, the rebel in the family. She was not going to follow any rule—neither God's, woman's nor man's. If Mama said, "Go right, Reba." She turned left. Reba laughed and told me, when I felt sorry for her because of the punishment, "It only hurt while it's going on."

I seldom got any whippings for I thought some rules were necessary for order.

Reba said, "If you take my turn washing dishes, I will pay you."

I wanted us to have something we shared without arguing, so I partly agreed. "No, Reba. I don't want you to pay me money. I rather have a Black doll." Reba looked at me like I was crazy. Well, maybe I was. Then Reba began to explain the ins and outs of the shoplifting, I stopped listening. Even hearing the rules made me fearful. I told her, "I will wash the dishes. You can pay me with clothes, books, a hairbrush and a Black doll." I liked new stuff too.

Reba quickly reminded me, "I told you before! They don't sell Black dolls in the stores."

About a week later when Reba came home in the evening, she motioned for me to follow her in the bedroom. Opening a large shopping bag, she watched my reactions. "Here is a dress, a bunch of coloring pens for drawing, a sketch pad and a big, thick book without words. Just dates and lines."

"Thanks for everything. But what is this?" Pointing to the book with blank paper.

"This is a real diary. You don't have to write your little secrets in notepads and on notebook paper no more. It even has a lock and key."

When Mama saw me with a new dress on for supper, she demanded, "Where did you get that dress?"

I told a story. "Miss Doris gave it to me when I spent the weekend with her. I was just trying it on."

"You're lying. When I picked you up, you didn't have anything in your hands."

My story blew up in my face when she saw me washing dishes after we ate. "Who told you to wash dishes? You're breaking the few plates we do have! The plastic drinking cups are greasy as hell! And the cooking pots still have burnt food at the bottom of them! It is Reba's turn! Where is that gal?"

* * *

Before the year was over, my sixteen-year-old brother, Paul, was arrested for shoplifting. Mama told Aunt Naomi about the situation. He didn't go to the reformatory school because Aunt Naomi helped our family out. She performed a ritual and paid the reduced fine. After the case was settled, she visited the family and told us, "I believed strongly in something called 'karma'. Or in other words, you reap what you sow." Without hesitation, she reminded the Love family, "The seed of crime bears bitter fruit. Crime does not pay."

I never considered what could happen when a thief was caught. I guess Daddy hadn't learned about 'karma' either. He told his thieving children, right in front of Aunt Naomi, "Naomi don't know what she's talking about. She is just saying what the radio character the *Shadow* says when the show goes off."

The Shadow was a popular radio show that we had listened to every week before we got a television.

But Aunt Naomi still warned the family, "Shoplifting, burglary, dropping out of school, drinking too much alcohol, divorce, debt, poverty and teen pregnancy are failing to control some desire. A failure to control the desire for anything can lead to bad consequences."

I believed Aunt Naomi. Washing dishes for pretty objects was over when Mama discovered Reba was giving me stolen items. Soon Mama said, "Since you want to wash dishes so badly, when you turn twelve, your weekly term will start."

My desire for free clothes ended after Paul's arrest. With my godmama's and Nora's help, I learned how to sew and make my own creative designs. I wanted to be a fashion plate also.

Was what had happened to Nora because of a failure to control something? I didn't have a name for this out-of-control behavior. All I knew was that our family practiced using the outside stuff to hide the inside truth. Our lies and secrets hid the unnamed pain. Our tall slender bodies dressed the lies up real pretty. I wasn't sure how the rest of the Love children continued to bring food, clothes, toys, radios, bicycles and rolling skates home without being questioned by Mama or Daddy. I guess Nora was right. Mama and Daddy were not good parents.

I do remember Mama's reaction when she made me tell her the truth. "Yes. Reba stole the dress so I would wash dishes for her."

I was shocked that she didn't condemn the thief or the stealing. Instead, my mama told me, "Don't wear that good dress around the house."

It didn't make sense to me. *Was I crazy?* No. Statements like this convinced me that there was something off in my Mama. Having to tell Mama that Reba was stealing my clothes so I would do her chores didn't make my friendship with my sister any better either.

Chapter 17

Losing My Mama and Other Turning Points at 12

I recalled the first time I noticed my mama's strange behavior. It was one fall morning after my daddy had left for work. The school children had gone to school. Even though I was six, I was home because Mama had forgotten to enroll me in school. "How can you forget something so important?" I had asked her. First, I thought Mama had forgotten because she didn't love me. But that day I discovered that something else was spinning a web of confusion inside of her, sealing Mama off from the real world.

After Mama fed Willie Earl, she went outside on the front porch. She sat on the steps in the warm sun for a while, examining the fallen leaves. After a long time, I opened the door. "Mama," I said, "Willie Earl's crying."

"Give him his bottle." I did not interrupt her escape. She continued the inspection.

"There's no milk in it."

"Make him some."

"I tried to make some, but I can't find a can of milk. Anyway, Daddy said he's too old to be drinking milk out of a bottle."

"Mind your own business. Go tell Miss Harriet to make the baby some milk for me."

I ran across the yard to Miss Harriet's house. She was sitting at the kitchen table, cutting up cabbages. I blurted out, "Mama said the baby's crying. She wants you to make him some milk. Mama's been sitting on the steps since my daddy went to work. I'm hungry, too."

Miss Harriet jumped up, threw the bowl of cabbage in the sink, grabbed her sweater, and tore out her backdoor to our house.

Mama still sat in the same place. Miss Harriet looked my mama over. "Emma, what's the matter?" Miss Harriet frowned at the situation.

Mama answered, "I feel like having a cigarette." I didn't even know that mama smoked.

"Let me see 'bout the baby first. Come on in the house. And then we'll talk 'bout a cigarette."

Miss Harriet took Willie Earl and me home with her until my daddy got home. She gave us a bologna sandwich and some red Kool Aid. After we ate, my brother took a nap and I sat on her couch and watched our house through the screened window. Mama sat on the porch all day.

When Daddy came home and saw what was going on, he threatened Mama from the front door. "If you continue to act like this, you're going to lose me and the children. And you'd better stop feeding Willie Earl bottle milk. That boy wants real food! And damn it! Stop calling him a baby. He just turned four!"

His threats made Mama come in the house. As Mama slowly awoke from the daze, her fiery temper arose. In the bedroom she ranted and raved. "Damn you! It's all your fault! Ya out in the streets six nights a week! I know you ain't up to no good! You make enough money to buy us a house, but we live in Shantytown. In a rundown cracker box shotgun house! We ain't even got back steps for the kit....!"

Before Mama finished her sentence, Daddy hissed at her, "You're one crazy bitch!"

Usually my daddy calling my mama 'crazy' would make her call him something like, 'a lying dog'. This made them even in their name-calling. Mama jerked around, facing Daddy. "Now, Abraham, I've already told you I ain't gonna be nobody's bitch."

She ran in the closet and came out with Daddy's pride and joy. His long, shiny double-barrel shotgun. She sounded like she had lost her mind! Mama shrieked, "I got your bitch! I'll kill my children and myself 'fore I let you have them! Ain't no other bitch or hoe will raise my young'uns!"

The barrel of the shotgun was pointed straight at my daddy's lying lips. I wanted to run outside, but the fear of death glued my feet to the worn linoleum floor.

Daddy's huge shoulders stood up straight and his eyes began to jerk. Looking like a superman, he leaped over Willie Earl's toys in the middle of the floor and wrestled my wacky mama down to the bed. My wild daddy twisted the shotgun from my unglued mama and flung it under the bed.

Daddy went berserk! He slapped Mama so hard that Willie Earl started to cry! I screamed, "Don't you hit my mama again! She's unhappy 'cause you don't love her no more. She told Miss Harriet that yesterday. And she said she missed her son, Timothy Earl, who's with his evil daddy."

Daddy pointed to me. "You talk too damn much! And where is everybody, anyway?"

"They came come home and left as soon as they made some peanut butter and jelly sandwiches. Mama said they were roadrunners. Just like you. Always out in the streets!"

The slap calmed Mama down. She stayed in the bed for three days and refused to get up. Miss Harriet continued to babysit Mama, Willie Earl and me until the weekend. I was glad. For I was afraid that Mama would find some way to keep her threat. Daddy didn't even go to church for two Sundays. And he stayed home every night for about three weeks. Then the argument started again when he went out on a Friday night. The fights made my mama withdraw from reality even more and increased my fear of life.

I think my mama had what Aunt Naomi called 'a nervous breakdown'. After that episode, something in her was broken. *But what did I know?* At that time, I was only six.

For the next five years, Mama sank more into her depression. She cooked her wifely supper and left without telling us where she was going. After Willie Earl and I started school, Mama would not be home when we came from school. The older children ate whatever was there and left. There was no one to ask, "Where is my mama?" I needed to be raised. There was no one to say, "Follow the house rules."

I told Aunt Naomi about the situation. She said, "Everybody in this house do what they think they are big enough to do. It ain't right!"

By 1956, everybody in the house became roadrunners like Daddy, except me. I read books to escape the insanity and the loneliness. My mama's strange disappearing behavior increased, along with my growing feeling of being abandoned.

One late afternoon when Daddy had finished his Bible study class, he rushed into the living room. My mama was stretched across the couch, looking like soggy soap. "This crying and insane talk's driving me out of my mind. I'm at the end of my rope! Get dressed! I made an appointment at the Kinston Clinic for someone to talk to you. She'll be here in an hour."

At 3:00 p.m., Nurse Ellen knocked on our door. Miss Ellen was Mama's midwife's daughter and a family friend. Daddy let her in and gave her a seat in his chair. The nurse went straight to the point. She said, "I am an ex-WAC, a midwife and a registered nurse. I have worked with Emma for a long time. I came to counsel her about her long-term depression. Could I speak with Emma alone?"

Our anxious family had gathered around the nurse like she was a miracle worker. The Love family slowly left the front room, hoping that the nurse had the magic in her big white pocketbook. Everybody disappeared to a silent waiting place. After two hours with my mama, Nurse Ellen called us back into the room. We sat as family. Sealed together in our sorrow.

Looking around at our anxious family, the skilled nurse spoke. "The doctor at the clinic says Emma is suffering from what is called postpartum depression. Her irritability and extreme mood swings may be related to imbalance in her hormones. In some women, it lasts a few weeks after birth. Emma's last child is about ten years old, so I think it's something else. What signs have you all noticed?"

Daddy spoke for us. "Emma seems to be stressed and confused most of the time. She cries a lot. It seems to run in cycles. Sometimes, she's okay. Her usual organized self. Other times, she either rages like a maniac or gets moody and shuts up inside. This has been going on for years. There have been times when Emma claims she sees things that are not there. Or says she is about to die."

"What I haven't said yet, is that Emma has had three pregnancies where she lost three children. Women whose children die during birth suffer many effects. Like loss of sleep and appetite; sometimes anxiety. Some become hypochondriac and mistake any minor ailment as a death sentence. Other women even hallucinate. They see these dead children in various places. Sometimes they think they hear the child crying."

"What can you do about it?" Daddy had a lost look in his big brown scared eyes.

"Many women recover with counseling and medication. Some women need psychiatric hospitalization. A supportive, loving home helps. Everybody in the house can help in some way."

Miss Ellen's words made me want to work on fully forgiving Mama.

In the bright light of the Saturday afternoon, Mama's moon lips were dry and parched. Her starry eyes were sunken down in the shadow of her soul. Unlike the fashion plate mama I knew, her clothes were a mess. Baggy, rough-dried and stained with old coffee. Lying on her left side on the couch, facing us, her bony hand scratched through her tangled hair. I thought, but was too scared to say, *The itch is the pain in her heart that cries from her losses. It can't be scratched away.* I knew this because I had the itch too. When my itch became inflamed, I burned something to scratch the pain.

The words that sprang from Mama's mind cracked the wall of silence as she struggled to speak. "I do miss Timothy Earl and the children who didn't live. But one of them is still around. I got a glimpse of her the other day when I was making the bed. First saw her years ago. She refuses to die."

After a long pause, she added, "Abraham thinks I am crazy anyway. So, I never told anyone. I think I would like Abraham to die."

The crazy part of me jumped over the same cracked wall with Mama. I screamed, "She's right! It's my twin. She lives through me! Reverend Love don't have to die. You should leave him!" I hadn't intended to go that far and call him 'Reverend Love'. But I saw the full damage he had done to my mama. I had been calling him 'Reverend Love' when Nora and I joked about his hypocrisy. That day I dared to speak it out! I surprised myself when I said, "Leave him."

Miss Ellen was floored! "Emma, you and your daughter both might need some long-term counseling."

Daddy grabbed me by my arm. "What you mean calling me Reverend Love? I am your daddy. Don't make me sound like a stranger!"

I didn't care what he thought. He show didn't care about us!

Standing up for my mama did not lessen her chronic depression and her thoughts about dying. From the time I was five until I was sixteen, Mama had summoned us children around the bed to announce that this was her last day. The last time Mama gathered us together, we were so stupefied with fear that we couldn't talk. We were scared that she was going to die this time. As she looked at each of her children, she gave individual instructions.

"Nora, that young man that you're seeing has another girlfriend. Watch yourself with him."

Nora kept her head down.

"Paul, you have a gift with poems. Finish school, go to college and become a professor. Stop trying to be like your daddy."

Paul knew Mama was right. He said nothing to defend himself.

"Reba, a hard head makes a sore behind. You're smart in your own special way. Find something to sell rather than steal."

Reba, always quick to give a smart answer, did not fight the truth, this time.

"Little Doris, stop being so serious. Learn how to play. Go get your life."

She knew me better than I knew myself. I looked at her with fear and silence.

"Willie Earl, you have a gift with words also, but don't use them to trick people. Become a lawyer."

He looked out the window. I could see tears forming in his eyes.

"And Nora, watch out for Reba and Doris. And sew clothes and learn how to provide for your own self. Stop looking to men."

Nora looked at the clock on the dresser as she ignored Mama's warning about her boyfriend. She had a date.

We left the gloomy room, feeling motherless and alone.

After this deathwatch, Mama's illness became full bloom. My once well-dressed mama either lay on the coach in a trance, disheveled and slobbering. Other times, she straggled through the house in mismatched clothes, ranting and cussing at the invisible guests in her mind. Sometimes, she made efforts to restore order in her house—once a source of glowing pride for her.

Her warnings, "Y'all better clean your room, Paul, take the trash out, or Nora, what time did you come home last night?" went as far as her memory lingered. Mama's mental flights of escape and forgetfulness made it difficult to remember to evict the intruder from her mind or to manage her house, which was crumbling. *Mama was the foundation. If she falls, do we fall too?* Even Aunt Naomi's herb and rituals couldn't remove the invader.

Fear for Mama's life and our safety forced Daddy to take Mama to the Cherry Hospital in Goldsboro, North Carolina, the state asylum for the 'Colored' mentally ill. When he took her away, sadness and darkness surrounded the house like a tent of death. The emptiness left me stuffed with despair. Sometimes I felt as mummified as Mama talked. I had tried to remember to swim upstream, but I floundered in the space left by Mama's absence.

Mama was in and out of the 'crazy house', as we called it, over a period of years. When Mama came home for a visit, she was on some type of medication that kept her sluggish and often bedridden. After finally relaxing my obsession with the 'secret', my mama's mental condition became another thing to worry about and hide. It was another turning point. *Was life just a series of turning points and secrets?*

* * *

As I was slowly losing my mama to insanity, other important changes took place as I left childhood. The disruptive element in our family during my fifth year returned in a shocking way when I turned twelve. Nora was hurt when she was twelve. I feared that one day I would be hurt, too. I had graduated from elementary school on a Friday. The next day I was excited that school was out. The thing I feared most came true. It happened on a Saturday, my favorite day of the week.

Reverend Love had called from upstairs and asked, "Rabbit, are you still here? Bring me some soap."

Why was he talking to me? I couldn't stand to hear his voice. I had found my Bermuda shorts and finished dressing. I started to slip quietly out the backdoor. *Time to go!* Out of habit, Daddy's Good Little Girl Doris obediently answered, "Yes. I was just getting ready to leave."

Oops! I forgot I am not Daddy's Good Little Girl anymore. I shouldn't have answered. But I had.

"Okay, Reverend Love." *At least I didn't forget his new name.* He still did not like the idea of me calling him Reverend Love. I persisted, without fail, to remind him of his devilish deeds by calling him that name. He knew it was not connected with honor and respect. But his hypocrisy.

The only sound was the calmness of the midday Southern sun as it sketched shadows on the window screens. The radio was not on because Daddy didn't allow worldly music in his house. All children had gone off to their own fun. Mama was home from the hospital and had recovered enough to be out doing her Saturday chores. It was hard for Mama to be crazy on Saturday. She had too many things to do. Daddy called this being 'out in the streets'—going to the cleaners, the shoe shop, the fish market and beauty shop, picking up layaways, visiting the sick and, according to Daddy, meeting a man.

In fact, it was this silence that reminded me that there no one was home, but me and 'Reverend Love'.

I quickly fetched him the Ivory soap. I knocked on the bathroom door, stepped to the side and said, "Here is the soap." He flung the door wide open! He was buck naked! *It* looked like a big, barbecued sausage that was going to pop if you stuck a fork in it. I froze with terror! I was hot, cold, and as mad as ten raving wolves. In my mind I instantly cursed him. *Let the bad man disease eat away your lustful eyes and your gross private parts. May your lying tongue choke you to death. And then may you burn on a cross like a slaughtered hog in hell!*

Rabbit was quick, but I was not quick enough to catch the soap as it floated out of my hand, slipped through his crooked fingers, and landed in the toilet with a loud wallop! He wanted me to see his strange looking thing. It looked like a one-eyed monster sticking out of his stomach! The mad dog was showing signs of rabies. The foam from Reverend Love's mouth settled in the corners of his mouth.

With my mama in and out of the hospital, Nora and the rest of my road running family often left me home alone. As I began to have breasts that I could no longer hide, he turned his evil imaginations toward me. The maniacal look in his daring eyes made me feel exposed, violated and terrorized. In the excitement of graduation from elementary school and the beginning of summer school break, the danger that lurked in our house had been forgotten.

Like the Ivory soap, I floated down the stairs which had grown three times longer. A revengeful daze led me quietly out of the back door. When my racing heart calmed, I eased around to the front porch. My friend Carolyn had taken a seat on the porch swing, swinging and waiting. Carolyn looked like my twin in her blue Bermuda short set. The same age, height, size, skin tone. And two ponytails like mine. Carolyn and her parents had moved into the projects a week after we left the alley. In fact, half of the people in Downing Alley soon changed the shotgun houses for one of the three 'Colored' projects.

An impatient Carolyn asked, "What in the world took you so long? We're going to miss the Saturday cartoon hour."

I thought, *Hopefully, she can't see that, unlike Ivory soap, I am no longer pure.* Mute, I looked at her. I was afraid if I spoke, I would drift off and join the pure beautiful wandering clouds.

That was the day I lost respect for Reverend Love. I spent the rest of the time I lived in his house, dodging him and his one-eyed monster. After the soap incident, I continued to follow Nora's lead and called him, 'Reverend Love'—to remind me and him of his hypocrisy, his womanizing and his lustful behavior toward his children. Nora had shared with me, "Your daddy's behavior is the opposite of God and love. He's the devil carrying a Bible and quoting scriptures. And he's supposed to be a minister!"

I agreed with Nora. He was a monster. When I discussed him with others, I said, "Daddy" or "my daddy" instead of "Reverend Love". I didn't want to confuse them. But I was no longer confused.

* * *

Soon after we had moved into the projects, another memorable change occurred during my twelfth year. My first period started at the end of the school day. Lucky for me, that day Mama was having a clear time. I also felt lucky because we had a full bathroom with a bathtub, and a smaller restroom, instead of the tiny water closet and the big aluminum wash tub in the alley. Nora was cleaning the bathtub and Mama was talking to her in the doorway. I interrupted them. "Nora, someone else is in the other toilet. I got to pee."

As I pulled my bloomers down, I saw blood on the seat of my bloomers. There was no pain, and I didn't remember cutting myself. "Mama, I am bleeding." I pointed to my private part.

"Nora, show Doris how to take care of herself."

Something in me snapped! I screamed! "I am tired of trying to make you mother me! I want you, my mama, to explain to me what's going on in my body! To talk to me about boys!"

Mama's face looked as blank as an unwritten diary.

I screamed, "Don't back away from me!"

She backed away from the toilet.

I screamed, "Don't leave me!"

My mama backed into the deep recesses of her mind.

I screamed, "It hurts when you disappear!"

My receding mama backed into the space between heaven and hell where no one could reach her.

I screamed, "I feel lost!"

I stopped the screams when it came to me that Mama was not backing away from me. Mama was backing away from the pain of her life. It was her way of surviving. I looked around the new toilet, the white porcelain tile, bright and shiny. My mama, who made all this sparkle possible, had gone to hide out on the gloomy side of the moon again.

Nora stooped down and felt around in the bottom drawer of the bathroom cabinet. She came out with a long white pad that looked like a padded napkin. From the drained look on Nora's face, I knew she was tired of my mama's behavior too. My sister/mama explained, "These Kotex have to be worn to protect your clothes from stains."

She showed me how to attach the napkin to a thin elastic belt. Then, shortly I heard the screen door close. Nora was gone to her cheating boyfriend.

I was left alone in the bathroom, blood running down my leg and with a twisted sanitary belt, almost as twisted as my budding womanhood and my twisted parents. That was my sex education.

My screams had started a raging fire inside of me as I sulked through the abandoned house. A voice gave me a way to express my rage on the outside. *Pour the leftover bacon grease on the stove, counter and the sink.* I obeyed without thinking or questioning the consequences. A stack of newspapers waiting for the trash can sat on the counter. *Spread the paper across the counter, the stove and in the sink. Strike a match for each area.* In a few seconds. Whoosh! The dry paper and the grease produced a small inferno in the kitchen! Fire danced across the stove, the countertop and the wall behind the stove. When the curtains started to burn, I ran out of the front door, down the street and sat in the cemetery, near my Grand Mama Quintanilla's tombstone, until suppertime.

That evening as we ate supper in the living room, Reverend Love blamed Mama. "I told you about leaving that grease can on the stove! Now I got to pay to get a new stove and get the wall fixed."

Mama insisted, "I never leave the grease on the stove! As soon as it cools down, I put it in the pantry and the cooked food in the oven, if I'm going out. Anyway, we needed a larger stove, and a new paint job wouldn't hurt."

My anger had simmered then. I saw a good way to hurt Daddy, in his wallet. I couldn't defend Mama this time, but I did help her get another stove and a fresh painting.

* * *

After the burnt stove was replaced and the kitchen was painted, Mama remembered her promise to me, "When you turn twelve year, you'll become part of the dish washing rotation."

I joined the dish washing crew. As Mama saw my ease in the kitchen, she got the idea that I should cook also. "You've been watching me cook for years. Let's see what you've learned."

Mama made me part of the cooking rotation crew, also. Soon, Daddy only wanted to eat my mama's cooking or mine. A talent had turned to a punishment! I asked why!

My mama told me, "Abraham said that Nora's cooking is too greasy, and Reba just slops her food together."

After I began my period, my mama told me, "You can't cook during this time. Abraham, studying to be a minister, feels that women are unclean during their monthly cycle. He practices Ezekiel 18:6, which states, 'The man who hath not come near to a menstruous woman …is just, he shall live.'"

I knew crazy, fanatical Bible interpretation made it the 'period' of separation. I was happy for a week off, but this isolation itself made me feel unclean and inadequate. Reverend Love encouraged this old Bible tradition. I had read the Bible, too. His behavior spoke of Ephesians 4:19, which states, "Who being past feeling have given themselves over unto lasciviousness, to work all uncleanness with greediness."

According to his belief, would Reverend Love go to hell when he died because of his sexual behavior toward his children?

During this growing up period, I had learned that children, especially girls, were "to be seen and not heard." Girls were treated the same way White people treated 'Colored' people. I had watched as a young child that the roles between boys and girls favored the boy and lessened the worth of the girl. The girls had to wash dishes, cook food and clean the house. My two brothers, the sons of the king, did not participate in the rotation cooking nor dish washing cycle. The boys had to take out trash, rake the yard and could go off and explore aimlessly for hours.

I dared to question Reverend Love about the unfairness in the assignments, "It's not fair. Taking out the trash and raking the yard only takes about half an hour. What girls have to do takes half of the day."

He roared, "You're just making an excuse to get out of your chores!"

"I want to be able to have some free time also."

As he angrily stomped away, he murmured, "You talk too much anyway."

I mumbled to his back, "Just as you forget to love and protect your children, I forget not to talk back."

I had wanted to find a way to escape some of this doubled-standard insanity!

Chapter 18

Finding a Safe Place

Reverend Love showing me his ugly thing was a turning point. I wanted to run away from everything. I decided to join the rest of the roadrunners and check out the forbidden streets. This was the first time I had ever left home without permission. I was tired of being a good girl. *Where would I go?* I wandered back to my old neighborhood. And an alley of shotgun houses.

Recently, the Love family had moved from the three-room-shot-gun-house-in-the-alley to the Greens Homes low-income public housing. We thought we were making progress. My mama's old antique mirror, the slave-carved crib, the broken shaving mirror pieces, my Princess mirror and my daddy's missing shotgun had come with us. Along with Mama's depression and my fear of being hurt by Reverend Love, many of the broken pieces of life continued to show up.

As soon as I had passed Downing Alley and three houses on the right, I saw an older girl named Janet sitting on her porch. The porch was almost as big as our house. It wrapped around both sides of the house and stopped at a rising chimney on one side and at the kitchen on the other. White chairs and various flowers and plants decorated the porch. There were hanging ferns, climbing ivy, and a swing that seated four. Janet's house sat on the street, not in an alley.

Janet called out to me. "Hey, Bookworm! I know you! You were the girl who used to read books while you waited your turn jumping rope."

"Yeah, but they didn't like to play with me. 'Cause they said I read too much! Do you live here? Are you the girl Janet who had to go in before it got dark?"

"That's me. That was a long-time age. I was twelve-years-old then. My grandmother is still strict, but she allows me to have friends on the porch. Where're you going? Do you want to sit with me on the porch and talk? I can get us a glass of lemonade."

My nosy self followed Janet into a magnificent house. I was looking and snooping at every turn. It was a large, tall white castle. Like the big estates that white people lived in up the hill. The interior had many rooms. A high fireplace, four bathrooms, a water toilet and a spiraling staircase. A living place with a library! Almost unimaginable! My new friend Janet was the only one in the neighborhood that I knew who had dictionaries and encyclopedias.

Janet looked at the book I had picked from the shelf, *A Tale of Two Cities* by Charles Dickens. She said, "I see you still like to read. You can always come over here and read and browse through my grandmother's library. I'll ask her. I'm sure she won't mind. How old are you anyhow?"

"Just turned twelve. A few days ago."

"Just twelve?" Janet examined my face closely. "You look and sound older. I've only a few girlfriends. Mama thinks they are too fast and boy crazy."

I asked Janet, "How do you get to live in a family home like this?"

"I have lived with my daddy's parents, my grandmother and grandfather, Mr. and Mrs. Allen since I was a baby. I call them 'Mama' and 'Daddy'. My father moved to California after the Korean war and got another wife."

"Where is your real mama?"

"My real mother lives a few blocks away in an alley where they sell moonshine liquor."

After Janet's grandmother initial questions about my family, she treated me like I was her new granddaughter. Besides, the first day she encouraged me to do my homework in the library. At home I did it on the kitchen table.

Janet's grandmother was the strictest person I had ever seen. I wished my family had some strict rules in our house. Like not cheating on your wife and not looking the other way when the children stole or not being sexual with children and not showing them your body parts. That day, I selected Janet's house for an oasis from the terror. It became my regular place of escape for me to eat, to read and have a safe house from the lurking nasty daddy.

One day, when Janet was cleaning, I asked her, "Can I help you clean up?" We changed sheets on four beds and dusted six rooms.

Later, as we did our homework in the library, Janet told me, "Mama will pay you if you help us to clean, cook, wash, iron and to take care of this rambling barn." Janet spread her arms all around and laughed. "I guess you call it a 'room and board' house."

"It show is big. I counted fourteen rooms, with ten bedrooms!"

"My grandmother rents rooms to her grown children who are local teachers, other 'Colored' teachers and civil servant workers who live in surrounding areas, but work in Kinston."

Janet presented a work plan to me as I put the books back on the shelf. I was helping Jean out every day anyway. *To be paid for what I liked doing?* I wanted to jump with joy, but I controlled my enthusiasm. My mama said I shouldn't be so quick with my feelings.

"Is this why y'all have a library, the dictionaries and books? I show will tell my mama. She won't care."

Then I thought, *This is not the place for lazy, alley talk. The right word is 'sure'. Not 'show'. These educated people do not tolerate alley talk and low living. In this household, married women are called Mrs. In my world, Miss. Why? Another mystery.*

About a week later, Janet told me, "Mama sees you as an innocent young girl who can go places with me. This is the only way I can attend any social outings. You're tall for your age and can fit my clothes and shoes. This way you can go to school dances and proms as my guest. Please ask your mama if you can go to the Christmas dance with me. Grasshopper, the guy next door, is going to be there. Also ask her if you can stay for dinner today."

"Okay. I'll have to talk to my mama about this." *Dinner? We say supper. A new way of talking.*

Around 5:00, after I finished my homework, I ran home to the projects to talk to Mama about the Allens. As I eased into her bedroom, I heard voices. I peeped in the dark room. The curtains were closed. Mama was stretched across the bed, talking to herself. The bedspread was twisted in a ball and clothes were strewn across the floor. Mama's deep expressive eyes looked like the face of a dead catfish that was left in the sun too long, blood-streaked, gray and puffy. The wrinkled, torn housedress was the same color of the dead catfish.

Mama looked through me and continued her conversation. "I tried to get you, but your daddy gave you to his sister up North." *Lord have mercy!* Mama was talking to Timothy Earl who was not there! Before I could even ask about the Christmas dance, I saw that the keeper of the inn was not in. I realized that Mama's lapses of memory and wanderings in the minds were increasing. Another visit from the Kinston Clinic would be coming.

I simply said to the room, "I'm going to be working for Miss Allen a lot. She invited me to dinner."

Mama's response made me feel like jumping off the Adkin Bridge.

"Nora, turn on the fan. It's burning up in here." It was a cold autumn's day. I walked back to Janet's house with scalding tears, leaving a dirty trace of sadness, hurt and confusion down my cheeks.

"What happened to your face?"

I lied. "A gnat flew in my eye."

Janet asked me, "Did Miss Emma say, '"Yes?"'"

I lied again. "She thinks it is a good idea."

"Okay. I'll tell Mama. Wash your face and hands in my bathroom. Mama wants you to stay and eat with us. This means you are totally accepted by Mama. She's a snob. She's been watching your behavior. Mama said you are teachable. We are going to help you. But try to be quiet. Mama believes that children should be heard, not seen."

"No problem. My mama believes the same thing."

After that, I silently joined in the family evening dinners, the after-dinner discussions and television watching in the den. I secretly became the "fly on the wall", as Mama called it, and absorbed the culture of middle-class 'Colored' people at mealtime.

By this time, I had learned to mind my own business, like my mama was often warning me to do. I had taken it further and learned to pretend I was not there. I had learned things listening to my mama and her friends talk privately, right in front of me. Now, during conversations that had to do with me, I could not have a voice, because I was not there.

Dinner was held in the spacious formal dining room. According to Janet, "Formal means linen tablecloths and napkins, plates, silverware, glasses and cups in various sizes in individual place settings." I had only seen this type of eating on television. The family included Janet, two aunts, two uncles, a cousin, the grandmother, the grandfather, four other roomers and the newly found self-appointed child—me. My name place card stated, 'Miss Doris Anne Love, Guest of Mrs. Allen'. Janet whispered to me, "Make sure you follow Mama's expected decorum. And watch me."

I listened to the group of well-dressed, educated 'Colored' people discussing 'The Negro Problem' like it was a separate problem from them. It was then that I saw that I was born into a nation, community, school, family and culture that had a pecking order. The poor, especially 'Colored' people in the South, were at the bottom of the social dump. The low-income people who lived in the rundown projects, the shanty towns and across the cemetery were blamed for their lowly living conditions.

The unemployment in the small Southern town was a favorite topic. One of the roomers was a regional employment official. Mr. Carter argued repeatedly, "Things would get better for the Negro if the Negro became educated and got better paying jobs."

All of Janet's aunts and uncles had become my aunts and uncles. Uncle Johnson argued with Mr. Carter. "Education is a key way to improve your life, but the 'poor' should not be blamed for poverty. Where do they get money for college?"

Reverend Love's low-income job qualified us for admission to the projects, but not to college. He maintained several income-making activities. He was not the exception to the family man who worked hard despite racism, to provide for his family.

I thought, *At least, these educated, light-skin 'Negroes' didn't call us or themselves 'Colored'! But we still aren't 'Negroes'! Is 'Negroland' a country, like France?* But I was there to observe and learn because the new 'Negroes' had a lot to teach me.

I knew how to be quiet and keep my mouth shut. But I had a problem figuring out how to get food on my plate and into my mouth. My mama always gave us all our food at one time. As Mrs. Allen passed the platter of food around. I wondered, *Do I put each food item on my plate?* Chicken, rice, corn, peas, cabbage, pork chops, cornbread, biscuits and a cut-up green vegetables with cucumbers and tomatoes dish. My plate became a tower of food!

Reverend Love or his Sunday guests always got the chicken leg, my favorite piece. I decided I wouldn't miss out on this opportunity. As I started with a bite off my chicken leg, Mr. Allen said, "Would you please bow your head so we can pray?" I should have watched Janet!

At home, we would also have our grace before we ate. I thought Janet and her family were Catholics. I guess even Catholics prayed before they ate too. I didn't know if I should continue to chew. Or should I swallow the big bite whole? I prayed that Mr. Allen would soon finish his prayer. I needed a drink of water. I was choking, my eyes were bulging, but I kept my mouth shut as I had been trained. Janet saw my situation and whispered, "Drink a little water." I was glad she poured it for me because I didn't know which glass to use. The water sent the stuck juicy chicken sliding down my eager throat. Prayer was over and it was time to eat.

I noticed right away that Janet cut her pork chop with a knife and fork. I was not going to try that. When I picked up my spoon, Mrs. Allen's eyes closed. She slightly kicked my leg under the table and pointed to the fork. I didn't know what to do with the cloth napkin. I didn't see Janet's until she wiped her mouth.

Anyway, it almost looked like a Kotex, so I didn't worry about it. My period was over last week.

A magnificent three-layer white icing, pineapple cake awaited at dessert time. This treat sat on a royal side buffet table. Two glass vases of multicolored fall flowers adorned each side of the buffet. 'Crystal' as Janet and Mrs. Allen informed me.

When it was time for dessert, Janet came in with matches and began to put candles on the cake. No one said anything. I became breathless, stunned and speechless. It was hard for me to say, "No. this can't be for me. My birthday was last week." I hadn't had a birthday celebration since I was five years old.

Everyone stood and sang, the "Happy Birthday Song." All eyes full of soft family love were for me. By the time they got to the third line, "Happy Birthday to Doris," I knew what I wanted to say. When they were finished singing the fourth line, "Happy Birthday to you," I opened my mouth to say it. All that came out was a well of hurt, salty tears mixed with surprise and joy. I didn't realize how deeply I was wounded on my fifth birthday. I had been smothering my feelings since then.

Without asking why I was crying so brokenly, the Allen family allowed me to cry. They all gathered around me in a healing family hug. Mrs. Allen assured me, "It is okay to cry. God gives us tears for balance. Holding it in makes you sick. It's good to cry. It hurts to be happy all the time, too." Everybody agreed and laughed.

As the river of emotion dried up, Janet said, "Doris, you have to blow out your candles so we can cut the cake. Your mama told me this was your favorite cake."

Later after dessert when my tears were emptied, I announced shyly, "I want to thank Mrs. Allen for inviting me for dinner and the birthday cake. The cake was almost as good as my mama's cakes. May I ask, who made it?"

Mrs. Allen smiled, "I ordered it from "Emma Love Catering Service." We all laughed again. Laughter and tears are needed in life. I had my share of tears. I wanted more laughter to balance the opposite, as Mrs. Allen said.

A creeping sense swept over me that it was time for me to leave my safe place and go home. I was not ready to go back to the projects.

But Aunt Naomi had taught me, "It is better to be asked to step up than to step down."

As I stood to leave, Janet stopped me. "Wait. Mama gave you this. And Uncle Johnson is treating us to the movies tomorrow." It was a gigantic overstuffed 'Happy Birthday' shopping bag. The fancy paper bag splashed pictures of glowing, yellowish orange birds of paradise across a green field. The handle was woven yellow silk ribbons. On each side of the bag was the name BRODY'S.

By the time I walked the three blocks home, I had already peeked in the shopping bag. The gift was zipped in a yellow silk sack. I ran straight upstairs to my empty room and laid the gift out on my bed. I was overcome with gratitude and wonder. It was a fur trimmed hooded black leather parka with matching fur trimmed gloves. Mama had told me, "'Brody's is the most expensive department store in town. This is where the rich White people and uppity siddity 'Colored' people shop.'"

I loved 'uppity siddity' clothes! This time the cat did not snatch my tongue. I screamed and screamed and screamed with unrestrained joy! There was no one home to hear me.

Of course, the next day, I wore my new fur trimmed hooded black leather parka with matching fur, trimmed gloves from Brody's to the movies. Janet and I met her across-the-lane lover at the 'Colored' theater. I knew the routine. I told Janet, "I am going to sit up front." Janet and Grasshopper sat upstairs in the dark balcony, the last two seats in the last row in the corner. When the shows were over, Grasshopper gave Janet a parting hug and took a different route home. On the way back Janet always asked me, "Doris, tell me the name of the movie, the characters and what the movie was about. You know Mama will want to know."

I reported like a good student. "It was a double feature. The first one was *Million Dollar Mermaid* with Esther Williams and Victor Mature. Esther Williams played a great swimmer who wore a one-piece bathing suit that caused a scandal. The main show was *The Ten Commandments* with Charleston Heston and Yul Brynner. It was the story of the life of Moses who led the exodus of the enslaved

Hebrews. That we read about in the Bible." The two movies gave the love-starved teens six hours to smooch.

Before we arrived at Janet's house, I decided to tell my self-adopted sister, "My daddy did some nasty things to Nora. He showed his private parts to me and he tries to touch my breast when he passes by me. I feel so ashamed when I have to ask him to buy me sanitary napkins."

Janet cursed. A secret game we shared. "That fucking bastard! Your daddy is your father. For him to try to be sexual with you is an abomination to God. He should be full of shame and sorrow—not you. If I told Uncle Johnson, he would have him disappeared on a long dark road. Do you want him killed?"

I didn't answer. Janet was silent for a moment. Then she said, "If I told Mama, she would think you're a 'ruined' girl. She may not let us be friends. This must be our secret. I will ask Mama to get you a supply of Kotex when she gets me my tampons."

"What in the hell is a tampon?" Then I got quiet again. "No. I didn't want him dead. I just want the fear and the hurt to end. Can Uncle Johnson have him burned up and or throw him in a river? I'm just joking." *Or was I?*

Janet reassured me by telling me her secret. "I have a sister that my mother gave away. I'm glad my grandmother got to me in time. You are the sister I can have. You two are probably the same age. We'll always be friends."

Finally, I told Janet about the real money problems at home. The next day, Mrs. Allen hired me as the rice cooker and the handy maid. I became an official part of her work staff, along with her housekeeper and her gardener.

As I became part of the Allen's household more, Janet finally told me other family secrets. A week later, after dinner, as we washed the dishes, Janet said, "Aunt Lola is an alcoholic. Uncle Joe is unemployed. Aunt Loretta and Uncle Johnson are getting a divorce. My cousin, their son, Carl hurts animals. He burned our cat. Mr. Carter tried to have sex with me. I didn't tell Mama. Look out for both. The last thing, you have to swear you won't mention it."

She became very serious. Almost scared looking. "I can keep a secret. Like a squirrel can hide a nut."

Janet almost whispered. "Mama cheats on Daddy when he is away working on the train. She spends some nights with Mr. Collins, the funeral homeowner. He is Aunt Loretta's real daddy. Everyone knows except Daddy. You promise?"

"I promise." I began to see that there was no perfect family. My many talks with Janet still left me full of hopelessness and sadness. But she did help me to remember it was not my fault.

I had just turned twelve years old when I aligned myself with my sixteen-year-old friend/sister Janet and her middle-class family. I hadn't experienced 'normal' love and calm family living in a long time. My mother loved me, but it was a little crazy because she was a little crazy. The conditions in the Allen household met the requirements of my dreams-good shelter, good food, good books, good intellectuals, good friends. They had all the elements of good living that I had imagined.

This family helped to save my life when I was a teenager. Without their showing up, I could have been a runaway, become an alcoholic or wound up in jail. My friendship with Janet was the way God provided safety for me. Their love and care were a valuable help as I dealt with my broken family and the suffering at home. I spent all my teen years there, soaking up how I thought intelligent people should live. I knew Mama couldn't help being sick, but I felt she had abandoned us in her sorrow. After many days of not seeing me, my mother's reply to where I was became a begrudging smirk, "She's over at her other family." I guess she felt abandoned also.

The other important thing that happened when I was twelve was Rabbit's return. Rabbit was gone for about seven years. Yet, when trouble came knocking again when I was twelve, Rabbit started to show herself again. When I left Janet's house on the night of my twelfth birthday dinner, she jumped in front of me and vibrated, "Are you ready to go to the river?"

When I got to the porch, Rabbit hovered around Mama's flower plot, sniffing daises. I didn't answer the question because I was afraid of what would happen at the river. I also didn't say anything because the cat had quickly snatched my tongue again. I went inside. Happy that the trickster was back. Rabbit had disappeared into a yellow snapdragon.

Chapter 19

Secret Arts: Herbal Medicine

When I knocked on her apartment, Aunt Naomi looked through the peephole and said, "Emma sent the right one." She opened the door and I walked into a minute living space. Apartment #5 contained a cot, a small table and two chairs, a wardrobe for clothes and an old radio. A tiny gas stove and a matching tiny ice box stood next to the kitchen sink area where dishes and clothes were washed.

And I thought our house was small! I had been in here many times, but today my eyes were wide open.

"I need someone to help me to prepare my healing herbs and calming salves. For my spirit work. I like your curiosity and you follow my directions."

I was fascinated with my strange aunt who had an orangish red complexion and wavy black hair like my daddy. Daddy cut his wavy hair, but Aunt Naomi wore two long braids down her back, like the Indians on television. Neither of them liked to talk about their family, but I had found out that their mama Tayanita was half Indian, a Cherokee.

"You and Emma have good souls. You can be workers." Aunt Naomi explained, "Working with herbs is a way, under God's guidance, to secure balance, power and safety. I am a trained worker. I have been doing this since I was a child your age."

I thought to myself, *You mean a thirteen-year-old child can learn how to do this?*

"Some children are born with the gift of the secret arts. As I was growing up, I knew children as young as five who had the call. I can tell when a person is called to do this work. Many are called, but few have clean hearts."

I was shocked! She had answered without me asking. There is something special about Aunt Naomi. *Was this why I was born into this family?*

Before we started to work, Aunt Naomi said, "Wash your hands and then I will pray. You can use the sink in here."

Near the sink was a long special built work counter that held dishes, pots and pans on the top shelf. Plants, herbs, bird feathers, roots, twigs, rocks, and other supplies for her secret arts were on the second shelf. On the bottom shelf of the work counter leaned a big bag of light brown lumpy dirt. 'Clay'. Aunt Naomi told me, "Pregnant women eat it."

She lit a white candle and burned a long skinny stick. The smell from the stick perfumed the room with a softness and put me in a very calm mood. Finally, Aunt Naomi waved a burning plant she called "sage" over the various materials on the counter. She had taught me that sage clears the room of old energies and invites the spirits in. Aunt Naomi picked up her small African statue, *Yemaya*, from the table, closed her eyes, held her head back and spoke some mysterious words. When she opened her eyes, they were red and had tears in the corner. I wanted to ask, *What is 'spirit'?* But something told me to wait. I would ask later.

Placing the statue back on the table, she said, "I did a reading about your daddy being a worker of the secret arts. The reading verified my feelings. Your daddy cannot suggest, prescribe or do any healing. He can only do what is given to him to do. Working with these roots, without permission from the spirit, can be harmful. He knows this but tries to do things his way. I do know you reap what you sow. I had already told Emma to watch out for him."

Spirit! There's that word again.

First, Aunt Nellie sprinkled some 'holy water' from a bottle on us. 'Florida Water' was written on the label. She walked over to each of the four corners of her box-shaped apartment. Then, with her finger, she touched her chest up, down, left, right. "This cleanse the room and protects the workers. Come over here and practice the same thing."

I was at her side before she had finished speaking. After I performed the cleaning ritual, Aunt Naomi said, "You did well. Continue to follow my directions and watch what I do. This is serious work." When she sat down at the worktable, I sat next to her. She opened a box of twelve black and white tiny, ointment tins. "Take every bit of salve out of the tin lids and mix it together with this stuff."

What is this stuff? This 'stuff' looked like grass, roots, small rocks and tar. It smelled like the tar that the road workers poured on the ground to make a street. It also smelled like Sulfur 8 that Mama used to make Nora and Reba's hair to grow. My hair was long, thick, and bushy, and according to Mama, "grew like weeds."

These thoughts took my concentration away from the chore at hand. When I remembered to pay attention to Aunt Naomi, I noticed that she re-scraped the little tins after I had finished with them. She also used the nail file and a toothpick. I only used the file. Aunt Naomi didn't tolerate waste. As I used both tools, each tin inside became clear enough to see my happy eyes in the fully scraped tins. Aunt Naomi looked at me and smiled.

Next, together we mixed the ointment salve and the 'stuff' together. Aunt Naomi divided the big basic batch into various portions, with specific medicines and herbs. Finally, as she made the individual packs, she said, "Little Doris, would you write the numbers and names on these labels? And stay out of your head and stay in the room."

The suggestion sent me straight to my head. She sounded like my teachers when they warned me about daydreaming during class. Was I that obvious?

Out of the silence, Aunt Naomi spoke, "My handmade mojo bags are made for protection, power and success. If the wearer decides harm and trickery, the results overtake him. Life returns what you send out."

Uhm. This must be important. She keeps on saying it. We worked with the herbs until Aunt Naomi said, "We can stop now. You are a good helper."

She gave me a sandwich and four new shiny quarters for my work. After I ate my sandwich, I asked, "What's 'spirit'?"

Aunt Naomi closed her eyes and waited. She listened, as if someone was talking to her. Finally, she breathed out, "Anything you can see, touch, taste, smell and feel with your heart is 'spirit'."

"Aunt Naomi, I have one more question." It seemed like I could ask Aunt Naomi anything. "What is the voice that speaks to me? Sometimes it speaks to me when I am sleeping or when I am playing. It's teaching me to calm down and when to ask my questions. It whispers in my ear a lot. It just told me to ask you this question."

Aunt Naomi was silent for a moment. Then she said, "The good voice is the part of God inside of you. That voice is God's spirit that's with you wherever you are. This is part of the soul that you can't see or touch, but you know it's there. You feel it in your heart. It's the part of God that makes you know that you know. You don't have to understand to know. Understand?"

She smiled softly and then lightly placed her hands over the heart area in my chest. My heart was calm and listening.

"The mean, ugly voice belongs to the devil. Before you ask Doris, the devil is the opposite of the good part of God. Because you can't see God or the devil, you have to be careful of the voice you obey."

Gee whiz! Do all adults talk in riddles?

Before I left, she shoved a brown grocery bag in my hand. "Go straight home and give the biggest cloth bag to only your mama. Emma already knows how to mix it. Tell her to use it for three days only. And sprinkle some of the herb from the wax paper in Abraham's shoes before he leaves the house. The small purple cloth bag is yours."

Excited about my new shiny quarters and the lesson with Aunt Naomi, I ran home to give Mama the supplies. She met me at the door. When I showed her the money I made, she blew up! Her face frowned up and her voice was too loud for the small hallway. "Is that all she gave you for three hours of work? I told you she was stingy!"

I gave Mama the bags and the instructions. "Aunt Naomi said you would know what to do. Use it for three days. Sprinkle some herbs from the wax paper in Daddy's shoes."

I didn't tell Mama about my purple mojo's bag that Aunt Naomi had given me. Even though my happy feelings sagged a little, I was glad Mama sent me to Aunt Naomi. I said nothing else.

"Doris. This is our secret. Don't tell your daddy. He don't have love like he should. This helps us out. I have company. Evangelist Thelma's in the kitchen. Go get the mail."

I came back and stood in the hallway, quiet and invisible, holding the mail and my curiosity. I stayed in the background until they finished talking. I heard my mama ask Evangelist Thelma, "What can I do about Abraham trying to use some roots from the Snow Hill conjurer man to block me? He still tries to use herbs, despite Naomi's warning."

Evangelist Thelma advised, "His heart is seared with a hot iron. Use some body fluid. Spit, blood, or pee. Write his full name on a piece of brown paper. Put the fluid on the paper and let it dry for a few days. Then burn it. Bury it near a tree when you finish."

When they began to whisper, I went upstairs. Soon Evangelist Thelma left. I watched her walking down the street, leaving a trail of magic, mystery and majesty behind her.

When Nora came home, I told her, "Evangelist Thelma came to see my mama today."

Before I got a chance to tell her what I had learned, she exploded! "You know I don't believe in that devil mess. I can't stand Evangelist Thelma! All her long white spooky clothes! With her witchy self! And you don't need to be concerned about it."

Nora was mad! I couldn't tell her that I had l just learned new uses for spit, blood and pee. She didn't know that Aunt Naomi was a skilled healer, respected herbalist, and the leader of a network of spiritual herbalists. My aunt had told Mama and me, "I use herbs to heal burns, cuts, broken limbs, skin breakouts, coughs, colds, tooth and earaches, women troubles, pregnancy problems and all spiritual and emotional problems." Aunt Naomi insisted, "Most life problems start in the heart, the soul and the gut."

I couldn't tell Nora that my mama and I were already in training to be workers of 'the secret arts'. Aunt Naomi taught us her secret medicine whenever we went to her house or when she came to ours. Mama and I never talked about this to each other.

Mama and I had an unspoken agreement. *This is to be our secret.* This secret sealed our love for each other and made our relationship special. I knew then that I had chosen the right mama.

Secret medicines, spell-making and luck-crossing were other unnamed influences in the Love's household. Good and bad. God and evil. Jesus or Devil. Aunt Naomi would help me to learn the differences. I had to understand!

Chapter 20

Getting Religion: Jesus Medicine

I was thirteen, the year of the born-again experience. It happened on a Saturday morning during the summer. The night before, Mama and Daddy had a violent argument. It was Friday, but there was not going to be any family fun. Something else had come up. During supper, Mama screamed at him, "You are the biggest hypocrite in the world! I don't believe your lies about some business that can only be handled at night. You lie more than a Philadelphia lawyer!" These were her words for a skilled liar.

Daddy, trying to deny his 'roaming eyes' as Cousin Babs called it, snapped, "You're just too possessive! A man can't sit up under his woman all the time!" He left the house, bound for Jay's Juke Joint on Sugar Hill and the waitress named Claribel.

Even if he came home late Friday night or early Saturday morning, every Saturday Daddy spent time alone in the bedroom. He still studied his Sunday School lesson and read his Gideon Bible. He had taken it from a motel when he went to Oak City to 'see his family', the story he told Mama.

On this Saturday, from the kitchen, my mama, Nora and I heard my daddy scream at the top of his lungs, "God, please forgive me for my sins! I am your son! I want to come home to you!"

Mama turned to me and said, "Stay here." Nora was ironing. The other children were out in the streets, somewhere doing what project children do on a Saturday—playing ball, at the movies or shoplifting. Even though it was a summer day, it was not warm. The dark clouds hung low in the distant sky. I could feel that something was about to happen.

By the time Mama took her pies out of the stove and put more in, I reached their bedroom upstairs first. I turned quickly and jumped down the stairs before she came up. I was glad he didn't see me. I knew he would like the idea of me seeing his ugly 'thing', anyway.

"Emma! I'm on fire! The Lord is calling me to repent of my sins! I want to be washed clean! These sins are heavy!" Daddy's groans and pleas were heard throughout our project apartment.

Mama came into their bedroom. This time I walked behind her. Mama quickly pushed me toward the door. Too late. I had already seen *it*. I stood in the door sideways so I could peep out of my left eye.

"Abraham, calm down and put your clothes back on."

The bedroom looked like it had been hit by a hurricane. Papers, pillows and ashtrays were lying everywhere. Two empty moonshine jars littered the floor. The bedspread was hanging over the door, covering the ancient mirror. Mama immediately took the bedspread off her most prized piece of furniture. Then she folded the crumbled spread across the bottom of the bed.

In the middle of the bed was the motel bible. A large gold cross, the same length of the Bible, kept it opened to Psalm 23. The dresser had been flung open and letters were strewn everywhere. Some letters had scattered under the bed. The big aluminum tub that we used to bathe in, before we had a bathtub, filled with water, sat in the middle of the floor. Daddy was standing there, as naked as an elephant, with his thing sticking out almost as long as an elephant's nose. He knew that mixing his own herbal concoction was a no-no.

Daddy dropped the mixture on the bed. As he scooted around on the floor, he found some of his clothes and struggled to put them back on. He continued, "Lord, I want to do your will. I will preach your word and tell your people the truth."

After Mama looked over the damages, she softly suggested, "Abraham, let me get the deacons from the church to help in your baptism. I think you would prefer to be baptized in the Neuse River than this little tub. Besides, you will get water all over the new linoleum you just bought." That thought calmed Daddy down.

He nodded his wobbly head, "Okay."

Standing sideways in the doorway, I could hear my daddy reading from the Bible, "The Lord is my shepherd. I shall...."

Mama's voice drowned Daddy's out. "Doris, get some clean clothes for your daddy off the clothesline. Tell Nora to iron two white sheets for the baptism clothes. Go tell Deacon McCoy at First Baptist that we need the baptism committee to take your daddy and me to the Adkin River right behind the Adkin High School so he can get baptized. I'm going to get baptized again."

Mama gritted her teeth as she remembered, "I told you to wait in the kitchen!"

My imagination leaped! *The Adkin River is the river I can go to! My friend Rabbit and the Love Voice had told me to go to a river.* It ran behind Miss Doris's house. Maybe today would be the day I could go there to see if it was the right one.

As nosy as Mama knew me to be, she was not surprised to see me following her. She knew she could count on me to do all her immediate chores that required action and secrecy. Mama also recognized right away that baptism might change the whole direction of our family. There was no time to waste and argue with me. As Mama always said, "Strike while the fire is hot!" Daddy wanting to give his life over to God was the answer to her prayer. It was like a miracle! He was calling for a change in his sinful life.

Maybe the baptism would stop him from hurting Nora, Reba and me. Last year, Nora had stayed away from home for most of the year, living with a boyfriend. When she came home, she was very much pregnant. Two weeks ago, when Nora and I were washing dishes, my daddy came in the kitchen.

I saw him mumble something to her. When he saw me, he told her, "Go outside and get my hammer for me in my truck."

It didn't feel right so I went behind Nora. When my daddy saw me standing there with Nora, he snatched the hammer and said to me, "You think you are so smart."

I didn't know if this was the first time he had tried anything with Nora again. But now my daddy knew I was watching him. Plus, Nora had already said a long time ago, "Mr. Abraham will be in trouble if he tries to mess with me again."

The next week my daddy decided to turn his life over to God. Mama and I jumped into action to make our life better.

According to Aunt Naomi, "Abraham don't have a calling to work with herbs, nor a clean heart or an ear to hear." Mama knew that the herbs Daddy was mixing for his tub baptism would cause him harm.

Aunt Naomi always stressed to her students and clients, "It is not wise for those of unclean desires and thoughts to mix Jesus' medicine and root medicine. It's an abomination to try to trick God!"

But I was surprised at my daddy's great outpouring of emotion and feeling. I realized that even Daddy had a soul. Mama had said everyone had a soul, even people who kill and men who didn't take care of their children. As I stood at the clothesline, I could hear Daddy crying, "Lord, I want to serve you. I am willing to give up my cigarettes, alcohol, gambling and women. I want to be a decent daddy and a faithful husband. Lord, help my stingy spirit. Forgive me for stealing my boss man's change every day."

Part of me wanted to laugh and cry at the same time. I took all the clothes off the line so I could hear him confess his secret sins from the bedroom window. Besides, it looked like it was going to rain. Outside the window I heard him cry out and repent many wrongdoings. I waited for him to say he was sorry he hurt Nora. He never did. I had to admit to myself, *Mama, you are right. I am so nosy.*

Inside, I told Nora, "My mama wants you to iron the clothes and white sheets for my daddy's baptism and hers, too. She's going to get baptized again."

Nora rolled her eyes and snatched the clothes. "Sis, I've told you my secret. And now you're acting just as crazy as Mama. Both of you act like nothing happened. I don't believe your daddy's sincere. You know what happened two weeks ago when he was trying to get me alone outside. Now this week he's turning his life over to God? Bullshit! Bullshit! Bullshit!"

We could hear Mama and Daddy singing together, "Jesus keep me near the Cross." To me, it made sense that Mama would help Daddy in getting baptized. Baptism would make his heart clean. It wouldn't hurt. Maybe, it will draw our family closer together. I still understood how Nora felt.

The singing continued, "There's a precious fountain, free to all, a healing stream flows from Calvary mountain."

Then I ran out of the projects. The First Baptist 'Colored' Church was on the corner, two blocks from where we lived. I was there in a flash. Saturday was the day that the faithful followers came down to the church to clean, to bring fresh flowers and to prepare for Sunday's service. I gave the message to Deacon McCoy, who sat on the front row, sorting the Sunday School books. On fire for God, he lit up with enthusiasm as he announced to the faithful members, "Mr. Abraham wants to turn his life over to Jesus! He is begging to go to the Adkin River to be baptized! Miss Emma wants to join the army of the Lord, also. I need two deacons and two missionaries to help with the baptism."

I left the church and stopped at the corner store to buy me some penny candy. When I got back home, Deacon McCoy and a line of deacons, missionaries, Mama and Daddy filed out of our house. Mama was wearing a white head rag. Aunt Naomi had taught us some things required sacrifice. I knew Mama didn't want her hair wet. But she would be real upset getting her hair filled with river trash. Mama must surely be in love with Daddy and Jesus to sacrifice her hair and get in the muddy river water. She had just gotten her hair done at the beauty parlor the day before.

As the baptism procession marched to the car, the 'Thank you Jesus!', 'the 'hallelujahs!' and loud church music hushed. Now, all the neighbors at home could hear my daddy pleading with God, "Lord, deliver me. I am tired of being bound to my sins. I will not run from you anymore. I want to be saved!" *Imagine! Daddy confessing his sins in public and going to get baptized!*

After his car was filled with Mama, Daddy and the baptism committee, Deacon McCoy's passion for the Lord exploded. His voice cried out, singing, "At the cross, at the cross, where I first saw the light." He drove off, as my mama would say, 'like a bat out of hell', to wash away my parents' sins. I knew that the few who didn't go to witness the baptism would sing, dance and shout until they wore themselves out.

Other church members were sitting in their cars behind Deacon McCoy's car, waiting to help in the work of the Lord. When I saw our neighbors, Miss Harriet and Mr. Clyde getting in their car to follow Deacon McCoy's caravan, I ran up to their car. "Please," I begged, "can I go? I have never seen anyone get baptized."

"Get in! Your mama won't mind!" shouted Miss Harriet as she turned in her front seat to unlock the back door. I jumped into the car and looked back. Suddenly, the clouds rolled away. And the sun began to shine its full strength. The harsh winds left town. The warm summer drizzling rain dried up like scattered raisins. Everything in heaven and earth agreed to this baptism, except my sister Nora.

When we reached the Adkin River, the parking area behind the school was crowded with cars. Everybody had unloaded and was waiting. The singing started again. This time, soft and soothing. It was the Sunday School song that Daddy had taught us, "Yes, Jesus, Loves Me."

Mama had told me that 'the banks' were both sides of the river where the water and the ground met. The water was a muddy gray. It made no sound. It just sat there, dark and still. I had thought about the river many times and now I was here.

"Follow me," Deacon McCoy said to Daddy. He turned to Evangelist Graham. "Do you have his sheet, the baptism clothes and the safety pins?" Deacon McCoy, a good leader, made being a deacon a prized position. The efficient Evangelist Graham gave him Daddy's brown paper sack. Deacon McCoy took Daddy behind a big pine tree.

I turned to follow the two missionaries who led Mama away from the crowd. Evangelist Graham stopped me.

"Stay with Miss Harriet."

Soon my mama disappeared up a small hill. I was mad, but I obeyed. Then I saw Mama and Daddy being led to the banks of the river—Deacon McCoy with my daddy and Evangelist Graham with my mama. The church people wore white baptism uniforms. Mama and Daddy were dressed in white clothes that were pinned with white sheets over them.

At the edge of the river, the baptism team stopped. Deacon McCoy spoke to Daddy,

"Abraham Jacob Love, do you know why you are being baptized?"

"I want my sins forgiven and removed. Tired of the sin business. I want the Holy Ghost so I can live for God."

"Are you now ready to accept God as your Savior and his son, Jesus Christ?"

"Yes, I am."

Suddenly, he dipped my daddy down in the water and held him there for a moment. Daddy came up splashing and speaking some strange words. Daddy and Deacon McCoy soon came out of the water. Daddy jumped up in the air and down in the sand, shouting, "Thank you Jesus! Hallelujah!" over and over until he fell to his knees.

My mama was baptized next, but the feeling from it was different. To answer why she was getting baptized, she quoted a scripture. With a strong clear voice Mama spoke, "Jesus said, 'Where two or three are gathered together in His name, he would be in the midst.' I am doing this to help my family."

There was no sign of the veil of darkness that would fall on her sometimes. On that day I knew that Mama really cared for us. I felt like dancing the way other people were shouting and doing the holy dance. My mama's honest answer had caught everybody's attention. The Adkin River became as quiet as the watery place from which Daddy had just stepped out of.

Deacon McCoy slowly lowered Mama into the cool, healing water. She rose from the dark silent water, flapping her arms wildly. We heard a loud piercing scream come from the newly baptized Sister Emma Lee Love. As they approached the bank, Deacon McCoy saw that the crowd also was caught up with the spirit on the banks of the Adkin. The dancing, singing and shouting went on as Mama and Daddy disappeared behind trees and changed into dry clothes.

By the time Mama came out of the water, I felt like I had already been baptized into something. Whatever it was, it was hard to explain. I didn't know anything about baptism, but I knew I didn't want to be baptized by Daddy's brothers in the church. All those men with the searching eyes and the roaming hands! I didn't trust them!

We rode back with our neighbors. Mr. Clyde said to Daddy, "I told Deacon McCoy that me and Harriet want to get baptized in the spring."

Later, my daddy, Reba, Willie Earl and I sat at the kitchen table, waiting for supper. Paul was out somewhere, and Nora was gone again. But she had left the supper on top of the stove. I knew Willie Earl felt special because supper was canned spaghetti and meatballs, which was his favorite. But I felt like something special had already happened that day on the banks of the Adkin Canal.

When my mama finally came in the kitchen, she had changed clothes. The swish of her pink long, polished cotton dress and the clop of her pink mule slippers turned our heads toward her. As Mama sat down, she turned her head, tied in a matching pink cotton scarf, to my daddy. We children turned our attention in the same direction. He had changed into his studying clothes. He was now wearing a pair of matching beige cotton pajamas and house robe. His new padded house shoes squeaked a little as he came in the kitchen. Mama and Daddy exchanged a strange look and secret smile with each other. When they held hands at the table, I said to myself. *Daddy ain't going out tonight!*

Pretending to roll her eyes, Mama turned to her three children, but gave us her magical rainbow smile. As she picked up her fork, she said. "Y'all the nosiest bunch of children I've ever seen!"

Willie Earl's favorite food, canned spaghetti and meatballs, was especially good that day because it was served and eaten in peace. Even Nora's cornbread wasn't greasy.

Mama's calling us nosy reminded me of the letters that were scattered under the bed during Daddy's getting religion experience. *I'll definitely get them. At my first chance.*

* * *

For a while after the baptism, Mama and Daddy didn't disagree about anything. Daddy awoke every day, making breakfast and speaking the scripture, "This is the day that the Lord has made. I will rejoice and be glad in it."

And Mama woke up and stayed on earth all day in her right mind. A week after the baptism, Mama said, "Abraham, I want to go to the beach this summer." The next weekend Daddy piled the whole family into his almost new station wagon and drove us to Topsail Beach. Daddy had replaced his old troublesome car after the gas tank mysteriously caught on fire. I had nothing to do with this fire.

On the way, Daddy warned, "Topsail is a new segregated part of the beach near Wilmington, built for 'Colored' people. Stay on the 'Colored' side and everything will be fine."

Our favorite part of the beach was the large outside wooden dance floor, near the water. Daddy told us, "It is okay to dance, but stay near the outside on the 'Colored' side. This way so we can keep an eye out on you. Me and your mama will be wading in the ocean water."

White and 'Colored' people danced to the same music on the same dance floor. But double white heavy ropes in the middle of the dance floor separated the White dancers from the 'Colored' dancers. As soon as my daddy's head disappeared, Paul shouted, "Y'all better follow me."

Paul, Reba, Willie Earl and I danced over to the spot where my daddy had told us not to go. The area was near the middle of the dance floor with the double white ropes divider.

We danced by ourselves to a song that my daddy didn't want us to listen to. "Hucklebuckle." Paul was flinging his arms and feet in a wild, crazy way. He didn't see me, and I didn't see Willie Earl. We were all caught up in the music and the "Hucklebuck". Soon each side of the dance floor spread out into an almost half circle like a horseshoe. I eased my way toward the middle to see what was going on.

Near the middle of the floor in a semi-circle, only two people were dancing. On the White side, a White teenage boy with long shaggy hair was twisting and grinding near the ropes. His tee shirt read: 'Carolina Shag.' Directly across from him on the 'Colored' side was my sister, wobbling like a duck and doing the Hucklebuck! Reba had told me earlier about 'Taking the floor' where everyone else would stop dancing and gather around and watch one couple's special dance steps.

Reba was a talented dancer who introduced the latest dances to audiences in school gyms, recreation centers, liquor houses, night clubs and juke joints. At this segregated beach, Reba and her dance partner couldn't cross the double white ropes divider. But together, they took the floor on separate sides of the rope. Reba, full of natural talent and fifteen years of rebellion, and her White partner, trained in ballet, jazz, hillbilly and sixteen years of segregation, danced as if they had danced together forever, somewhere in another world where all colors were beautiful, mingled and equal.

Suddenly, someone cut the ropes and the line of separation disappeared. Everybody was doing the Hucklebuck in one space. Reba's partner began to move the front of his body against her back as she rubbed her big butt against his front. The whole dance floor found partners, not by race, but by age, height and who was nearby. All joined Reba and her partner in following the song's directions. "Do the Hucklebuck. Do the Hucklebuck, wiggle like a snake and wobble like a duck."

When the long song ended, the manager realized the ropes were gone. The jukebox was disconnected. The dance floor was shut down for 'repairs'.

Stopping at the Dairy Queen on the way home topped the day off. Daddy ordered special treats for everybody. Banana splits! But what made the whole day unforgettable was the Hucklebuck dance.

As we rode back in the car, Reba spoke out and said, "In our house, dancing is a sin. The White guy that I danced with told me that young White people come to the beach to hear Carolina Beach Shag music and to dance. And guess what shag music is? Another name for rock and roll, swing, rhythm and blues music. 'Colored' music. Because of segregation, they can't be around our popular Black music and our amazing dancing. Their parents think it a sin to dance with us!"

We waited for Daddy's comments. His face was as blank as a moonless sky. Mama looked straight ahead. To end the discussion, Reba said, "Thank you, Daddy, for allowing us to sin today!"

We burst out laughing. Even Daddy had to smile.

Later, we found out that Willie Earl had taken one piece of the cut ropes without being noticed. His souvenir of how we had integrated Top Sail Beach for ten minutes in 1957 hung over his bed for years.

After a fun day at the beach, Daddy promised, "I intend for us to do more things as a family."

Sad to say, this was one of the few family outings.

* * *

After his new life with Jesus, Daddy became an evangelist who traveled everywhere, preaching the word of God. His time away from home increased. "Emma, I have to preach at a church on the other side of Durham on Wednesday night. On Thursday nights, I will be the guest minister in Greenville." He then began to use his church preaching as the main reason for going out of town and being out at night. I saw Daddy studying the Bible often, but he usually went out of town to preach or teach. Daddy still didn't take his 'First Lady' or their children that the 'Lord had blessed him with.'

After my daddy had been evangelizing for a short time, Mama took Willie Earl and me to hear Daddy preach his first sermon, at the First Baptist 'Colored' Church, his own church. The deacon board president called it a 'Trial Sermon'.

Paul refused to go. "I don't have nothing to wear."

Mama knew that Nora wouldn't come. Reba had begged, "Can I stay home with Nora? She said she would wash and straighten my hair."

Mama didn't have time to fight her willful children, so she agreed.

As we came in the church, I saw a lady wearing a white dress and glasses who look like my mama. The dress reminded me of the dress that the midwife Miss Ellen wore when she helped Nora. When the lady led us up front to sit and gave us fans, I said to myself, *Oh! My God! This is Miss Claribel! She's an usher at my daddy's church!* I was ready to go right then.

Mama, the fashion plate, well-represented Reverend Abraham Love that day. She was super-coordinated with her pale green dress, dark green patent leather pocketbook, matching green patent leather shoes, fancy green lace gloves and a beautiful matching green fan. Her hat, twisted puffs of pale and dark green netting, flowed over her face, like a shield. She stood up, slung her long green puffed netted scarf over her right shoulder. And looked directly at Daddy, sitting on the pulpit with Reverend Murphy, the pastor and Deacon McCoy, the board president. My daddy was dressed in his Sunday best suit, "sharp as a tack" as Mama would say. "An African king, ready to rule his kingdom."

But the queen was not happy with the king. Looking through the veil of her hat, Mama told us, in her pissed-off voice, "Let's go." She threw the fan in her twin's face. Miss Claribel's glasses flipped from her surprised eyes, danced across the empty bench and landed in the middle aisle of the church. Willie Earl and I stepped on them as we followed my mama out of the church.

I whispered to Willie Earl, "I know they're talking about us, but we don't care. We showed that home wrecker that we were tired of her stuff."

Mama had called her that. But Mama didn't know Willie Earl and I had crushed Miss Claribel's glasses. That was our secret.

When I awoke the next morning, I found out that the church deacon board had approved him. On the dresser in the living room, sat a piece of paper. It read, "First Baptist Colored Church of Kinston, North Carolina ordains Reverend Abraham Jacob Love as a minister and a servant of the Lord Jesus Christ." It was dated August 21, 1958. Reverend Murphy and Deacon McCoy had signed it. Now this would make him a real minister.

He's still a jackleg preacher! I thought to myself, *Nora is right. This is fake.*

Mama never went back to First Baptist 'Colored' Church. I followed Mama's example and went to my mama's church. I liked her church until I saw Mr. Brown holding Mama's hands for a long time after the handshake was over. My mama was looking at him the same way she used to look at my daddy. I rushed up and snatched her hand. "Mama! I am hungry. Can't we go eat?"

At least, Daddy's baptism got me going to church more. It was a place where I could learn about the God of my family and the community. I felt hopeful because a protective force seemed to be around me. Going to church helped me to stopped feeling so alone. While I was struggling with the name 'Colored', the people in church did not see themselves as 'niggers' or 'Colored'. They saw themselves as God's children.

Daddy had taped a picture of Jesus, hanging on a cross, to the wall next to the front door. When you stepped into our house, Jesus on the cross greeted you. Sometimes the members' dumb faith in the White man with the blond hair and blue eyes made me mad. The leaders in the church taught, "Without faith, it is impossible to please God." *We don't live in their neighborhood, go to their schools or churches. They don't like us! And their father is our God?* I was only 14. But I had enough sense to know that this didn't make good sense. This was upsetting to me.

The Jesus medicine just didn't work on Daddy. The church's idea of one man, one woman did not match my daddy's need for more than one woman, more than one family and children outside his marriage to Mama. Consequently, my mama's and the church's criticism of my daddy running around with other women created a network of unrest and hypocrisy in the Love household. Cousin Babs had called it "adultery". Daddy didn't give a heck what my mama thought, how his sister felt, what the church taught or what the neighbors said.

And I don't think that God is mad with me if I don't believe in their 'bad religion'.

PART V.
BREAKING THE CYCLES OF SECRETS

Chapter 21

Finding Voice at 14

By the time I was fourteen, the frightening memory of my daddy showing me his ding-a-ling, resurfaced again. I wanted to scream out to the world about Reverend Love and his unspeakable deed. Breaking the cycles of pain and loss became my goal. Later, as his lasciviousness continued, I decided to tell my ninth-grade homeroom teacher, Miss Freeman. But I didn't know how to frame such a tabooed discussion of my 'shameful secret'. I didn't want her to think less of me. After all, Miss Freeman was one of the few people in life who seemed to recognize the path that I was on.

Miss Freeman's youthful fashion, creative teaching and soothing words reminded me of a younger Mama. Her delicate spirit bonded me to her in a most important way. There was something deep and healing inside of her. In her presence I felt the possibility of wholeness for me and Mama. Her quiet fire was used to open students' minds. Maybe, Miss Freeman could teach me how to use my raging fire wiser.

I always suspected that Miss Freeman was a hidden counselor or a licensed minister. The class was constantly participating in self-improvement activities in our homeroom. After a week Miss Freeman announced, "I am going to record each student's voice. This way, you will get a chance to listen to how you sound when you talk. Be open to the idea that everyone has a voice. And everyone has something to say. Each person's voice has its own unique sound in the world. Your voice gives life passion and fire."

Each of us gave a brief speech as our voices were taped. Homeroom was short. Three students would be recorded per homeroom. The first time I heard my own voice on tape was in one of the homeroom's recording sessions.

Feedback was encouraged. One student commented, "Doris, I like the way you organize your thoughts and make your points clear. It's always interesting to talk with you. You should be a writer. You tell good stories."

Another classmate, a band member noted, "You should be a radio announcer because of the timbre of your voice."

"What is 'timbre?'"

I wanted to know.

"Timbre is the pitch and tone that is vibrated as we use our lips, tongues and vocal cords to produce sound. It is the fire and passion we speak from."

Miss Freeman was a skilled teacher.

Fire? Passion? Um.

Carolyn, my good friend sitting in the desk next to me in the class added, "You should be a teacher, nurse or a doctor because of the healing sound of your voice."

The bell for the next class rang. "Doris, please stay after homeroom. I will give you a note to class later."

Our homeroom filed out and Period 2 class came in. "Let's go to the teachers' workroom and finish." Miss Freeman motioned to me.

Carolyn whispered to me as I left, "You're going to get a reading—a short quick lesson on your purpose and self-confidence. I got mine yesterday. It was a reading of life!" She gave me a thumbs up.

I was glad we were alone. Maybe now would be a good time to tell her. As we talked, my teacher pointed out some of my reactions. "Why is it hard for you to accept compliments? When Carolyn suggested that you should be a nurse, teacher, or a doctor because of the healing sound of your voice, you looked shocked and uncomfortable."

"I did like what she said. But I was shocked at the nasal, high pitch of my voice. I was also embarrassed at the emotions that sounded from my voice. I guess I always put too much emphasis on my discomfort and not my probable gifts."

"Doris, remember that exercise was to listen to the sound of your physical voice. There is another side to our voice. Some say it is like God speaking through us. I am telling you this because I feel you are familiar with this aspect of your voice. Fear will keep your voice locked up."

"Is it the same voice that tells me what to say, write or think? I call it the "Love Voice?"

"When you get in touch with that voice, you will get in touch with your own power."

I knew Miss Freeman was right. I had wanted to say to my amazingly smart teacher, *My voice is hidden away in my secret fear of being raped by my daddy. Behind this fear is the belief of not being loved, protected and valued. And behind that fear is the fear that I won't achieve my dreams.* But trying to protect my broken family, I didn't voice this.

Instead, I told Miss Freeman something less dangerous. "My fear of success started when I began to feel that I was not worthy of success. I thought that if I thought I was worthy of a good life, my family would think I was trying to be better than them. Their frequent insults messed up my self-esteem. Even as I think about it now, I often lag behind in my achievements because I want to be loved and accepted."

Miss Freeman *read* me right there. "Being loved does not mean ignoring your dreams, talents or voice. After everyone gets his physical voice taped, we are going to talk about this voice of power that lies inside of us. I call it your soul. I don't know how you know this, but you already seem to know about the soul."

"You're right. I talked about it with my aunt who is a healer."

"I suggest you join the school newspaper so you can begin to express your opinion more. You have a lot to say. When you write, you get to tell and show your soul thoughts and deepest secrets."

"Does writing connect me to the soul that the church says will burn if it sins?"

"This is becoming too complicated. We will talk about some of this in our voice practice during homeroom. The minister over the Youth Department can help you better with those concerns."

My teacher went to Mama's church.

Miss Freeman looked at the clock and said, "It's almost time for recess. Sign up for journalism next year. But, if you continue to practice ignoring the inner voice, you will never find your voice and your power."

By the time I finally decided to tell Miss Freeman the truth about the loss of my voice, another bell rang. Miss Freeman's planning period was over. I still had not told her my full story which would end some of the secrets. But she knew the reading wasn't over. "Doris, we have to talk more. I sense you are not telling me about the real origin of your basic fears and your self-esteem issues. I will give you a note to excuse missing your gym class."

After the break, I went back to my classroom for French IA, taught by my favorite teacher, Miss Freeman. From the reading, I had learned I had a right to my own voice and a right to ask questions and express opinions. Finding my voice and figuring out when to speak or be quiet wouldn't be easy.

* * *

In the morning homeroom discussion, the voice exercises opened me up to the idea of speaking out about my secret. At lunch, a way to change the situation began to form in my mind. As I walked home from school, Rabbit appeared along the curb. Her almost formless figure urged me, *Tell it!* At the red light she crossed in front of a speeding car. *Don't let him get away with it.* At a block from home, she hissed, *Speak up for yourself.* As she hopscotched on the sidewalk in front of me, she sniffed, *Speak up for yourself.* Rabbit urged me all the way home, *Tell it! Tell it! Tell it! This will stop it!*

I decided to walk through the 'Colored' cemetery on Midnight Lane before I turned down my street in the projects. I needed time to think. Along with the 'Colored' church, the cemetery was the most segregated place in town. *Was heaven the same way?* I didn't think so. The plant kingdom did not follow such limited thinking. Overgrown weeping willow trees, with their sweeping, low branches, mingled with lengthy spider webs. Tall Spanish moss plants with curved leaves grew chain-like stems which crisscrossed the surrounding plants and tombstones.

Aunt Naomi, always a teacher, had told me, "The dead spirits gather under the sprawling weeping willow tree in the center of the cemetery at night." In the late afternoon, I could feel the creepiness of the graveyard dead in the old 'Colored' segregated cemetery. She had taught me, "Unrevealed secrets and untold stories are a common denomination on the other side. They pray for a chance to come back." A bright yellowish white light surrounded me, and I realized that I had to confront my demon devil daddy, Reverend Love. Today! This will break the cycles of secrets and pain!

A great wind whirled through the cemetery as I looked for Grandmama Quintilla's grave. I found it near the sidewalk. She hollered out from her steel vault tombstone, *Make it known! Tell the truth!* Great Grandmama Beulah, lounging in her final resting place under a massive, towering oak tree, joined in, *My child, stop it today!*

Mama always said, "Grandmama Beulah was as majestic and as strong as any oak tree." When I looked at the oak tree, I felt the massive presence of my great grandmama.

Rabbit appeared, cawing like an angry crow, resting on top of a tombstone that read, 'Rest in Peace. Mildred Sutton, daughter of Marva and John Sutton, 1891-1895'. A small voice from this grave whimpered, *Write it out for me. I didn't live long enough to learn how to write.* That was Rabbit's story, too.

I ran out of the mournful, spooky cemetery! The haunting cries from the spirits of the dead convinced me to confront Reverend Love when he came home from work. I would not let another day go by without speaking up for myself. And for others. Rabbit, who arrived home before me, was sitting in Reverend Love's truck when he parked it. Rabbit, who couldn't be seen by others, always appeared in places that made me laugh. There was no laughter today.

For a long time, I had reacted to this nameless, unspeakable sex stuff by pretending that I didn't know, just like my mama. Mama shut it out by going crazy. My soul screamed! *I will no longer let this family drive me out of my mind! I will no longer pretend that we live in a normal household! I will not remain quiet! I am not defenseless!*

I knew in that moment that I would use my voice and my truth to stop the hurt and the pain. I had to do it for my beloved sister/mama Nora, who had suffered greatly.

As I walked the short distance home, my mind was full of turmoil about how to carry out my decision. I looked up as I crossed the street a block from my house. My friend, Milton Williams, moved from the opposite side, came toward me, and joined me. We walked together, without saying a word. When we got to my house, I saw my daddy's work truck. I called it house, but it was the Love apartment in the projects. Mama made it feel like a home. I whispered out loud, "Damn! he's home. Please stay here until I check to see if anyone else is here! If he is here alone, I can't be here by myself."

I knew Mama was home that day, but I didn't know if her mind was present.

Milton demanded, "What's the matter?"

Known for his own personal turmoil, Milton was a champion for the underdogs, the downcast and the 'dark skinners'. On the football field, he released his anger by crashing, crushing and destroying any opponent in his path. That day he was calm and caring as he listened to my fearful, secret dilemma.

That moment I knew Milton was one person who wouldn't judge, misunderstand, or reject me. I spoke the words that would literally change my life. "He wants to have sex with me. He's always brushing against me, touching my breast or feeling my thighs at supper! Can't take it! Wanna kill him right now!"

"Who're you talking about?"

"Oh, I'm sorry. I never talk about it. Just the thought of him sends me into a red-hot fury. I'm talking about my daddy. I call him 'Reverend Love', even to his face, sometimes. He's a minister and a hypocrite. Yes, my daddy does sexual stuff to his children. My mama is sick so she can't help. I'm just tired of maneuvering to keep him off me. In a matter of time, he will eventually rape me."

Oh my God! I said it out loud!

Milton immediately jumped into action. "I will stay here until you tell me it's okay. Or until someone else comes. From now on, go to the library after school and do your homework. If I can't come for you after practice, go to a friend's house. And come by the recreation center later. Then I can walk you home. By that time, someone should be there. Please let me know if he tries anything else. If this doesn't work, we'll have to take it to the next level."

The plan was so perfect. I felt so much relief that I joked, "What is the next step? Murder? Set him on fire?"

"Whatever you need for me to do." We laughed. He may have been joking, but I was almost at the point of mayhem, arson and daddicide.

Before I stepped into my yard, the Love Voice gave me exactly what to say. In long determined strides, I walked up to my 'daddy' as he got out of his work truck. My loud, powerful voice on fire, announced, "If you ever try to touch me or show me your ugly ding-a-ling again, I am going to tell Emma Love your wife-my mama, my teacher Miss Freeman, your church members at Sweet Deliverance Temple of Faith, your sister Aunt Naomi, Miss Doris, my god mama and my friend and classmate, the football star Milton Williams about your inappropriate behavior!"

When I had mentioned 'Milton', Reverend Love's eyes went into a roll. Milton's reputation for a quick temper was all over town. Everyone knew that Milton had beat up three basketball players when they were 'playing the dozens'. The guys had jokingly called his mama a 'crippled witch on a broken broomstick'.

Reverend Love was speechless. I was glad I saw how Reverend Love was affected by the name. The name of Milton caused him to drop his head, which seemed to become weary and heavy. Some defeat flashed in Reverend Love's large, startled eyes. As Mama would say, "He knew a new sheriff was in town."

"Milton told me to tell you, 'If you try anything nasty with me again, his team will jump you, that the last time better be the last time!' He also said, 'You'd better stop trying to fuck with Nora, you nasty pervert! Or he'll put his foot so far up your behind and leave something there to remember him by.'"

My using Milton's curse word was a sure sign that his control and abuse were about to end.

I walked in the house, exhausted. Things looked the same as the evening before. In her right mind that day, Mama was putting supper on the table. When Reverend Love finally dragged his bewildered self into the well-maintained government project, he knew that a change had already taken place in the Love household. He winced when he saw me settled in his rocking chair, doing my French homework. Daddy went in the kitchen and sat at the table.

"You home early?" Mama acknowledged his presence. Her greeting was not returned. Reverend Love had shrunk down from the king of his castle to a bankrupted landlord. He knew he was no longer Lord over his family. He could sense that it was time to count his losses. I wondered, *What had I said this time? I had threatened before.* But we both knew—Milton.

I could hear him as he started his Ain't it a Shame Game? *"Ain't it a shame that Paul's threatening to drop out of school and move to New York? Ain't it a shame that Nora has two babies she don't take care of? Ain't it a shame that Reba and Willie Earl are out in the streets?*

Reverend Love, Nora's favorite name for him, realized that he was losing the control he once had over his family. He snapped at Mama, "It is a shame! We don't even own a house!"

I wanted to snap back, *It's your shame. With all the money you make. Not Mama's. Ain't it a shame how you mistreat your family?* But I had done what I was given to do.

I looked around to find Rabbit. I saw her oozing out the door, as toothpaste does when the tube is pressed too hard. It was a sure sign that her time was running out. The form was becoming formless. *I am almost done. Come to the banks of the river so it can be completed.*

Bring the broken mirror. Her message was received in my stomach and rang from my head to my toes with a sound of urgency.

I eased out on the porch to waved 'okay' to Milton who was standing down at the corner, on alert. From that day, my life was never the same. A great turning point had happened.

* * *

After my conversation with Miss Freeman, I wrote every day to find and express my voice. And like Miss Freeman said, 'to release some emotions.' The writing below had partly motivated me to tell Milton about my secret, horrific life as a teenager, living in a house of sexual abuse.

The incident below characterizes the turbulent life in a troubled family. This was the type of private writing that I wrote in my secret diary to pen the terror. I wrote this in the third person objective voice. My English teacher had said, "This is a good way to stand outside of a story to tell it." The title is taken from a saying that Mama and Grandmama used to point to the great wisdom in life that lies hidden below the surface of things. Aunt Naomi used it when she spoke of the truth that underlies all motives. Daddy used it to conceal a lie.

"All Goodbyes Ain't Gone: All Shut-Eyes Ain't Sleep" Doris Anne Love

Cut out that light and go to bed! was the oft-repeated cry of Hattie's mother. Mrs. Taylor was a mere shadow of the former vivacious woman who was bedraggled at the many chores she had managed to almost complete at the end of another frazzled day. Trying to please the Lord of the house, she was seething. She was absolutely tired of fighting with her husband Reverend Taylor about the 'high light bills'. One of her husband's constant complaints was that he was going to the poorhouse because of their wastefulness. The family's daily use of water, gas, lights, food and, probably, air and space.

Mrs. Taylor mused, *Hattie will just have to go to bed when everyone else. There would be no more last minute almost-forgotten homework or hand washing of her pair of once-white bobby socks for gym tomorrow.* She would even have to turn her small bedstand light off and join the rest of the household.

In the dark stillness of the room, Hattie searched for her brother's flashlight. With the heavy, old quilt pulled over her head, she hurriedly translated the French verb "faire" into the imparfait and the passé compose. *Mama don't realize that I have a lot of homework*, fretted Hattie. *These college prep classes require more hours studying than Laura's business courses.*

Wham! The door flung open; the overhead light flicked on; and the older sister Phyllis staggered in. Pretty drunk with it only being a Tuesday night. *Ma! Hattie is reading under the covers again!*

Mrs. Taylor's voice floated upstairs. *I'm not telling you again! Cut the hell out reading that crap and go to sleep!* Before the mother had finished her nightly cry, Phyllis had passed out cold.

With the shade pulled up, the streetlight cast a pale yellowish glow on the forbidden magazine. Hattie furtively devoured it in the squat, upper bedroom that she shared with her snoring sister. She sped through the story. Hattie wondered, before her mother made her nightly rounds to see if all the windows, doors, lights, children were secured, *if the girl in the feature story of the month in the True Romance Magazine received the money to terminate the intrusive pregnancy.*

Just as Hattie finished the story, leaving the unwed mother five months pregnant and going off to a home for unwed mothers, the patrolling Mrs. Taylor pushed against the door fortified with boxes, entered the half-lit room, and announced, *I knew those shades had not been pulled down.* No mention was made of the stack of boxes or Hattie's unusual bed wear.

At last, Hattie gave in to the will of her nagging mother and frugal father and allowed the night to settle about her. She waited for sleep, which eluded her like it always did when she sought it. And she always did. She pressed her eyes tight and prayed that whoever watched over the sky at night would protect her also. There was no sheep to be counted and no milk to be warmed. Hattie simply hoped that sheer weariness would bring sleep. For she had not slept for over an hour in one stretch in four years whenever she was home since....

And as faithful as the night itself comes, after Hattie had locked the door again, re-stacked the boxes at the door, mummified herself in some old jeans, a sweatshirt, a sweater, two blankets and the old, frayed quilt, the familiar scraping of metal against metal clanged in her ear. He used a cloth hanger to unlock the door! Fear raced down her throat and erupted in nauseous waves of hatred and hopelessness in her stomach. *What do you want? Get out of here. I'm going to tell Mama.*

Reverend Taylor chanted his litany from the Bible, *And Lot went up out of Zoar and dwelt in a cave, he and his two daughters. And the firstborn said unto the younger, "Our father is old. Come, let us make our father drink wine, and we will lie with him, that we may preserve seed of our father."*

Just before the rooster crowed next door, Hattie woke up again from one of her many nocturnal naps. A cold, sticky, unfamiliar substance ran from the edge of her mouth, mingled with sleep tears on their way to her ear.

This barricade of clothes had kept the fondler away from her private parts. The only body part exposed was the face. During a catatonic nap, the mouth was used by the lust-driven daddy to stimulate his penis. The fluids from his release were the evidence that he had found an entrance.

In the end, Hattie was raped in the mouth. It was written as a story, but the plot was true. Names were changed to protect the innocent and hide the guilty.

After the incident, I desperately wanted Reverend Love punished! My imagination prayed that he would be laid low, stretched wide and beat between his legs with barbed wire, until his thing fell into the lake of fire, along with his screaming body. I was crazy mad, from his intrusive, ungodly behaviors.

Chapter 22

Launching Out into the Deep

I felt so much relief when I had finally told my Aunt Naomi about Rabbit. One time when my aunt came over, I explained, "My twin's spirit Rabbit first came to me years ago. The spirit of Rabbit had followed me through my childhood. She wants to bring good luck in our family."

"You told me a little before. I bought and cleansed your new Princess Mirror so you could do this type of work for your family. And part of this is releasing her."

"'Replace the broken shaving mirror and put the broken one in the river' was Rabbit's call to me. 'The bad luck can be washed away by placing the pieces in a river flowing in a southerly direction.'" These fateful words of Rabbit followed me through my childhood and early teen years. Rabbit had been gone for several years, but when she came back, she was saying the same thing, "*Go to the river.*"

"I will let you know when's the best time to do your work." Aunt Naomi offered.

"Aunt Naomi, now, every time Rabbit shows up, she seems to be growing fainter and fainter, dissolving into a form that will eventually blended into nothingness. I can barely distinguish her at night or in the blazing sun. I don't know when I should do this, but I know I'm ready."

Before Aunt Naomi left, she said, "This will be big turning point for you. Your life is about to change."

The confrontation with my perverted daddy increased my confidence to tackle the release of my secret spirit friend. By the tenth grade, I knew it was time to go. Going to the Adkin River was required for me to start the family healing. I had been putting off going to the river for a long time.

***

During the hurricane season in the fall of October 1961, due to a tropical storm off the coast of North Carolina, a hurricane watch was announced. It dismissed school early. Mama was on the alert for her children to come home and get out of the weather. I rushed into the house to escape the stinging rain and the bitter winds. I took off my drenched coat and turned around to speak to Mama. Sitting on the couch, Mama and Aunt Naomi were staring at me from a place of deep thought. The only sound was the sharp, boom of thunder.

Aunt Naomi stood up and said, "I told Emma today is a good day to go to the river. Mother Earth's giving her blessings and clearing out old things and reversing negative trends. I want to do this to help my brother's family."

As always, I looked to my mama for approval. Mama didn't say anything. She nodded. Somehow my mama understood the seriousness of my going to the river. Of course, by now I had long resigned myself to the fact that only I could see Rabbit. Others thought I was crazy, just like Mama. But she and I were students of the secret arts. We knew that this was possible. Mama had a wide mind too.

Rabbit, sitting on the couch, jumped up and stood at the door. Both of us knew it was time. I am ready. I guess she was too.

Aunt Naomi continued. "Get your mirrors and let's go before the winds get too strong! The weatherman reported that we won't feel the full blast of the storm 'til early 'morrow morning. Still, put on all your rainwear."

I had already chosen the Neuse River the year 'Daddy' was baptized. It flowed in the required southerly direction. On one of her frequent visits to the house, I'd asked Cousin Babs, a history teacher, about the Neuse River and the water behind the school. She had told me, "Kinston was developed in a high, steep land area, just above the Neuse River. The river's name comes from some Indians living in the area, Neusiok, which means 'peace'. Some call the water behind the school, the Adkin River. It's not a river, but it connects to the Neuse. It's a canal. A canal is a waterway that brings water to some of the farms in this area. The canal was named for the land developer who owned the land."

Eager to get more information, I had asked Cousin Babs, "What was his name?"

"Adkin." We both laugh.

When Aunt Cousin Babs finished the history lesson, she said, "It seems that some of those native people mixed with our people from West Africa."

Hearing this connected me to the Adkin Canal, the Neuse River and the native people forever. Aunt Naomi was here at the suggested time and I was now ready.

My mama, who saved everything, including S & H Green Stamps, fancy shopping bags and funeral programs, rambled in the hall closet to make sure I was fully prepared for the storm. She came out and said, "Here. Put on your Grandmama's old rainwear. It comes with a big green and purple raincoat and matching hat, oversize green galoshes and a green and purple umbrella. May be a little long, but you're tall. Mama wore this the stormy day you were born. It's endured many rainstorms and hurricanes. Still in perfect condition."

Aunt Naomi wore her deceased husband's army rain outfit—an olive-green wool raincoat, a metal combat hat, her fishing shoes, and a long clear plastic raincoat from the secondhand store. When I saw what Aunt Naomi was wearing, I laughed out loud. "Aunt Naomi, you look like a German stormtrooper."

From the corner of her eyes, I saw her lips turned up into a slight smile. "And you look like a walking ad for Grape Nuts Cereal. In fact, we're both stormtroopers today. We are about to kick evil in the ass!"

She was right. But her words shifted my attention. I had never heard Aunt Naomi say a cuss word. Mama was the cusser in the family. Things were already changing.

We left the safety of our house and marched straight into the known path of a hurricane. Both of us bundled up and bent over, looking like two Quasimodos, twin humpbacks of Notre Dame. I had bought the book, the *Humpback of Notre Dame*, in a secondhand store. Some of my life experiences were as disfigured as the main character Quasimodo's deformed body. All of us—Quasimodo, Aunt Naomi and I—were outcasts who struggled to gain acceptance in a disapproving society.

We followed the path of the Neuse River near the cemetery. We could see the loose sandy banks, muddy water and swaying trees. The thicket of underbush made the watercourse hard to see. I chose the part of the river, the *Adkin Canal* (thanks to Cousin Babs), that ran behind Adkin High School.

As we traveled to the banks of the Adkin, I asked my Aunt Naomi, "What is so magical about a river?"

"First of all, the river can describe the life of a person from its birth to its death. You started out happily on your path—clear, pure and sparkling like a diamond. We know your childhood was abruptly ended and you entered the struggles of life too soon."

Aunt Naomi's pause turned into a lesson.

"Just as a river flows up and down, round and about a destined path, so does your life. Your experiences will take you on a voyage over mountains, peaks and secretive, underground living, shotgun houses, hurt, poverty, racism, sorrow and remorse. When you accepted your calling at five, the whole course of your life changed."

I wanted to ask a question, but I knew if I were silent, I would hear the answer.

"A burning desire to learn about life and ancestral energies led you down many entwining roads, with many twists and turns, experiences and lessons. Now you are about to cross over into young adulthood. Just as a river eventually flows into a larger body of water, like a sea or an ocean, you will launch out into an ocean of new experiences. Your life will continue to flow onto greater lessons."

At the water's edge, Aunt Naomi taught me. "Our ancestors saw life as a circle, and we all return to the Source in the end. Life is also a school that uses experiences to teach."

"But why did my twin tell me, *Go to the water.* Why is the river used?"

"Healing spirits live around mountains, rivers, wells, trees, and springs. The river water is healing. Some spirits can be evil, but Rabbit is a helpful spirit."

I asked. "Why don't many people believe this? Most people think what you think, say and do is of the devil."

"Africans and Native Americans believe you can use the forces of nature to influence the future, find lost objects, bring luck or perform healings. The church condemns the practice, but do some of the same things, blindly. Many 'Colored' women suffer because they are ignorant of their obligation to continue the work of the ancient mothers."

"What do they say about twins?"

"Many African people regard twins as special, almost sacred beings. The spirit of your twin was a gift from your ancestors. Twins represent the duality, the tension or balance between opposing forces that's part of life. The spirit world knew your soul was open to other dimensions. Your twin Rabbit was sent for you only. Rabbit's what some call a guardian angel. Rabbit is a trickster figure in some African tales. The spirit told me to train you as a light worker so you could get the full benefit of having divine help. So, let's get the work done!"

Finally, we reached Adkin High School and the Adkin Canal. When we saw the wooden bridge that linked the school to the large, open Adkin Park, Aunt Naomi shouted over the whistling wind, "Let's stand on the bridge!"

Standing on the bridge, remembering the past, I also thought of Hurricane Hazel of October 1954 when I was ten years. It was the worst hurricane that I had experienced. After the hurricane waters subsided, a little girl's body floated down the Adkin Canal. The trickle of water in her backyard became a whirling pool of death and decay. Even though she lived blocks away, her lifeless body was found tangled in some weeds behind the high school. We had been warned to stay away from the flooding Adkin, but I had followed Nora and Reba there.

Aunt Naomi spoke through the growing storm. "Doris, move closer to me so you can hear better."

I shouted, "Okay."

When I moved near her, Aunt Naomi continued, "Look into your mirror as I talk. All the time imagine where you have been, where you are now and where you want to go."

The increasing wind and cold rain sliced through the solemn trees and sloshed against the banks of the Adkin. Bent on shaky knees I took my Princess Mirror out of my carrying bag. When I looked in the flooded mirror, the first thing I saw was a faint image of Rabbit, waving goodbye.

After a short pause, Aunt Naomi said, "Let's get started before the bridge falls down."

From out of nowhere, Aunt Naomi began to laugh. She laughed so uncontrollably that the bridge began to sway rhythmically with the roar of the laughter. I had never heard my aunt laugh. The most I have gotten from her was a raspy, throat grunt. But never boisterous, unrestrained laughter. The wailing wind changed its mournful solo into a riotous duet with Aunt Naomi.

It was then that I realized that Aunt Naomi was being possessed by the spirit of the river goddesses, *Yemaya* and Oya. Aunt Naomi had taught me in one of her classes, "*Yemaya* is "the mother of the world" and "the mother of the fish." She protects children and provides stability and security in our lives. *Oya* governs the winds, hurricanes and change. She brings about the 'winds of change' in our life. During ceremony, ritual or praise, the energies may mount us, take over our bodies and minds. Trust them and don't fear their presence."

I lost myself in the magic mirror and the images that flashed by. For once I had no more questions.

When Aunt Naomi came to herself, she took some apples, small slices of watermelon, black-eyed peas and pieces of dried pork skin from her sack. Then shared them with me. I remembered in the class, she had also told me, "The many seeds in watermelon, which is *Yemaya's* favorite food, represent the expansive range of her motherhood and her power."

That's why the old wives' tales say that a woman who had a baby ate a watermelon seed. It makes sense. I guess Aunt Naomi and Mama had tapped into something.

"Please join me as we invoke the spirit of the ancestors to join us as we honor the waters, the mothers and life. Here is a small piece of peyote that Native North Americans used in their spiritual rituals. Hospitals have used peyote for mental treatment. Others used it during meditation. It can bring peace and healing. It's a natural medicine from a dried cactus plant."

"Peyote! Wait now! Is this stuff legal? Is it safe?"

"Yes, this is safe. I promised your mama that you would be given a minimal dosage, if any. I ate a small piece when we left your house. I wanted to hear if you were ready."

"Is that why you were laughing so wildly? I want to laugh too. I am ready."

"The peyote can reveal a lot of hang-ups that keep us blocked from our real emotions. When the mind is freed, you can open up to God and your true self."

"Is it sold in the State ABC liquor stores?"

"No. You get it from a trained spiritual herbalist and healer. This medicine should be taken under regulated spiritual guidance. You can bite a piece of apple along with it for it is as bitter as quinine."

"I trust what you know. And I trust that Mama is thinking in her right mind again."

"Just as I needed to laugh, you need to laugh too. You are just sixteen. Aren't you tired of all these grown folk situations? Find your own life. Find yourself a boyfriend. And give thanks for your new life that is waiting around the bend of the river. Now, let us share our abundance and gratitude with the Great Mother."

Aunt Naomi threw her food offerings in the river. I did the same. As she chewed her spiritual medicine slowly, I followed her lead. To build up my nerves, I exhaled deeply. I bit off an apple and chewed on the small piece of peyote. It tasted like a dried piece of stick soaked in grapefruit peelings, sugar and peppers.

But at that moment, I struggled to maintain my balance on the shaky, whining bridge. A ferocious north wind slapped me in the face as I caught my magic Princess Mirror. Steadying myself, I clutched the looking glass tightly in my hands and wiped the drenched mirror off with the sleeve of my sloshy raincoat. I caught a misty picture of Rabbit in the muddy canal down below.

"Where did Rabbit come from?" I couldn't wait.

Aunt Naomi answered, "Like I have taught you, we actually live in two worlds. The spiritual and the physical. Rabbit is spirit. 'Cause you are so connected to Spirit, your strong imagination drew her to you."

"You mean I created her with my thoughts?"

"The creative power of your imagination, daydreaming and visualizing drew Rabbit to you."

"Why do I have to release Rabbit?"

"You, Rabbit and your soul are all connected and a part of the Source. You can't be separated from your source. Rabbit is simply part of your soul, seeking expression and experience. Her time is up on this plane of existence. You have reached a place where it's time to stand on your own."

Aunt Naomi anointed both of us and threw herbal dust to the north, south, east and west. "Let's go join Rabbit on the bank so she can be released also. It's better to go down than to be thrown down. Do you have the broken mirror?"

Again, Aunt Naomi burst out in another incoherent peal of laughter, laughing wholeheartedly, waving her long arms over her head. She did a hand dance with the rain. Her hands became a helicopter suspended in mid-air.

Do I have the mirrors? I didn't answer. Partly because I knew it was rhetorical. My English teacher said that some questions are just asked for the effect. Not for an answer. I carefully put my cherished mirror back in the original box it came in. Then I wrapped the box in a towel selected for its storage. The broken shaving mirror pieces had been wrapped in an old towel. They waited to be released.

The other reason I didn't answer was because I felt some fear. I had just heard that God and I are one. That was a helluva leap for a

16-year-old! Who had been taught that God sits high and looks down on us lowly creatures. I had to ignore the surging storm, spiraling winds and hellish rain as I felt in my bag for the wrapped towel. Aunt Naomi had given me some hallucinogenic medicine that was on its way to my stomach and brain. No turning back. I followed Aunt Naomi down from the bridge. Again, both of us, still the Quasimodo twins, crouched and slouched from the assaults of the pounding rain.

As we left the bridge and stood on the bank, I began to get in the flow. I was drawn into some strange place that made me feel soft and fluffy on the inside. Meanwhile, the fierce hurricane winds didn't let up. They splashed and smashed up every limb, tree and bush on both sides of the canal. The fear of the ferocious storm lessened as I shifted my attention on my baptism into a new life.

Aunt Naomi took a tambourine out of her large spiritual sack and said to me, "Music and dance were also part of our ancestors' worship practices. The plantation system did its best to wipe away our culture, arts, song, drums, from our memory. This is what I do as a spirit worker. I create a sacred spiritual space apart from the mainstream religion where we can re-member our sacred selves."

Not a word from me! I surprised myself!

Aunt Naomi announced, "Take out the broken pieces of the mirror and drop them under the bridge over there."

She pointed southward.

Ready to begin a new chapter in my life, I stood on the banks of the Adkin Canal and unwrapped the shattered mirror which was broken into fourteen pieces. I carefully took a piece of the broken mirror and slid it toward the trembling bridge. As each fragment disappeared, I called an ancestor or family member's name. "Henry Love! Tayanita Love! Grandma Quintilla! Pap Wallace! Grand Mu Beulah! Henry Moses! Abraham! Emma! Timothy Earl! Nora! Reba! Paul! Willie Earl! Doris!"

When I finished, Aunt Naomi concluded also. "It is our desire to stick with, as much as possible, the religious beliefs and rituals of our African ancestors. To do so, we are going to end with a water dance. We will honor our ancestors, release the spirit of Rabbit and welcome your new life. After the ritual dance, you will no longer be able to see Rabbit, but you can continue to call upon her from the spirit world in times of great need."

Is the spell on my family broken?

As if to confirm the ritual, the broken pieces of mirror came from the bottom of the river and floated together on top of the water. The Love Voice or by now it could have been the peyote, sounded inside of me, near my right breast. *For you, the fourteen pieces represent the new life you will create from the broken pieces of your past.* The spiritual medicine was working rapidly and telling me about my life. The fourteen pieces of the broken mirror scattered light across the Adkin Canal, which was now swollen and running over into its banks.

Another insight came to me. *Just as the broken mirror still has light, my life still has light.* The Love Voice spoke, *Rest assured that the spiritual cleaning is removing some of the taints and stains of the brokenness. But who you are can't be broken.*

The brokenness in my life drowned in the watery graves of the river. As I imagined my expanding life, I slipped out of my mind. The melodious clanging together of the flashing mirror pieces in the choppy water became hypnotic. I began to dance in the escalating hurricane waters to honor life, my ancestors and Rabbit. My ancestors flashed before me, giving me words of comfort and cure. Mama Tayanita, my daddy's mama, standing on the right bank, assured me. *My family is Indian. We have used peyote for hundreds of years in our ceremonies.*

When I saw Rabbit, a strange overwhelming sense of gratitude and love flooded my mind. Rabbit vibed, *Don't think I am not with you. I will be with you always. The ordinary world of form keeps the ignorant-trapped and unaware. Our time together helped you go past the five senses.*

Rabbit was as filled with divine wisdom as I was with earthy innocence. She sent me a last reminder, *Never accept anything for its face value.* Then Rabbit was gone! I used the idea of being always connected with my friend to fully release her to formless spirit. I had been expecting to be sad about her leaving. The exact opposite had happened. I was surprised at the ease I let her go. There was no loss.

I had gained so much from the experience. I remembered I met her when both of us were formless. She merely returned to the Source. First.

I wanted to share these almost unbelievable insights with my aunt, but she was caught up in her own world of sacred ritual and medicine. Soon I fell under the rain dance energy. My once humorless aunt, danced, twisted, pranced, swirled, spun, jigged and laughed on the banks of the Adkin. We alternated playing the tambourine and became wild women, wise women, herb women, girl women, market women, earth women, men women who found our way home again.

Aunt Naomi, the worker of light and me, the apprentice light worker, shapeshifted into hens, tigers, elephants, jaguars, rats, mineral, soil, rock, tree, bird, sun, sky and moon until we became one with all forces of nature. The skilled worker of the sacred arts eventually assumed the stance of the queen of the jungle. Aunt Naomi howled with a chilling growl as a roaring lioness mounted her. Head held high, she pranced around the banks of the Adkin with shrieks and explosions of abandoned lion laughter.

Whoops and giggles overtook me as the laughing hyena possessed me. I laughed, chuckled, chattered and convulsed in a loud pitch until I collapsed on the banks of the Adkin. Over and over, I gyrated in the wet sand and the sloshing water. Hyena energy rolled and spurted out peals of human-sounding laughter from me. My once suppressed joy released a deluge of earthshaking, unbound laughter.

Wham! The bridge snapped, sending rusty nails, unpinned bolts and splintered timber in all four directions—all on the journey to the Neuse River and the ocean, sailing on with the tide of life. For safety, Aunt Naomi ended the water ritual. Total darkness fell as the continuous torrential rain and the clashing river smashed the mirrors into hundreds of shards. Sparkling bits of the mirror found a resting place in the bottom murkiness. Other shiny bits traveled the seven seas.

Spent, Aunt Naomi rose from the banks and headed back to the projects. I followed. Wordlessly.

* * *

When we arrived home, Reverend Love's evening/weekend car was not there. I was used to his nightly escapades. His new shiny work truck was parked in the back on the street. Our front porch was littered with bent trash cans, shredded plants, my mama's beloved flowers and scattered newspapers. The netted seats of our two plastic lawn chairs were shredded and strewn down the sidewalk. Mama's cherished porch swing had looped itself over its pole. It was hanging in a dangerous, awkward position.

When I reached for the doorknob, Aunt Naomi took my hand and held it. My teeth were chattering, but I knew she had something significant to say. I ignored my freezing, shivering self. "We always know what to do, but we don't have self-confidence to believe in ourselves. Trust what you feel. You will understand this better by and by. Let's go in. I'm spending the night. 'Cause it's too dangerous to try to walk any longer in this raging storm."

In Mama's house everybody went to bed early when God was doing his work. A hurricane was definitely the masterful handiwork of the Lord. No lights. No television. No talking. And no supper. Always slow to fall asleep, I lay in the dark, restless, and still feeling incomplete.

Maybe, if I peed. I went to the bathroom. After I flushed the toilet, I moved the window curtain aside. Reverend Love's truck was sitting across the street, near the tall magnolia tree that was swaying its body and waving its giant hands in the wind. The new chrome around the truck lights was beaming in the dark. A feeling that wouldn't go away came again, this time with an old familiar voice- *Burn it. This will complete the release.*

Getting back in the bed, I felt Aunt Naomi's *Trust what you feel.* I eased out of bed and put on my galoshes again and Grandmama's raincoat over my sleep clothes. I quietly gathered my supply bag from under the bed. Then I crept downstairs to go out the kitchen door.

The plan to do it when only Reverend Love was home hadn't worked. He was gone so much that it was hard to catch him, day or night. I had seen on television another way to carry out my plan. One day Daddy was watching his favorite kind of show-war movies. I realized I could use the simple method in the war story.

Something was telling me this is the day. And tonight is the right time. I eased the kitchen door open and went outside to carry out my plan.

Daddy kept his extra supplies in the backyard makeshift shed for his shade tree mechanic customers. I took a gallon of his gasoline and a small can of motor oil. The hurricane was increasing its force and it had started to rain again. The flashing lightning made a clear path. Leaving the backyard, I bent down to avoid the whooshing winds and ran to the truck. His new 1961 Apache Chevrolet truck was never locked. No one dared to touch Reverend Love's possessions.

I jumped in on the passenger side and dumped out the contents of my supply bag—a box of self-strike matches, an old raggedy dish towel and torn paper. I carefully re-imagined the war scene on television. *First, the matches were put in a safe place. The front right pocket. The soldier opened the gasoline and poured some of the gas around the walls of the enemy's truck. And then on the driver's seat where he had placed the old towel. Next, he unscrewed the motor oil, and poured it in the gasoline container. After that, part of the saturated dish towel was crammed down in the can, leaving the other part sticking out.* The smell of the new car mingled with the smell of oil and gas. I began to sweat like I had run a mile.

I rolled down the window. Seeing no one, I got out of the truck, cautiously. No one was foolish enough to be out in this kind of weather but me. To complete the mission, I reached into my pocket for the matches. The scene in the movie became hazy. I had followed the actions exactly until now. I forgot the torn paper. I was on my own. Instinctively, I lit the match and threw it through the window.

I ran for the safety of the kitchen. As I eased the cracked door open, I looked over my shoulder. White smoke and a fireball were forming inside the truck. Through the kitchen windowpane, I watched the spreading flames lapping up the leather seats and the dashboard of the truck. Upstairs, in the bathroom, I took a final look out the bathroom window. Boom! Sounds from the exploding truck windows filled the night. Flying shards of glass joined the lightning as they both zigzagged the sky.

I left Grandmama Quintilla's soggy raincoat in the chair in my room and returned to the security of my bed. Kaboomalumalum! House-rocking thunder! This was one time I didn't want to see or know what was happening. Laying there remembering the burning truck, I realized I had to curb my enthusiasm for fire. I liked fires the same way I like to read. Both instantly took me out of myself. This must be what Mama means when she says, "You let your imagination run away with you."

She was right. I just couldn't stand the day-to-day sadness and loss. Fires allowed others to share some of the burden. Eventually, I fell asleep, satisfied that the burning was big enough to release the pressure and bring some balance. My plan had worked.

The next morning when I woke up, the events from last night encircled me like a cozy blanket wrapped around my shoulders. I eased into the kitchen and gazed out the window. The gray sky, streaked with stripes of light, gradually admitted a little sun. Suddenly I lost my breath! The new 1961 Apache Chevrolet truck was barely recognized. Across the back of the burned-out shell of the truck, lay the once magnificent magnolia tree. It was burned to cinders also.

Aunt Naomi, who got up with the dawn, had made some herbal tea. She and Mama were enjoying their tea. Mama welcomed me into the kitchen. "How's we be doing? I am getting ready to fry some fish for breakfast. Have yourself a cup of tea and some tea cakes that your Aunt Naomi made."

"Good. I feel like things are looking up." I smiled as I reached for a cup and my treat. In fact, I was in seventh heaven. Especially since Mama was home from the hospital and alert. I was also happy that the burnings could stop. I sat at the table as Aunt Naomi went to the sink to help Mama clean fish. Mama and Aunt Naomi were talking about something that had happened during the storm last night. I pretended not to hear.

Mama said, loud enough to Aunt Naomi so I could hear, "Abraham will be shocked when he come home. That big tree in the back was struck by lightning. The lightning split the tree in half. And the burning tree set his new truck on fire. Both the split tree and his new truck burned to the ground." Mama used her secret arts trickery to be undetected. I saw her smile before she put her mask on.

The wrathful hurricane had closed power lines, burst windows, collapsed fire hydrants, split trees and set trucks on fire. During the storm, my soul had found release. By noon, the Neuse, no longer raging, flowed her peaceful course again. This bustling stream of water meandered several miles and linked the town to many experiences and memories. The river continued to traverse many neighborhoods, races, cultures and history. The banks of the Adkin stood solid. And Daddy would share the burden with his tight wallet.

Chapter 23

Only Sixteen

Mama had come home from the mental hospital for the last time when I was sixteen. During her sporadic absences, I missed her soft presence and her healing mama-smell. When she entered the front door, she was still as pretty as the spring daffodils in the front yard. Her head and the air around her had cleared. Instead of the stale scent of burned tobacco, she smelled like Dove soap and Blue Gardenia perfume. Mama never smoked another cigarette.

Her swaying, roses-smelling hair matched the bounce in her determined steps. The wide smile returned; it was warm and bright. Her attire—a fashionable dress, low-heel pumps and matching handbag, with a small pillbox hat—reflected the new life that awaited all of us.

The first day she came home, Mama made some scrumptious cheese buttermilk biscuits. After I sopped two biscuits with molasses mixed with bacon grease, I washed the dishes. The peace and love of being in the kitchen with my mama again flooded me with warm memories.

We were both lost in our rambling thoughts. Mama broke the silence. "Had an eye-opening revelation about myself and my life when I was in Goldsboro. Something happened I can't explain. One day my mind was dark and confused. The next morning the cloudy thoughts had been swept away. I realized just because your daddy didn't love his family anymore, I could still love myself and my life."

BREAKING THE CYCLES OF PAIN: SOUL SECRETS

From then on Mama grew back into her same old industrious, sharp-tongued, beautiful self.

Even though Reverend Love was no longer prowling the house at night, he still had an unsettled spirit that kept him restless and grouchy. By the time Nora was twenty, she had two children, my niece, Betty, and my nephew, Leonard. Nora had been so tired of his creepy shenanigans that she disappeared for long periods of time. When Nora didn't come home from partying for days, I fed the children when Daddy wasn't home. Sometimes I stole clothes for them. I loved and took care of them.

By this time Reverend Love was a stranger in his own house. "I have a Deacon Board meeting." The door slammed and the unholy reverend was gone for the night. Remembering his frustration that Nora 'left the children on her mama and Rabbit', he opened the door again and demanded, "You better not feed her children. Not with my food!"

My brother Willie Earl and I were his only children still at home. Reba had married a Marine and moved up North. Paul had stopped threatening and kept his word. He dropped out of school and moved to New York. There were fewer mouths to feed, but my mama and I had silently understood that 'Daddy' was still enraged that he could not get to Nora's 'goodies'.

Mama smilingly ignored the empty threats. "How would he know?" she asked me. "He's never home."

One day before Reverend Love left for work, he came into the kitchen and called my name, "Rabbit." Then, he fixed his gaze to the outside of my right ear and spoke, "I'm turning grocery shopping over to you. A dollar a day should be enough for supper. I have to save money for a truck."

At this point, I was glad he knew about shame. Shame made him talk to my ear. He could not stand to see the strong disconnect from him in my eyes. I also saw that he had divorced this family.

I didn't answer. I picked up my books off the kitchen table and walked toward the living room to go out the front door to leave for school. Mama, standing in the kitchen doorway listening, cried out,

"A dollar! How can we live on that a day? Did you forget? I was in the hospital so many times, I lost most of my customers!"

Reverend Love, ignoring Mama, turned his back to both of us, flipped through his wallet. Without turning around, he grunted, "Use this." And slung a crisp dollar bill toward the table. It landed on Mama's left foot. All her training about being a respectable lady, a good pastor's wife flew out the back door as Reverend Love opened the kitchen screen door. I stopped to watch the action.

As Mama would say later, "Something came over me and a pot appeared in my hand. It said, "Throw me." Reverend Love felt her furor as a small iron skillet hurled past his ear. By the time he saw the pot flying out of the back door, Mama had jumped on her unsuspecting husband's back. Both tumbled out the back door, fell off the narrow concrete kitchen porch and on to the ground. The jolted Reverend Love scrambled to pluck my outraged mama off him.

My determined mama was set to get his fat wallet. The holy, pious minister who said cussing was a sin, shrieked, "God damn it! Bitch, you're stone out of your fucking mind? Get your crazy, yellow ass off me! If you don't stop biting me, I am going to put your lights out, for good this time!"

He had miscalculated my mama's renewed vigor to react to him and her life. Mama clawed, scratched, mauled, and held on, like she was fighting for her life. I guess she was. "You are not going to treat me like one of your cheap dollar hoes. I made too many sacrifices to be tossed away like a used menstrual rag!"

Mama stopped biting his neck, but still clung to his back.

Reverend Love relented. "Okay! Damn it! $2.00!" Mama released her death grip and they both stood up, watching each other, like two panting mad dogs. My mama's bewildered husband staggered back in the kitchen, picked up the dollar bill on the floor and added another two dollars to the daily's allotment. This time, gently placing $3.00 on the table.

From upstairs we heard him call, "Emma, where is the mercurochrome? My back look like I've been fighting a tiger!"

Mama screamed upstairs to him, "I shoulda beat your ass down to a ropy mess."

I hoped she would leave him. But it was a good beginning. Reverend Love was late for work that day. He had tangled with a tigress, and he was the self-declared loser. I was glad that Mama jumped on him and demanded more for herself. This convinced me that she was ready for her life.

Some nights later, I went outside to lie on the ground to watch the moon and to think. The sky overhead was midnight black, sprinkled with silver diamond stars. Mama was sitting in her repaired porch swing. My speech interrupted the silence. "Mama, I always wanted to help my family. After my baptism and contact with my soul, I have decided, no more secrets and lies. Like George Washington when he chopped down his father's tree, I cannot tell a lie."

I left the cool soft grass and sat next to her on the swing. And I launched into my truth. "Mama, I shoplift to get clothes, shoes and food treats for the children and me. I want to get you something, but you may not agree to this creative idea. I guess I had caught the 'Tall bodies look good in beautiful clothes disease'. Plus 'full bellies make life better.'"

Mama didn't flinch. She said, "I was in such a dark place I didn't have the strength to deal with the house troublems. When I was your age, I would have felt guilty about stealing. And this is a way for you, 'specially, to get back at 'Whitey'".

After a forgiving smile, she added, "Don't get me wrong. I rather you didn't, but just be careful. But don't think I was so crazy I didn't know what y'all children were doing. I was too sad to resist most things. It seems like we both are growing up together. I am growing out of my old fears, and you are growing into who you always wanted to be."

Mama had never shared so much about herself. I was stunned and left wordless. For a while the crickets accentuated the silence. Then Mama continued, "Since we are being honest with each other, I have to tell you about the carved wooden crib. Mr. Brown, the owner of the fish market, and I were engaged way back before I met Nora's daddy or your daddy."

Mama's brave voice dropped to a whisper as she remembered the past. "Our families sharecropped on the same farm. His grandfather gave the crib to Lewis. During the Great Depression in the 30's, there were hard times in this country. You ain't seen hungry. Lewis gave the crib for Mama to keep when he moved up North to work."

She stood and placed her hands across her heart and said with an old affection, "He wanted to work and save money so we could marry."

What! I looked up at Mama in total shock. She was telling a family secret that I didn't have to pry out of her. I listened with my breath oozing through my stunned lips, which almost fell on my chin. *Lewis? Mr. Brown!*

Once Mama started, the floodgates of her earlier life opened. Pacing across the porch in the dark, she looked up at the sky, and she continued, "Meanwhile, the land suffered a drought, a hurricane and a flood. Mama's and Pop's tobacco crop didn't do well that year. The farmer was about to put us out, take all our furniture, including the fancy crib. Our broken-down horse. And even our old truck."

"How could he do that?"

"That's what sharecropping is. The farmer and the tenant share the loss. But not the profits. We wound up owing the tenant farmer whose land we lived and worked on."

"What did Grandma Quintilla do?"

"Now Nora's daddy, John Walker, heard about our troubles. He made a deal with your grandmama. He told her, 'If ya yella gal, Emma, will marry me, I will pay off Ole Man Jones and get all your things back. Ya family can live in one of my shotgun houses.' I made a sacrifice and married a devil. Don't put others before your dreams, Doris."

I interrupted. "I knew there was something between you and Mr. Brown! He was always giving you extra fish. And holding your hands at church too long. What happened to Mr. Brown?"

"He returned about a year later in a new car. Dressed like a professor and had plenty of money. Going up North had prospered him. When he found out what happened, Mama said, 'He cried like a child who had lost his mama.' Told Mama to give the crib to me. By then I was six months pregnant with Nora."

"Lewis told me later, 'I understand that you did it for family. I'll always carry you in my heart and look out for you'. He used his money to open his grocer/fish market. That's why he helps me. Especially now."

I said, "Witnessing you kick Daddy's butt created a sense of power in both of us. Confronting him helped us to destroy the power of ancient lies that we both had believed. That he had complete control of our lives. That he was unstoppable because he was a man. And that he was a man of God. Like Nora always said, they were all lies."

"The day I jumped your daddy, my habit of remaining silent in the face of questionable activities vanished. His decision to give me only a dollar a day for food unlocked the final rage that caused me to crawl in a hole and hide. I knew we deserved more."

Talking always puts things in order. I began to understand her more. Mama had endured many sorrows and carried secrets. She had made a great sacrifice of love for her family. This talk confirmed that Mama wasn't crazy.

After Mama shared her story with me, she ended the session by saying, "That was then. Now I am ready for my new life."

Mama joined me on the porch swing. We sat quietly in the mystery of family healing and love. Every now and then, an occasional lightning bug sparked a snap of yellowish orange light. In the darkness, Mama said, "Let's go inside. Even the stars are sleepy." We left the porch, both breathing a sigh of relief.

* * *

After my mama came to herself, I decided to concentrate on my life. At my baptism, my Aunt Naomi had reminded me, "You need to laugh more. You are only sixteen. Get away from family troubles. Get yourself a boyfriend. You're gifted with words and insight. Find your own life."

School? Writing? Boyfriend? I was determined to concentrate on school and writing stories. But soon, I noticed there was never enough food in the house. Breakfast had ceased the day after Mama jumped on Reverend Love. There was no lunch money on the kitchen table. One morning, after my rice and butter breakfast, I said, "I can see he's decided to stop taking care of us." I was still so angry with Reverend Love, I refused to call him "Daddy."

I looked cautiously at my recently released Mama, expecting some sadness. Instead, her beautiful moon-shaped lips spread across her glowing face. *My Mama! She was home again!* Mama's eyes blazed as she said, "I had made a decision too. I will not argue and beg no man to take care of me and my children! Two is easier to take care of than six."

Then she laughed. Not the crazy tormented hysterics. That made me hold my breath until the incoherent soliloquies faded. It was a soft chuckle from a soul recognition that she was responsible for her life.

"Mama, I'm so glad to hear this. I have a plan worked out in my head. Aunt Naomi buys day old bread from the bakery and she asks the butcher for the bones and the scraps from the butchered animals. She gets wilted vegetables for almost nothing. Bushels of potatoes and rice cost pennies. You know Mr. Brown gives us extra fish anytime you send me. When Reverend Love slaughters his hogs in the fall, try to get more meat to freeze. This way we can still feed Nora's children without him even knowing. He's never home anyway."

"How do you know all this?"

"Watching Aunt Naomi's thrifty shopping and Miss Doris's resourceful cooking prepared me for this limited budget. You cook on Monday, Wednesday, Friday and Sunday and I alternate. Even when he doesn't give us anything, Jean's grandmother increased my cleaning time. We'll always have some money."

"All this will surely help. You always come up with good ideas. I also decided to limit my cooking to fish dinners and sweet potato pies. Only on Fridays and Saturday.

"How will your customers get their food? Willie and I are involved in stuff at school on Fridays and Saturdays. I am a cheerleader. He's the sports newscaster for the school and the *Kinston Free Press*."

"No deliveries. I take fish orders and cook pickups scheduled during the week. I can bake extra pies. And sell more pies on the spot."

Mama reached into her pocketbook. It was empty now, but was once stuffed with money, before her total collapse. As I picked up my books off the counter, Mama squeezed two quarters in my closed hand and said, "Get yourself some lunch. I do know a sure way we can make some money in the summer. We can work in tobacco."

Mama wanted to talk more. "Mama, please tell me more later. I got to go. I'm going to be late." *Now, no food and working into tobacco! Why does it look like life always throws me a curve?*

* * *

I didn't hear anymore about the summer work until a few weeks later when school was out. Mama woke me up at 4:00 in the morning.

"Get up. Put on some old pants and a long-sleeved blouse. We're going to work today, 'puttin' in 'bacco'. Mr. Albert is going to pick us up at 5:00 to take us out in the country to his farm. You got the job through me. Mr. Albert said the 'Colored' teenagers are too lazy and destructive."

"What is 'putting in tobacco'?" I jumped up, right away. I was ready for new adventures in my new life that I was seeking.

"'Puttin' in 'bacco' requires a team. Men called 'croppers' work in the field. They break the tobacco off the tobacco plant. Women work under a shed. Your job will be to assemble bunches of green tobacco leaves and hand them to me, a 'looper'. The looper strings the tobacco around twine onto sticks that are placed on a wooden contraption called a 'horse'.

"Other workers, 'hangers', hang the tobacco to dry in the barn. All workers are called 'hands'." *Mama was such a good teacher.*

At 5:00 a.m. sharp, Mr. Albert rode up to the agreed place. The corner of the projects. At the intersection of Bright and Love Streets.

In his 'bacco truck to pick up his 'hands'. Hands on the back of the 'bacco truck' included Milton Williams and his mama. Miss Louise Williams and my mama grew up out in the country near each other.

Miss Williams spoke to everyone, "Good morning, folks. How yurs be doin', Emma?"

"Fair to middling, Louise."

Miss Williams reminded Mama, "Praise God! The bed you woke up on this mornin' was your restin' place and not yur coolin' board. Fairl' middlin' is shabb'." Then she announced to the four teenagers, their parents and the rest of the adults on the 'bacco truck, "We ain't having no mess from y'all chullins today. Don't want to hear 'bout low pay, discr'ination or 'the White man this' and 'the White man that'. We are here to work so we can pu' some food on the tabl'!"

According to my mama, Miss Louise had escaped death twice. She was born with polio and later had contracted a severe case of chicken pox as a child. It left pox holes in her face. Her husband left her with five children. Food in their house was scarce as polite White people.

Everyone I knew respected her but dreaded her presence because she didn't tolerate any joking or tomfoolery. She would give anyone 'a piece of her mind', as she was doing my mama right now.

I looked at Milton. His eyes said, "We all got problems."

In a few days I complained to my Mama, "'Puttin' in tobacco' is dirty work. The tobacco produces "tons" of tobacco tar. The sticky stuff builds up on your hands, clothes, faces and lips. You also have to be on guard for Black widow spiders, snakes, crickets, horse flies and big worms, camouflaged and resting under the cool of the big leaves."

Mama joked, "North Carolina is called the 'World's Foremost Tobacco Center'. Don't you want to make some of this summer money? This is the time that women and even children get to work."

The look of disgust answered the question. "I want to try picking cotton with you the next time you go."

The next week I went picking cotton with Mama. The same *hands* were sitting in the back of the truck, including Milton. At lunch sitting under a tobacco barn, the teens ate canned Vienna sausages, soda cracker and drank Pepsi Colas. This used up all our earnings at the farmer's store. I began to complain, "My mama never told me that the temperature gets over 100 degrees in the shade. I didn't know you had to leave earlier and to start earlier because of the hot sun."

Milton understood exactly what I was saying, "Bending over hurts my back and they want you to pluck the cotton with both hands."

I picked up my complaint. "My hands are raw. I got pricked a thousand times. I'm quitting. As my aunt would say, 'I would rather drink muddy water and sleep in a hollow log' before I pick another cotton bud.'"

The other two teenagers agreed. When lunch was over, I told the adults getting ready to go back to work, "The teenagers are through with cotton. Picking cotton's too hard."

Miss Williams' eyes shot fire swords at me as she spoke to the boss for the adults. He had eaten his lunch in the big house. "The young folks refuse to go back to work. They say it is too hot and too hard. They're worn plumb out!"

The angry farmer, who owned acres of crops, snapped, "This is why I don't want to give jobs to 'Colored' teenagers. They are lazy and can't stand any discomfiture. Y'all just an ignorant, dark, ugly doomed people. They'll have to wait for knockoff time to go back to those miserable projects."

We didn't know what 'discomfiture' was and weren't trying to find out. I was glad that the 'cotton picking' picking cotton was out of my life forever. The other two teenagers ran up the hill behind the farmhouse to dip in the Neuse River and wait their time out. A grove of magnolia trees grew near the banks.

Milton and I lounged under the ancient, shady magnolia tree, with its showy white flowers and attractive large leaves. We talked about school, sports, music and our love of singing. As we sang, Sam Cook's song, "Only Sixteen", we made our own version. "We were only sixteen, and we loved each other so. We were not too young to fall in love and we were old enough to know."

Milton eased his muscular arm, developed from football situps, around my waist and said, "I like your style. You are not afraid to think for yourself. I also like smart girls. Can I be your boyfriend? Will you be my girlfriend?" We sealed the passionate questions with a long, starving kiss.

The other teens were scolded by their mamas on our way home, especially Milton. Not me. Mama agreed with my decision. "You're right. Cotton will tear your ass up. Back in Mama's and Grandmama's time, to get all that cotton, our folks' fingers were covered in blood."

"Mama, I'm glad you see why young people are now rebelling against this backbreaking, demoralizing, low paying slave labor system. It's got to be changed. I know I'm going to college, so I won't have to do this kind of work. I wasn't born to be a 'field nigger.'"

I didn't mention my new-found love to Mama. It was a way for me to gain some independence from her. And I'm sure Milton didn't mention his new love to Miss Williams. Her anger would have sprewed out quickly! Especially after I made myself spokesperson for the teens. "Doris may be a good gir' and smar' in school, but she's as dark and as po' as you. Find y'urself one of them ligh' skinned girls. The ones that live in the new 'Colored' tract homes. Behind y'all school.'"

I felt sorry for him after he told me this and more things about his strange, sad mama. To know his mama was to fear her or avoid her. Milton lived with the fear of her wrath. She wasn't my mama. Avoiding her was easy for me.

Milton never told his mama his truth. The truth was that Milton and I had become friends before working in tobacco. He had helped me with my 'daddy' situation. Our sensitivity to each other's suffering fired our passion. Milton was my earliest idea of a soul mate. It was easy to love Milton. He felt familiar and comfortable to be around. Like me, he was intelligent and secretive. Both of us longed for love and acceptance. And both of us, outsiders in our own lives, felt stronger when we were together. Both of us had daddy issues. My mama had told me, "The only man we ever saw around Miss Williams' house was the mailman."

Milton's father never showed up. Often, I wished mine hadn't. Lying under the magnolia tree, I had asked, "Milton, where is your daddy?" A dark shadow fell across his face. His response to my question was silence and withdrawal. When he finally spoke, he said with hurt and finality, "The door to that is locked and Mama threw away the key."

There was no need to press further. Milton and my mama used the same techniques to cope—silence and denial. From what I had seen from his mother, I knew Milton had some mama issues also.

* * *

I had developed my own ways to cope and survive. I lived in a world of secrets that divided my life into separate parts. Home, I was the obedient child who loved books and learning. I was fearful of my 'daddy' and had a crazy mama. At school I was the smart, sarcastic, outspoken student who lived in the projects. Milton and I found an escape outlet from our tragic lives in each other. Milton knew my story right away. The details of his story always remained a mystery.

Milton's strategy for me to escape my father's roving eyes and groping hands made us inseparable. He faithfully followed his plans. When school was out, I went by home to check in with Mama. If she was home. "Mama, I'm going to Janet to do my homework. I may have to go to the library." When Milton first helped me, Mama's mind was sometimes as blank as Milton's homework paper before he met me. When Mama found herself again, we continue our routine. Coming to the library and seeing me doing homework, Milton started doing his. His horseplay in class decreased and his grades improved.

Even before Milton, I had a routine. After my homework was completed at the library or Janet's house, Janet and I would eat dinner and wash the dishes. Next, we would sit on the porch and watch the teenagers going in the recreation center. Soon, I was ready to join the dancing and fun across the street. And Janet was too.

One day before Janet graduated from high school, I asked Mrs. Allen, "Can Janet go across the street to the Center with me?"

She blasted me like I had asked her if Janet could go to a nightclub and have a cocktail.

Mrs. Allen ranted, "That Center is a hotbed of savage music, lustful dancing and a meeting place for teen sex. We raise Janet in a decent house! We play respectful church music or sometimes classical music on the Victrola!"

If you think Janet wants to play Old Maid Cards, you're as crazy as my mama! Of course, I didn't share these thoughts. I still like the Friday gumbo and I needed money.

After Milton started helping me, I began to disappear after dinner from the Allen's and live a completely hidden life. I walked down two blocks from the Allen's house, crossed the street and walked down another street next to the old projects. I entered the door of the Center not facing Bright Street. This way Miss Allen couldn't see me. Milton was waiting for me.

Milton and I met at the Center sometimes, but our favorite place to socialize and dance was at a teen club called the Algiers, on a side street off Sugar Hill. The club was open on Friday, Saturday and Sunday nights. It was full of young people from 13 years to 20. The dimly lit joint sold fried fish and chicken sandwiches, sodas, ice cream and cookies. Its main feature was a jukebox that played all the old and current hits.

In the close darkness, Milton and I danced, twisted, cha-chaed. The song, "Bring It on Home to Me," by Sam Cook or "The Wedding Song" by Etta James stirred our deep emotions and we were aflamed with our young love and awakened passion. Overhead lights blinked at 11:00 and all lovers went to their own hideaways—love nests in secret fields, the old icehouse, the stone yard, the cemetery, and other unsuspected private public places. Before returning home.

Ironically, my mama provided the perfect place for a lover's lane for me and Milton. Our favorite place for romancing was where Mama did housework when Reverend Love's money stopped. Mama said to me one morning, "Miss Levitz needs a housesitter on some weekends. Do you want to make some money?"

"Does the family need some money? Did your husband decided to start taking care of us again?"

Mama just smiled. "Of course. When do I start?"

I told Milton at school, "After school, come to the house where my mama works. I am going to be housesitting for them. They also want a 'boy' to cut the grass once a week."

By the time Mama finished working that day, Milton was already cutting grass. By dark, the Levitz went out of town.

I housesat the large twelve-room mansion. Miss Levitz's instructions were clear: "We will be gone from Friday evening to Sunday afternoon. Water the houseplants. Pay the milkman and collect the milk, newspaper and mail. Turn the outside lights on at night and off during the day. You can watch the television in the kitchen. Food is in the refrigerator on the back porch. Sleep in the maid's room in the basement. No company or loud music."

This long list of directions made me feel like a 'Colored' servant. Still, it was a good place for what we had in mind. During one house sitting venture, we made the decision to go all the way. Our hot deep-throated kisses and heavy exploration of body parts wanted full expression of our love and longing. In the maid's room, when I spread the cover back on the maid's bed, Milton asked me, "How do you feel about doing this?"

"A little scared." No one had ever talked to me about the actual sex act. I lied. I was as nervous as a crook being arrested.

As Milton lay down next to me, he said gently, "Just relax and let me kiss you." His kisses coaxed me and took me to unknown places. When he entered me, he owned me. I wanted to lose myself in him. As we did it, we found each other. It took several sessions before my pain became secondary to our pleasure. We were in a big white mansion surrounded by a golf course, overlooking the town that brought my first love and me fully together. For days, I said to myself, *I did it! I did it! I hope it can't be seen on my face.* Now I knew what the big to-do was about.

When I turned seventeen, as much as it rubbed me the wrong way, I talked to Reverend Love about dating a boy. The adults called it 'courting'. If I didn't inform him of my intentions, the busybody neighbors would. One nosy neighbor warned me, "I know your mama has had a hard time keeping up with things. Don't be walking and holding Miss Williams' son's hand and kissing on him. I'm watching you. You don't want me to tell Reverend Love, do you?"

"I'm sorry, ma'am. I won't do that again." I had learned how to lie, be tactful and use my smartness to aid me. Truth seemed to get me in more trouble.

I had not dared to call him 'Reverend Love' in this situation. The next morning after the warning from my nosy neighbor, I asked, "Daddy, can I go to the movie with Miss Williams' son, Milton?" Milton's name caused him to flinch as if something poisonous had bitten him. His instinctive reaction ended the conversation as soon as it had begun. Daddy almost ran out the back door to his truck. The door slammed and the old truck's angry, loud motor disturbed the morning's silence. He had replaced the burnt truck for an older model.

Two days later, my daddy spoke to me as he was leaving for work, "I guess you're old enough to have a boyfriend. But I don't want no hanky panky."

At the end of the week on a Friday evening, Milton came over before Reverend Love left for the night. Mama was visiting a sick choir member. Knowing that Milton was coming, Reverend Love got dressed, picked up his Bible satchel and waited on the couch. After the knock on the door, I said, "Come in." A little shaky.

Milton, tall, dark, and handsome, strolled in the room and walked directly up to Reverend Love. He extended his hand and spoke, "Good evening, Mr. Abraham." My daddy ignored it.

Fidgeting with his case, my daddy asked, "How's your mama doing? Give her my regards." Then he went straight to the point. "Doris tells me you want to take her out sometimes."

He paused. Milton shifted his feet. I looked out the window. Daddy shot out of his seat and stood face to face with Milton. Staring across at him, he sneered, "Do you also go out with other girls?"

Milton glanced at me before he spoke. I wished my 'daddy' hadn't been so blunt, but I surely wanted to hear the answer. "No. I like Doris a lot. I talk with girls, but Doris is the only one I am interested in."

"It is okay with me, but only on the weekends and no hanky-panky. She must be home by 11:00. Doris wants to do well in life. Don't bring trouble to her." As he turned toward the door to go, Reverend Love joked as he reminded me, "Home by 'leven, you go to heaven, home by twelve, you go to hell."

He laughed at his own made-up rhyme. He was teasing, but I knew he was serious. I smiled to myself. *And you've already secured your place in hell because of your sinful and demon dogs' ways.*

Miss Williams didn't know that po' dark Doris Love was Milton's muse. I inspired him to do better. His mama didn't know "We were now seventeen, and we loved each other so. We weren't too young to fall in love and we thought we were old enough to know."

Soon, things about Milton and his secrets would unravel.

Chapter 24

Senior Year

After I registered in my 12th Grade homeroom, the teacher advisor of the school paper sent for me to come to the library. My heart was beating like I was under arrest. I thought Miss Caldwell, the librarian, and the newspaper sponsor, had seen me kissing Milton goodbye behind the school. This was our everyday parting ritual. When he left for football practice at the Adkin Park, which was across the repaired Adkin bridge. Instead, Miss Caldwell told me, "After reading your articles for the last two years and watching your composing skills, I am appointing you as editor of our school paper."

Thank you, Jesus! I had followed Miss Freeman's suggestion and had enrolled in the journalism club in the tenth grade.

In a creative writing assignment in Journalism III, I wrote an editorial that I wanted to publish in the school paper. I didn't realize it was the opposite viewpoint of my journalism teacher. When Miss Caldwell returned the paper to me, she bellowed, "No way will I publish this! Do you want to get me fined or fired?"

I examined my article carefully:

> *The educational system in North Carolina did more than an adequate job in programming its graduates to maintain little control over 'Colored' life. The learning material seldom included 'Negro' writings and influence. Most 'Negro' teachers dared*

BREAKING THE CYCLES OF PAIN: SOUL SECRETS

not openly expose 'Negro' students too heavily to 'Colored'/ 'Negro'/'Black'/African culture or history. Occasionally, a few teachers would suggest for extra reading, authors like Lorraine Hansberry or Gwendolyn Brooks. White male writers as Hawthorne, Thoreau, Hemingway, Dickens and Shakespeare are taught and touted. White women writers, like Emily Dickinson and Sylvia Plathe were ranked just below them.

"The Creation" by James Weldon Johnson was permissible, perhaps because of its religious nature. Yet all the teachers took pride in singing and requiring students to know and sing the Negro National Anthem—"Lift Every Voice and Sing"— written by the same writer and set to music by his brother John Rosamond Johnson. While it is a good starting point, many educational changes are needed so our people can expand our own vision for ourselves.

Education in the South was designed to teach White supremacy and Black inferiority. Its success manifests in the preference for light skin over 'those of a darker hue' in the society and in this 'Colored' school. This programmed thinking continues to create stereotypes, disharmony, and feelings of hopelessness for those who look most African. These practices reflect the plans of institutional racism.

By the twelfth grade, I realize that the role-assignment had already been set up. The smart girls became teachers or nurses; the boys joined the armed services or went to college on sports scholarships. Others took their places as rank-and-file workers and became mothers and fathers and taxpayers in the South or fled for safety up North. The rest remained n'er-do-wells—school dropouts, drunks, unmarried women and negligent fathers. They are at the bottom of society and often live 'in the bottom.'

"You have totally forgotten the good practices for students interested in writing and journalism. Your lead story is too long and your whole paper is too personal!" The advisor was livid!

My paper had more slashes and red marks than a bleeding soldier. I didn't care. This was my appraisal of my educational experience. After twelve years of being fully immersed in it. I wanted to write to express my experiences and feelings about it. I wouldn't use my writing for lying and covering up truth. Even after getting a 'D' on the paper, I still felt the same way.

Many teachers, like the journalism teacher Miss Caldwell, motivated us to conform and comply. Miss Caldwell demanded, "Remove the single quotations from around the word 'Colored'. She sounded like a seventh grade English grammar book as she quoted the rules: "'Quotation marks are marks used in pairs to set off a quotation or a phrase. The singular quotation is used to quote quotations within quotations.'"

"I know the rules. I got A's in English 9, 10 and 11. I used the single quotations to make a point. It's startling for me as a person from African to be given a name that has no connection to a country. I want to call attention to the fact that I am not buying into the names and the meaning attributed to those names."

"You can do it my way or remain the unpublished editor of the school paper. Besides, it's heresy to suggest that we teachers play a role in the continued brainwashing of our people."

I said to myself, *But they never teach us about our culture, about money, our soul or how to be free.* I bit my tongue as I cried silent unshed tears of anger and despair.

I was struggling to stay in a respectful position, but she was pushing me. "Please, Miss Caldwell. I am not criticizing teachers. Their accomplishments and lifestyles are my models for success. 'Colored' teachers themselves were educated in racist institutions. They taught us the same programmed educational, social and economic ideas taught to them." My teacher's silence was louder than my plea.

"Still, your constant, negative critique of my writing does not mean that I can't write. I guess I must control my emotions and my passion."

My stunned teacher Miss Caldwell didn't respond to my attempt to reconcile.

After many fights about toning down my opinion, I had written an editorial that met her standards. Here is part of the editorial article that was approved as an editor in 1963:

"Our Place in Life"
Doris Love, Editor

"How many of you have seriously thought about your place in this world of progress and change? I dare say many of us have been so busy indulging in other activities that sometimes we forget to give special thoughts to the problem of finding our station in life. This situation, if left unattended, may prove more and more confusing and uncertain as time goes on.

When we think of the future, we should think of the roles we will portray in society. We will be mothers and fathers, teachers, physicians, nurses, lawyers, plumbers, carpenters, and other workers. These professions require skill, integrity, initiative, punctuality, and other finer traits of character and leadership. To be able to meet the challenges and responsibilities of adult life, we must prepare ourselves now.

We must become capable of conquering all difficult tasks we encounter. We should know the Right and live by it. Learning to give and to take shows advancing signs of maturity. Selfishness has no place in a successful life. Never shift your obligations *to others. You must fulfill them. Do not permit your responsibilities to become other's burdens. Lastly, follow the Golden Rules of friendship, honesty and love. Thus, when we travel along life's way, we will have acquired essentials for a happy and wholesome life."*

After the article was published, the journalism teacher praised the article. "Well, Doris, you did it. You finally wrote an article that wasn't so confrontational and accusatory."

"But Miss Caldwell, the editorial is so boring and adult-sounding. I am shocked and not pleased at the narrow middle class viewpoint I used. I thought the sentences were clumsy, but you're not just concerned with grammar."

"You know that your probing voice offends the middle-class community, White and Colored folks in the town. Compromise is a key element in life. You will understand it better, by and by."

When I controlled my rebellious, independent-thinking nature, my writing and my life were dull and flat. I knew Miss Cardwell didn't get it. What I wanted to be was not supported by my family nor recognized by the school. And certainly not by the racist society. Nor had it been revealed to me, but I was forever seeking an avenue of expression.

At the time of writing that editorial, I was doing the very thing that my teachers and my 'daddy' said would get me in trouble. I joined the NAACP, participated in the local civil rights protests and had followed Aunt Naomi's advice. I had gotten a boyfriend.

* * *

Three months before graduation, Miss Freeman, now my Conversational French 4 teacher, stopped me in the lunchroom. *"Bonjour,* (Good day) *Doris. Mon estudiante devoue.* (My favorite student.) Would you come by my room when school is out? I have a brief meeting. I'll be back in my room at 3:30. It won't take long. I know you have some after school activities."

"Oui, avec plaisir." (Yes, with pleasure.) I wondered, *How does she know I have some after school activities?* Miss Freeman was like a spy. *Un espion.* She seemed to know students' affairs. Without even trying. And her habit of speaking in French outside of the classroom made me a little nervous. When the bell dismissed school, I flew down the hall. Soared between loitering students and around the over-conscientious Student Hall Patrols (SHP) who over-enthusiastically gave tickets for traveling down the halls too fast. If they had not been 'Colored', they would be hired as police officers when they graduated. A 'SHP' lost me as I ducked in the gym.

The leader opened the registration table for the 5:00 protest meeting. It was Miss Freeman. *Bon après-midi. Comment-allez vous?* (Good afternoon. How are you?)

I remembered quickly. *"Je vais bien. Merci. Et vous?"* (I am well. Thanks. And you?)

"Comme si, Comme ca." (I'm okay.)

After that test, we acted like we never met.

I signed up to participate in the pre-protest training.

Later, I stood in front of Room 204 and waited. I followed my favorite teacher into her classroom. Miss Freeman, wearing a eye-catching, pale yellow dress trimmed with white lace, sat at her desk. She said, *"S'il vous plait, asseyez-vous."* (Have a seat, please.) I sat in the student desk *(pupitre)* next to *(le bureau du professor),* the teacher's desk. French is so formal and polite.

What does she want?

Miss Freeman asked, "Doris, did you study about the underground railroad during slavery in your history class?"

"No, but I read about Harriet Tubman. At the new 'Colored' library, the librarian showed me a book to read about her life."

"Bon! (Good!) That's one thing I appreciate about you. You're so resourceful. A born scholar! Harriet Tubman was a great fighter for our people. I want you to know all your options also."

Waiting to hear more from her. I didn't say anything. "There is still a lessening of the social and racial effects of slavery in the North. This is where Harriet Tubman was taking our people. That's why many students who graduate from Adkin, migrate and take liberating paths that lead to Washington, D. C., New York, New Jersey and Pennsylvania. Others follow the 'North Star' even further up the road to Connecticut and Massachusetts for better social and economic opportunities. You can go to college here, but I don't think this is a safe environment for you to settle in."

I answered, "I choose to deal with the immediate struggle for liberation of my people in my hometown. I studied the history and culture of African people very early in life. In and out of school. I want to go to college here in the South and move somewhere else. Maybe out West to California. Wherever I wind up, I will fight for my people."

"What do your parents think about your participating in the sit-ins and demonstrations?"

"I just can't ignore the love for Mother Africa and my people. It was born in me. It was my mama who first made me aware of racism and segregation. She took me on a tour of the 'White' only, 'Colored' only signs throughout Kinston. This taught me that people of African descent are second rated, second considered and second classed in this town. And in the world. The change must start with each of us. Right now. Here today. My mama is glad that I have joined the movement. Who are you to ask me to retrain my ideas? You were in the gym recruiting."

"I'm not saying, 'Don't fight', but don't lose your possible scholarship fighting and get stuck in this narrow town. Just be careful of your outspoken radical views. I am getting married next year and moving to upstate New York."

"On the other hand, my 'daddy' is totally against the boycotts. He told me, 'Rabbit, stay out of that mess. It has nothing to do with us.' 'Rabbit' is my nickname."

She tried to hide her polite smile. "That's a funny nickname. What did you say?"

"I disagreed and found the courage to let him know. I said to him, "It has everything to do with us. And all Black people having a good life! Whatever happens to one person happens to all people." I told him. "This time you nor Mama can silence me on this. If the young people don't do it, who will?"

He didn't see me in the crowd of students on television. I realized he didn't recognize that I am growing up. After a short moment, I concluded, "I cannot not do what I am called to do."

Miss Freeman stood up, openly smiling her approval. "I knew you felt like this. I have something for you."

She went in the cloakroom and took out a big bulky package and a small, neatly wrapped one. Both covered with graduation paper decorated with graduation blue hats, diplomas and blue smiling balloons.

"These are for you. Doris, you are my all-time exceptional student. *Garde ton sperme, ecris tes livres et surveille ta bouche. Comprenez-vous?* (Do you understand?) Keep your spunk, write your books and monitor your mouth."

We both laughed out loud.

"*Oui.* Can I open them now? But how will I get them home?"

"I will bring them to your house after the protest. I hope you aren't in jail."

We laughed again. This time not so fully.

The big package—a piece of luggage and the red-and-white gingham checkered, two- piece pajamas in the wrappings—surprised me. The cat had such a grip on my tongue that it hurt inside my chest and I wanted to cry. First, I had to stop believing the old tale that the cat could grab my tongue to silence me and keep me from expressing myself. It wasn't a cat; it was my fear of what would happen when I spoke out. The new thought drowned the cat that day. I decided I would continue to tell the truth so I could heal my life and stop crying.

I finally spoke. "This is my first real luggage. The well-crafted Samsonite brings shame to my large shopping bag that I traveled with before. *Merci beacoup* (Thank you very much) for the pajamas. I'll save them for college. You won't be disappointed."

"*N'en pense rien.* (Think nothing of it.) Even before you spoke, I could see the words of gratitude pouring from your eyes."

"Also, I am so grateful to you because I had never considered that I could lose my scholarship by seeking justice. You taught me that everyone has a voice. Part of our journey in life is learning when and how to use it. You helped me to realize that my love of writing is a good outlet for me. It gives me *ma voix." (my voice.)*

Miss Freeman smiled. *"Bien parle."* (Well spoken.)

I said to myself, *Je suis heureux notre conversation est fini."* (I am glad our conversation is over.)

* * *

An hour later, I attended the NAACP meeting at the St. John Baptist Church for the pre-protest training. There were sixty restless demonstrators in the church basement. I counted forty teenagers, fifteen adults and five children under twelve. The meeting was started with prayer by a minister. The minister stood up from the pulpit. "My name is Reverend Bryant. I am the assistant pastor here at St. John's. All heads please bow. "God, we put our petition before you again. Lead us as we set forth to claim our given divine right to life, liberty and the pursuit of happiness. Help us to be as wise as a serpent, gentle as a dove."

The minister ended by saying. "Lord, you said in your word that a little child would lead them. We give thanks for victory, in Jesus' name. Amen."

Miss Freeman sat with most of the trainers on the first row. One of the trainers, the high school music teacher who stood in front, asked, "Do your parents know that you are here?"

Few hands went up. Everyone in my row said, "No."

"We understand that some of your parents are afraid for their jobs and your safety. But we know there must be some sacrifices made. Meeting and planning our strategies of action can prevent a lot of chaos and unnecessary suffering. This is not just about Kinston, but about South Africa where apartheid controls the daily life of the people. People everywhere are demanding an end to this segregated, unequal way of living."

Then, one of the college students who wore thick eyeglasses and who dressed like Milton, came to the front of the room, and introduced himself. "I'm Kevin Gardner. I'm a junior at Shaw University. And a member of the NAACP who helps to organize. Born and raised here in Kinston, across from the cemetery. I participate in sit-ins, sit-downs and demonstrations all over North Carolina. The first thing we'll do tonight is match up a little person with a big person. Can anyone think of a reason we would do this?"

Before the question was answered, Kevin went into action. He made eight teams with an adult leader, adults, teens and children. We moved and sat with our team leader. In small groups the adult leaders explained the rules of protest. The strategy for the next downtown protest at the Paramount Theater was always the same. "No fighting. No violence. Keep your hands to yourself. Turn the other cheek." This would be a challenge for some.

At the mention of the White theater, the anxious people like me, breathed a sigh of release. Now we knew our battleground. Police. Angry White taunts. Paddy wagons. Jail.

Reverend Bryant ended the meeting. "Join me in singing, 'We Shall Overcome.'" The song fired us up. We left, united in our determination for freedom and equality.

At the next day demonstration, I was encouraged when I spoke to Miss Freeman, my French teacher, Mr. Holmes, my next-door neighbor, Mr. Brown, the fish market owner, as I met up with my group and team leader Kevin Gardner, the Shaw University student. Under the team leaders' directions, over two hundred exuberant adults, students, and children orderly marched down the main street, Queen Street. The song "I Shall Not Be Moved" echoed the throughout the area and reflected our immediate demand for freedom. On the way to the theater, I saw my friend, Carolyn, standing on the opposite sidewalk, a single 'Colored' observer, watching with a group of frowning, angry White faces. I motioned for her to join us. She put her hands in a thumbs down position.

During the protest, each participant walked up to the ticket window and put the movie fee in front of the ticket clerk. We were instructed to say, "I want to buy a ticket for the 4:00 show."

The angry clerk mumbled, "We don't sell tickets to 'Coloreds'. Go further down on Queen and Bright Street."

This refusal went on about an hour until the window was closed and the theater manager came to the window and posted a sign,

'SOLD OUT'. As the police began to arrest all the adult leaders, a message circulated about a debriefing at the church at 8:00 that night.

Carolyn and I walked home together. I asked my friend why she didn't join us. She snarled, "I ain't going to be like a nigger, begging no White folks for nothing."

To show her how dumb she sounded, I mocked her, "And no White person gonna give no nigger nothin' if the nigger don't demand it!"

When I reached home, my graduation gifts had been placed on the couch, waiting for me. Miss Freeman's sister had dropped them off. Miss Freeman went to jail; I didn't.

Despite my nervous teachers, my curious friends and family warnings, I continued to participate in many sit-ins and civil rights marches. I went to jail several times during the summers of 1962 and 1963. In jail we were bailed out mysteriously, and always released before supper.

I felt very alive when I participated in the daily protests at the local segregated White theater, drug store and department stores. The same feeling came upon me when I wrote in my journal. And when I burned out my frustration. Or when I was with Milton, who never participated 'cause of his mama's warnings of certain consequences, if he did. I walked for him.

Reverend Love was wrong about his assertion that participating in the civil rights movement would lead to a decline. The greatest possible decline had already taken place in my life. And he was responsible.

* * *

A few weeks before graduation, Milton disappeared for three days. When he showed up in French 4B, he whispered to me as he passed my desk, "Come to the Circle at 7:00." Located in the old projects where Milton live, the Circle was a ring of bricks that created a seating area around a massive magnolia tree. It was a few feet from the recreation center. Milton and I had used it as a meeting up spot.

Later, sitting on the Circle, waiting, I felt some dread and fear. Milton walked up, looking like sadness was his only friend.

Without the usual hug and kiss, Milton blurted out, "I've been to South Carolina. Got an underage girl pregnant. You see. Had to get married. The father carried his shotgun with his Bible."

"Wait. Slow down. Now.... you've been where?"

"In South Carolina you can get married, really young with a parent consent." He nervously scrambled the story.

"What do you mean? You got married!" I jumped up screaming.

"I didn't even want to be with her, but Mama kept insisting, 'Find a girl from a good family! Her family is rich and well established in the town.' And I certainly didn't want to marry her. She has no conversation. No mind of her own. Don't even like to sing. Her father, Reverend Cowan, threatened to put the law on me. She is only fourteen."

"Is the girl Geraldine Cowan?" Light-skinned Geraldine's parents owned a hamburger joint, a grocery store, a beauty shop and a church. This was the type of girl that Miss Williams wanted for Milton. In that moment, I knew he was lost to me forever.

"How did you find out?"

I ignored the question. It didn't matter.

As Milton described the gun the irate father carried, tears flooded my face. They trickled down my neck until they formed a necklace of tears at the top of my sweater. I slowly opened a bottle of black shoe polish. "You're a black lying sack of dog shit! And a fucking cheat! You're just like my 'daddy'! Go back to your black, dominating, mammy and your yellow stupid wife!"

Buying shoe polish was a good excuse to get out of the house after dark to see a boy. The polish blackened my lover's baseball shirt, his lying face, and our interrupted love.

As he screamed "I'm so sorry!" I continued cussing.

"Sorry my ass! You weren't sorry fucking her!" I kicked him in his balls and he went to his knees like he was praying. I ran all the way home. Crying. Cussing. Planning revenge. If I had known where Reverend Love's shotgun was, this would have been my weapon of choice. Instead, I used my own weapon and knew its location.

The house was empty and I was glad. In the bathroom without the bathtub, I sat on the closed toilet seat. I changed Sam Cook's lyrics by myself with my new fountain pen that was a graduation gift.

"We were eighteen and we're in love and he was too young to know. That love is a gift from Heaven above. And money cannot replace love's glow."

After I had written the new lyrics on a brown paper bag, I wrote Milton's name on the bag. *"You lying bastard!"*

Filled with rage, I stabbed the bag eighteen times. *"I hope you get run over by a eighteen-wheeler truck!"* Next, I tore the brown bag with our poem into eighteen pieces and reached into the cabinet drawer. Then found a match and lit the shreds in the wastebasket. The burning paper set the straw waste basket and all its contents on fire. I was enchanted by the growing fire. This was my secret weapon. *I hope you burn in hell for two lifetimes!* Flames leaped from the melting curtains to the thinly plastered wall to the cheap wooden frame wall. The sudden realization of what I had done caused me to dash some Ajax cleanser on the sizzling fire. I silently closed the door on the smoldering flames and went over Carolyn's house. For some reason, I felt a little satisfied.

The next day, no one could figure out what happened in the bathroom. No one ever saw any connections between the fires. The fires remained a mystery.

When I thought back, I remembered that my teacher Miss Freeman had tried to warn me. She had stopped me at her desk at the beginning of the eleventh grade. "I know you are doing Milton's homework. He may be your first boyfriend, but you are not his only girl. I have been meaning to give you this. Milton left this on his desk on Valentine's Day."

She reached into her desk drawer and handed me a small valentine card. The folded envelope read, 'Milton Williams to Geraldine Cowan'. Inside the Valentine card, a couple was kissing in the middle of a bumblebee hive. The writing stated, 'Bee my Valentine.' It was signed, 'Love you, Milton. Will you bee my girl?' The same phrase used to snag me when I was in the tenth grade!

There had been other clues. In the second semester of the eleventh grade, one day at the beginning of lunch, I bumped into Milton, rushing down the hall toward the junior high side of the building. If the SHPs had seen him, he would have been issued two tickets. One for speeding and another one for being in an area forbidden to high school students during lunch. The junior high school lunch ended when the high school lunch began. I stopped him. "Milton, you can have one of my sandwiches. Both Lois and Frances brought me lunch today." I would let them see my schoolwork if they bought me a sandwich for lunch. Food was still scarce in our house.

He hesitated and seemed a little nervous. "My friend's family have a hamburger stand. Sometimes they send me leftover food. I'm going to see if there's anything today."

First, I thought, "Oh, we have so many things in common." Then a voice spoke to me. *That nervousness is covering a lie.*

"Who is your friend? Who is they?"

In a flash, Milton disappeared into the off-limits area. He was rushing to collect his secret lunch from his secret friend that he had kept secret. I knew something was up, but I had learned from Mama to ignore and pretend that I didn't know. Alone in our own world, Milton and I had talked about our childhood, the poverty, living in the projects, being Black and our future. We shared our hurts and our dreams. We were close friends who pushed each other to want more and be more. But Milton never shared his involvement with the underage, middle-class, light-skinned girl who gave him food. And probably money. And now, I knew for sure, some honey.

But what we shared was Milton's fantasy: "When we graduate, you'll go to college and I will go in the Air Force. We can get married and have our own house, our own car and our own life. We can live in New York or Washington, D.C. Then no one can tell us what to do."

I felt the same about him. I knew he really cared for me. Because I had no idea how to have a relationship with the opposite sex, I believed everything he had said. I chose to ignore my gut feelings about Milton. I had decided that the Valentine card didn't mean anything. I forgot what Mama had told me, "Know when they open their mouth, they're lying."

Brokenhearted, with another secret to hide, I graduated high school in June 1963 with honors in English and French.

Testing scores identified me to the National Merit Scholarship Foundation as an academically talented Negro student. I received a scholarship to a historically black college, Livingstone College in Salisbury, North Carolina. Mama and my godmama came to the graduation. As usual, Reverend Love was missing in action.

When school was out, I saved as much money as possible for college expenses by performing 'maid services', babysitting, ironing, cleaning, and working in tobacco—without Milton. Summer, in full bloom, protested my despair. The smell of magnolias filled the summer breeze with its intoxicating fragrances all over town. The sidewalks were lined with different size magnolias trees. The scent from the trees followed me everywhere I went. Sad memories of Milton lingered with every breathe I inhaled.

The old folks always said, "The tea from the bark of a magnolia tree can cure headaches, cramps and sometimes, a lover's remorse." *Maybe I need to make me some magnolia tea for my broken heart.* I never made the tea.

One Friday afternoon in late June, when I finished my chores at the Allens, the scent lured me across the street to the Circle. Milton was sitting on the Circle, resting after a game of basketball with the basketball regulars. Sweat poured down his surprised face. He dropped the high-top tennis shoe he was tying when I stood in front of him. I smiled my mama's moon smile and the gloom evaporated. "You are here." Both of us said at the same time. My anger and disgust didn't stop my heart. I was a fool in love.

He said, "Let's go for a walk so we can talk." Finishing with his shoes, he grabbed my hand.

"I have to housesit for Miss Levitz, beginning at 6:00. It's 3:30 now."

We walked up on Sugar Hill and shared a fried chicken sandwich and a Pepsi. As we started to walk uptown toward the Levitz home, Milton began to talk. "She is still living at home. We don't have room. Besides, she don't want to live in the projects. Anyway, I don't have money to take care of her. I wish I hadn't listened to my mama. My life is really screwed up!"

"And mine is fucked! I thought you were real." I usually controlled my cussing around Milton but since his betrayal, I didn't give a fuck what he thought. Anyway, he knew I had a little fire in me.

He didn't realize how I fought everyday not to go to his mama's project house and cuss her out. I wanted to break every window, burn down her hedges and the rattrap of a rundown project unit she lived in. I didn't want to get in trouble and get stuck in the awful town. But still I wanted all to suffer who made me suffer.

"The way I feel about you is real. But now I don't know what to do."

"So real that while you were loving me, you were loving the silly little rich girl too! And going along with your mama's bullshit like a sissy!"

He dropped his sorry head. Then nothing further was said.

At my destination, I took the key out from the secret place and unlocked the door. When Milton turned to leave, his goodbye kiss turned into many. His kisses stole the bitterness and pain from my heart. In the ugliness of betrayal, I still sensed some beauty in our love. I wondered, *How can there be both?* In the process of untangling our love, we said our goodbye with a fiery love encounter in the 'maid's room' in the grand mansion. In the furnace of dissolving passion, I became pregnant.

Mama, who was now in complete recovery and as alert as a watch dog, told me one late August morning, "Last night your daddy dreamed of fish. He's always right about this. When was the last time you had your monthly?"

I started to lie, but the partly digested spicy collards and vinegary neckbones from dinner churned in my stomach and ran up my throat. I bolted for the back door and heaved in the backyard until my inners almost dumped. Mama waited for me to return. Back in the kitchen, I said, "I'm sorry, Mama. I didn't want it to happen like this." I left in tears.

After a week of dodging Reverend Love, I decided. *The hide and seek game is over. I don't care what Reverend Love thinks about the pregnancy. He needs to look at his own filthy life.* Mama was in the kitchen making Reverend Love some breakfast. Grits and ham. Suddenly, he had begun to buy groceries. As he gobbled down his breakfast, I came into the kitchen. The new situation had me hungry enough to eat straw. I couldn't wait for him to leave.

My 'daddy' barked at me, "You can't run forever. I know that there was something about that scoundrel that I didn't like. He is uppity, just like his mama. Always looking at you with a smirk on his face. Tell him that I said if I see him around here anymore, I will shoot his low-down ass!"

"But you can't just blame him!"

"He lied to me. I had asked him 'rectly if he took out other girls. You heard him say 'No'. I heard he's already gotten another girl pregnant!"

Mama said, "Just like you don't lie. This is the wrong time to keep him away. If he is trying to come around, let him."

I wanted to hate Milton, but I understood his situation, his poverty, no daddy and a controlling mama. My love and compassion for him remained, even though it was mixed with scorn and disappointment. As my clothes got tighter, I stopped thinking about ways to kill him. Milton never came back to my house when 'Daddy' was home, but we continued to meet in our secret places. His married status had not changed our hearts, nor our desires. The bond and passion that we shared together fueled a bottomless connection that made a final separation difficult.

My unexpected pregnancy in August 1963 threw my life into a spiral of despair and depression. In the same month, hearing about the March on Washington, D.C. where Black people rallied for civil and economics rights, did not cast the clouds away. At that point, I felt little inspiration when I heard the "I Have a Dream" speech by Martin Luther King over the radio. September 1963, Livingston College started, without me. On November 22, 1963, my world continued to slide into darkness. President John Kennedy was assassinated. Black Americans had thought he would bring justice to our miserable lives.

Four months later, my boyfriend, Milton, and I became the parents of a baby girl who brought some glimpses of hope for me. Kabari Williams was born in the bedroom downstairs that I had inherited from Nora when she moved out for the last time. The same midwife, Miss Ellen, who had delivered Nora's three children, caught Kabari when she entered the world. Up North and married, Reba had her babies in the hospital. No more Love babies would be delivered at home.

Milton's sister, 'Miss Snooty, Goody-Two Shoes Julie', and her mama looked down on me and my poor, backward family life. I was shocked when the sister showed up at our house the day after the birth. Julie walked into my bedroom, as casual and as cold as cash. She asked, "How much did it cost!"

"Maybe about $100.00, I think. You can ask Mama."

"No need to. Milton sent this." Julie gave me a wad of dollars. "What's her name?"

"Kabari."

"Kabari! That sounds like some African name."

"She is an African. And we are, too."

Julie rolled her eyes and shook her head at this 'crazy Nigger'. I unrolled the money and counted it out. It matched what Milton said he would send. Julie worked in an office downtown. She and Nora were the same age. Both worked the Marine night club circuit on Sugar Hill. According to Carolyn's grandmama, Julie was a 'Marine hustler', along with Nora and half of the young women in Kinston.

My father's calculation was off. Kabari's arrival upon earth was a divine gift and approved by the ancestors. When the midwife first placed Kabari in my arms, the love that I was longing for, looked up at me and twitched a slow smile. The clouds vanished. Becoming a mother was a catalyst of love and change. In fact, the birth of my child caused me to rise to a higher standard than I had ever imagined for myself. I did not get to use my National Merit Scholarship, but my academic prowess would open other venues as I continued to knock on the doors of learning.

Chapter 25

Go Back Where You Come From!

When Kabari was four months old, my sister, Reba, came home and stayed two weeks. After a few days of playing with Kabari, Reba said, "She is a smooth blend of her good-looking, conniving father and you and your smart self. Even though she can't talk, she talks with her eyes and her hands. Just like you. Too bad her daddy's a scoundrel."

"It's not like you haven't had some rascals in your life, too." *This is why Reba and I couldn't 'set horses' (get along). She's too cold-hearted.*

I spent hours lavishing my protective love and careful attention on Kabari. Both my mama and I showered her with soft lullabies and made-up songs. I wanted her to feel special and chosen. You could see she did by the way she smiled, hugged and made many happy sounds.

One day, Kabari wore a new outfit that Reba had given her. Reba said, "Kabari looks like the beautiful little Black princess dolls that you always wanted. And they didn't sell in the stores." Kabari's natural joy reminded me that I was not a bottom feeder or an outcast. I knew she was a gift that would propel me forward.

At the end of the first week, I knew Reba was infatuated with Kabari who had an easy way of being. Now, Reba, who always challenged and belittled me, wanted my prized possession. My persuasive, intimidating sister insisted, "Let me keep Kabari for a month. I have four boys and I want to see how it feels to have a little girl. I will take good care of her. This will give you time to search for a job."

Reba was gifted with using smooth words to get her way. She had gotten it from Reverend Love. I didn't know why we were angry with each other, but I wanted it to end. I did think this was a good way to bring us closer together. A week after Reba, my four rambunctious nephews and Kabari went back to Pittsburgh, I got a full-time job, working as a taxicab company dispatcher. I missed my baby, but I didn't regret my decision to allow Reba to take her. At first.

Reba didn't come back with Kabari on the agreed date. She telephoned me and said, "Anderson and I are breaking up. I don't have money to come home. I have to wait for another month until I get my allotment check."

I contacted Milton for some money so I could go up North to get Kabari. He snapped, "I told you not to let your sister take her. You know she's not reliable." Nor was he. "I won't have any extra money until next month."

His new family required all his money.

One morning before Reverend Love went to work, I asked him, "Would you give me some money so I can ride the bus and get Kabari from Reba?"

He snorted, "You didn't ask me if she should go. So why should I help you get her back?"

I begged, "Please, Daddy. I will pay you back every time I get paid, until I pay you off."

Reverend Love's only reply was, "You got yourself into this mess. So, get yourself out of it."

I had already begun to save money for my uncertain escape to a new life. Now I had to save money to get Kabari back before I could leave. I had no idea where I was going but I knew I would leave. My life was reduced to going to work and moping about my child, whom I had unwisely allowed my sister to take home up North to Pennsylvania.

Two weeks later, my buddy, Carolyn, came over to my house and invited me to go dancing with her and two other girlfriends Friday evening, two days away. She was dressed up like she had money. After Carolyn had a baby, she often went North. Finally, she began to work as a seamstress at the local shirt factory in Kinston. Willie Earl had graduated from high school and now lived in New York. Mama was cooking pies in the kitchen again and Reverend was reading his Bible in the living room. Things looked calm and normal. But a quiet storm was brewing.

Carolyn pulled me out to the backyard. "You got to get out of this depressing funk," she said. "Last week, Brenda, Susan and I went dancing down at the Blue Moon Café and Lounge. We had a ball."

"A café! Reverend Love says it's a juke joint!"

"And what is the matter with a juke joint? It's just a place where 'Colored' workers, off-duty Marines and 'Colored' travelers come to eat some home-cooked food, drink some liquor and relax. They can't drink, eat and stay at White people's places. Damn, you're getting so uptight. Anyway, since when did you let what your Daddy thought bother you?"

"But it's right smack dab in the middle of Sugar Hill. That's where all the Marines come when they leave the base! I don't want to be a Marine hustler!"

After my mistake of allowing my baby to go with Reba, I began to consider my decisions.

Trying to convince me, Carolyn said, "I remembered the saying Nora and her friends developed for the Marines: 'Some mama's son is going to be mine tonight and give me some money. Pay my rent. Buy some food, drinks, cigarettes, clothes, car. Have a relationship. Get a little love. Or even a marriage proposal tonight.'"

"My sister is an expert adviser and participant in the antics of Marine dating and seduction."

As we sat on the back porch I told Carolyn, "I'm surprised that so many women teachers and high school girls are involved with Marines."

Carolyn responded, "If you think about it, the average man don't have pocket money like Marines. Most of the hardworking men can barely take a woman out to eat. Those who do have spending money, or are educated, want a woman from a better side of town."

As we continued to make fun of the saying, 'Some mama's son is going to give me some money,' Mama interrupted our laughter. "At least the Marine hustlers get something out of it. Y'all give it away for free!"

We hadn't seen Mama standing in the kitchen door.

I stopped resisting. I wanted to have some fun, too. I loved to dance. Dancing and having fun could ease my missing Kabari.

"Carolyn, help me choose what to wear."

Maybe some mama's son would help me get Kabari back.

* * *

The Blue Moon Café's iridescent painted ceiling sparkled with yellow and blue moons against a black, star twinkling sky. The revolving overhead blue lights flashed on the diners, drinkers and dancers. Bluesy jukebox music penetrated the room and souls of the patrons. Near the backdoor, odors of hot fried fish/shrimps/ chicken, chopped barbecue, peppery collards, and Cole salad, made you want to eat, drink and be happy. The spirits in the juke joint were alive!

All who heard the call, "Come to Sugar Hill," came running. Every Marine who was on leave. Or who was off duty. Or who could find someone to cover his duty found their way to the jukes, clubs, speakeasies and liquor houses. Husbands lied about going to help with a flat tire. Wives pretended that they were visiting the sick and teenagers fibbed about a new babysitting job. All wanted to taste of the forbidden. Now I had joined the exodus into night life.

My three chatty friends and I had no idea that our group was under surveillance as soon as we entered the dimly lit room. A popular song, "The 'In-Crowd" by Dobie Gray was playing as we groped through the dark juke joint. We found desirable seating, the table next to the bar and the door. In case of a fight, we could hide behind the bar or run out of the door. The room was bathed with an air of mystery and expectancy. A general feeling of being chosen, being in the right place and being part of the magic permeated the Blue Moon. And it didn't escape me. All of us felt like, "This is the night that dreams can come true."

The waiter came over to our table. "The gentlemen with the white hat at the bar ordered you all drinks." Then he asked, "What do want?"

I had drunk some Boones Farm Wine and Kool aid with my brothers. And I had heard Nora talk about vodka and orange juice. I ordered, "Vodka and orange juice for all of us, please."

"On the rocks?"

"Could you put some ice with it?"

The bartender and the waiter knew everyone who came to the Blue Moon Cafe. They knew we were old enough to drink, but new to the game.

He walked away, saying under his breath, "Four virgin Screwdrivers on the rocks."

When I spotted the person at the bar who bought us drinks, I smiled, *Thanks*. His cocked beret spoke loudly of his personality. *Dapper Dan*, I mused. *About my age. Inherited the long taunt body from African and maybe Native American heritage and Marine training. Well-dressed like Reverend Love. But not churchy. As Mama would say, "Clean as hog chitlings." A college boy look! Sky blue herring bone sweater and coordinated with navy blue slacks. Royal blue penny loafers to match. His uniform's probably hanging in the barracks. Resting on its days off.*

I, too, was dressed for such a night. Reba's form-fitting aqua blue dress flowed down my body, like floating ice cream. The dress sat on top of a pair of navy-blue leather, sexy high-heeled shoes. The long sleeve expensive, tailored-made dress had elaborated stitching across the front. It was trimmed with white silk ribbon around the edges of the sleeves, circling the neck and running down the front of the dress. The outfit was shoplifted along with stolen shoes that my sister Reba had left when she had taken Kabari. *Was this a trade for my baby?* The princess dress was an ocean of me, ready to be explored and experienced by the dandy who kept looking my way.

"Dodayouseeakafinealookakamarineakaatheakabarakalaloo k ingakaatausaka?" I asked Carolyn in Pig Latin as his penetrating eyes pierced my heart and threw another boomerang in my unsteady life.

After his buddies arrived, the generous Marine led them to our table. As the tall immaculate men swaggered toward our table, the women in the room patted their hair and rehearsed their winning smiles. Men straightened their shoulders and adjusted their jackets. All knew that royalty was in the house.

Each person introduced himself/herself. Eddy. Bill. Paul. Jimmy. His friends and Jimmy. Carolyn. Brenda. Susan. Doris. My friends and me. Things felt a little awkward as each Marine scoped out each girl and the girls did the same to the Marines. I relaxed when I realized that Jimmy and I were top contenders for each other. There was nothing to worry about. Jimmy didn't know that he had already been chosen. Sometimes it takes a man a longer time to know or decide.

Later, Jimmy had asked me, "whatakakindofaka languakadoaka youakandakayourakafriendakaspeakak?"

We both laughed and answered together, "Pigakalataka."

His presence made breathing easier. I nodded approval to something felt, but unspoken. Another soulmate, right from the beginning. Aunt Naomi had said you can have more than one.

It was so amazing how the depression vanished when I met Jimmy. *Maybe he would be the Jim Dandy who would rescue me?*

* * *

On a rainy summer night of 1965, Corporal James Alfonzo Williams and I sat in his sleek silver and white 1957 Chevrolet Bel Aire car near the backdoor of the projects. We were discussing our blossoming relationship and how we could continue it. Jimmy had said, "I really like your smile, dignity and intelligence. But I received transfer orders to report to Seal Beach, California in six weeks."

After many moments of sharing lovers' embraces, intense lip and mouth explorations, I breathed, "I am devastated you have to leave." Coming out of the comfort of his embrace, I looked at the clock radio. 3:00 a.m.! We had talked three hours past the 12:00 curfew! I was frantic and I had been warned!

A nervous me jumped out of the car and scurried from front door to backdoor, trying to get into the house and away from the buckets of warm torrential falling water. As the summer rains drenched me, I realized that my niece had fallen asleep and forgotten to unlock the doors. Or Reverend Love had made a final lock check. I was resigned to my fate. Homeless and boyfriendless! At the back door, the idea came with a flash of rain that almost blinded me. *Use the kitchen window.*

From the back porch, I had climbed up on the oil drum and pushed the window open. The window screen fell into the kitchen on the counter with a dull bounce. The kitchen blazed with light; the clock on the stove indicated that it was 3:05 a.m., well past the assigned hour. My hair, clothes and shoes were leaking water in the sink like someone had turned the spigot on me.

"Go back where you come from!" shouted Reverend Love as I stepped through the kitchen window into the sink. I didn't answer him. I looked outside to see if the car was still there. My reply was to turn around and to stepped slowly out the same way I came in.

Wiping tears and chopping rain from my bowed head, I resignedly slumped back to the waiting car. "He told me to go back where I came from."

Jimmy told me, "Get back in the car." After a long silence, the honorable Marine decided, "You can come to live at my family house in Winston-Salem. It's about 185 miles away. About three hours. It'll be fine. Things will resolve themselves."

This was the incident that would catapult my life into the direction I had been envisioning. Since I started reading as a young child, I wanted to leave Ktown and go to college, but I didn't have a plan, money or support. Unforeseen events sped up the process. The curfew violation threw me out of my house and straight into the arms of destiny.

"Go back where you come from" became the rallying call of my life. This would be a theme that motivated me to be the best possible. I knew instinctively that it was a crossroad situation, a welcomed turning point this time!

Later in the day, my "Black knight in shining armor" and I went back to Reverend Love's house in the projects to get some of my clothes. I packed some clothes, my magic mirror and other valuables in my Samsonite luggage. I made sure I wore my necklace from Aunt Babs and hid my juju bag in the bottom of my pocketbook. Fate would have Reverend Love at home midmorning, totally off his usual work schedule.

The house was in an uproar. My mama was crying, "I'm tired of you running my children away."

Mama was not surprised about me leaving abruptly. She knew it was just a matter of time.

Reverend Love was visually upset. For the first time in a long time, I saw some real expression in his eyes. I could even hear some feeling in his voice.

"I never meant for you to actually leave home like this!" Reverend Love moaned as he pled with me to stay. "You can always stay in this house."

Feelings were expressed toward me that I had never experienced from my mama, nor Reverend Love.

As for my 'daddy', who was totally self-absorbed in his hypocritical preaching and lascivious tactics, any affection or help from him appeared suspect. I simply ignored his proposal. "Don't leave. You can come home whenever you decide."

I knew I would never look back and re-consider.

On the long, silent ride to another uncertain life, I mused about my daughter Kabari. Then I said to Jimmy, "My sister Reba has four boys. But she wanted to see how it was to mother a girl. She had insisted on keeping her for a month. It has been way past that time, and I haven't saved enough money to go get Kabari. And Reba still hasn't brought Kabari back. I said 'okay', not because I wanted to. I have always tried to make her accept me. My sister lived up North in Pennsylvania. It's another problem I must work on—pleasing people."

"It will turn out alright. We'll get Kabari back," Jimmy reassured me.

The heavy downpour accompanied us down the highway. Jimmy said quietly, "The rainstorm has not let up from the night before. Heavy winds and these violent rains are ripping everything in its path."

I agreed, "The disabled trucks and the abandoned cars on the edge of the highway look like a wrecked car museum. We better be careful."

Suddenly, through a sheet of rain, a green John Deere tractor careened out of nowhere and the driver lost control on our side of the highway.

"Jimmy!" I screamed.

To avoid the tractor hitting the car directly, Jimmy abruptly turned the steering wheel to the right. The Chevy went into a spin. It spun off the highway and flipped over several times before it dropped into a ditch, right side up, on four new and still perfect Goodyear tires. The collision of rubber, metal, glass, ground and rain ended in a ghastly silence.

I was caught up in a strange place of danger and safety. My life, a story of 'twixt and between', flashed before me. *Seeking peace and finding confusion. Driven from the house of secrets and straight into harm's way. Tired of being 'Colored' in a White world.* In the tornado-like rotation of the car, I was bubbled in a place of quiet terror and soft safety.

Coming back to my right mind, I heard Jimmy ask, "Baby, are you alright?"

Jimmy removed broken window glass as he crawled out of his window. As I struggled to open my door, I realized that the front doors were wedged with cow pasture grass. Jimmy's eyes were cloudy with concern for me as he pushed the tall grass and broken branches from my collapsed door. I stepped out of the car, still trembling and dazed. Jimmy said, with deep emotions, "I am so sorry. I promise that I won't let anything happen to you again. Marry me so I can take care of you forever."

Life presented a perfect solution for a challenging situation. Not totally calmed, but grateful for life and now a future, I slowly nodded. "Yes. I'm okay. And yes, I'll marry you."

Was I still in the trance?

A witness to the accident called a tow truck crew to handle the seemingly deadly disaster. The emergency crew towed the car out of the ditch, pulled out two dented fenders and two crushed doors. They moved cow pasture grass stuck in the hood and the bumpers of the car. As the driver surveyed the wreckage, he said to Jimmy and me, "You are lucky to be alive!"

In amazement, Jimmy and I looked at each other. We knew it!

Again, Jimmy called his mama. This time to let her know that he was not bringing his girlfriend home, but his fiancée. When Jimmy's mama got the news, she started the ball rolling. *Fiancée! Marriage!* By the time we arrived at the house, his family had been notified and everything was being planned. His mama's first question was, "Do your mama and daddy know where you are? And that you two are getting married?"

"Yes." We lied twice.

Then, Miss Lorene said, "Everything from the blood test to the wedding license to the possible wedding date is set up."

The family accepted me with instant and complete love. Mr. and Mrs. Williams became Moms and Pops. And I had eight additional sisters and brothers. My life was flowing upstream.

Later, when the initial shock of the sudden engagement wore off, we provided them with some of the details of the accident. We were careful to leave out the part that the car flipped several times and had to be pulled out of a ditch with the jaws of life wrecking equipment.

After the interrogation about the accident, Jimmy's moms announced, "Engaged couples cannot sleep together until marriage."

In a few days, Corporal James Alfonzo Williams Jr. and Doris Ann Love were legally married. Our wedding gift was a fifth of Southern Comfort whiskey from Jimmy's father, Mr. James Williams, Sr. After our family wedding feast, the whole family went to visit their relatives out in the country. Our marriage was consummated in Jimmy's sister's bed that she had given up for us. Soon Jimmy reported for duty as required. In a month or so, I joined my new husband when Naval housing became available in Long Beach, California.

Four months later, we newlyweds drove back to my hometown from California to meet with my sister, Reba. In the projects. I could hardly wait to reunite with my daughter after six months. Kabari screamed as she tried to remember me. And we cried as we clung to each other. "Never again will I leave you!" I promised my love child through hot, happy tears.

In that short period of time my mama had finally done what I had always implored her to do. To my surprise, she had left Reverend Love and roomed with my godmama Miss Doris. Reverend Love had gotten rid of all my books, diaries and other personal possessions. *But where was the antique crib?*

Despite the reversal and because of the reversal, I was exuberant. I had my wonderful child back in my arms. I'd married a loving, handsome, affectionate, intelligent man and we lived a promising life in California. My new husband had reminded me how the gods were smiling on us. "In Los Angeles, the weather is balmy. The people are progressive and the opportunities are everywhere. California's junior college system is free. Students only had to pay for books, and classes are transferable to a 4-year university. Most of all, there are no 'Colored' and White-water signs in California."

Jimmy was right. I still believe that truth and knowledge were the way out of prejudice, ignorance and poverty. I remain resolute that neither father, nor child, nor husband, nor racism or any system would block my desire and determination to learn the mysteries of life. This I carried deep inside of my soul.

* * *

A week later, on the way back to California, I contemplated the other situation I had experienced during the visit to my hometown. After we had picked up Kabari, I had said to Jimmy, "Drive me to the side of town near the cemetery. I want to see my sister Nora."

"Sis", as Nora sometimes affectionately called me, had knocked on Nora's door. I immediately stepped into my role as rescuer and protector. I opened the unlocked door and wandered through the dark, cold house. "Nora where are you?" A small light burned from an oil lamp in the bedroom. In the dimness, I asked myself, *Is that Kabari's crib? Trimmed with carved dancing rabbits and flying butterflies.* My godmama's husband, Mr. Eugene, a carpenter had re-stained it for me. *I was glad Nora had taken it before it was thrown out with the rest of my belongings.*

Looking closer, I prayed silently, *Lord ha' mercy.* I patted a damp sheet and blanket, looking for Nora's new second son. A familiar voice spoke, *Look in the far corner of the crib.* A small, hungry baby lay in squalor, protesting life with a weak, sad sob. I immediately picked up the fragile male child and rocked him in my arms. I cuddled and cooed him. I asked, "Where is your mama?" He answered with a shrieking wail. I put the irate baby on the disheveled bed on the opposite side of the room. Then I searched for clean dry diapers and crib sheets.

Recovering from the shock of the sad, dank house, my inner voice said to me, "*Decide a course of action. No time for sorrows.*"

Right away I got a fire going. I was good at starting fires. I found some kindling, small pieces of dried woods to get the fire started. The fire blazed as I added the coal in the wood stove. "*Burn the whole thing down. It's nothing but a shack!*" crossed through my mind as the flames added streaks of light in the room. "*No. Nora and her children wouldn't have anywhere to live.*" Part of me felt like burning my sister.

The thought was abandoned as I searched for clean sheets. Having no luck, I took the dingy sheet from the bed and tore it into two crib sheets and several diapers. *Lordy! Lordy! Lordy! How sad!* Tears rolled down my face as I removed the wet garments and bathed the baby with Avon lotion. Then dressed him in two "diapers" and swaddled the rest of his body in torn pieces of sheet. Buttoned in his mama's blouses, the baby's whole appearance changed. Although still whimpering, the abandoned baby appeared now to be wanted and loved. The soggy crib sheet was changed to a dry sheet. The blanket from the bed was doubled-spread across the crib.

There was no milk in the house. The crying child would have to drink some sugar water until I went to the store. As I rinsed the bottle out, I gagged. *What a shame!* The bottom of the baby bottle was caked with green and gray furry mold.

An ancient memory came to mind of my ancestors working in the tobacco fields. Forbidden to stop to nurse, they had feed the baby a sugar teat. I tore one of the "diapers" in half, knotted it in three sections and filled the twisted dampened middle knot with sugar. The baby sucked noisily as I inserted the knotted sugar teat into its eager mouth.

I wrapped the baby in my coat and took him outside where Jimmy and Kabari were waiting in his new 1965 gold and black Chevelle. Jimmy had left his restored 1957 Chevy with his mother in 1965 before he transferred to California. Having a car sent my mother-in-law on her own personal journey of transformation.

I explained the situation quietly to Jimmy. "My sister is not home. I made a fire and cleaned the wet baby. There is no milk."

Jimmy rushed to the local drug store to purchase diapers, milk, bottles and baby clothes. As soon as he returned, I re-dressed the baby in warm, new baby clothes and made milk for my little nephew. Full of weariness and a growing anger, I asked Jimmy, "Would you drive us around town to find my sister?"

Jimmy, ever ready to comfort me, answered, "Point the way." We traveled from one spot to another for several hours until it got dark, trying to locate the missing mama and her other three children. In the back seat, Kabari fell asleep when the sun went down.

I had hoped that Nora would be home when we returned. Disappointment greeted me as I deposited the fed baby back home in the warm room, dry bed and empty house. It was not an easy choice, but necessary so that I could find his mother. We left the sleeping baby, tucked in Kabari's crib. It was a family crib for sure now. Predictably, I found Nora lounging in a night club on Sugar Hill that we had been informed was her hangout. She was as drunk as 'Cooter Brown', a local saying for any public drunk.

After the initial greetings, I explained my reasons for being in Ktown. "I came to meet Reba, pick up Kabari and to see you and your children." Then I told Nora, "The house was cold and dark, the crib was wet, and the baby was hungry." I knew she knew this, and

I knew she didn't know how to care. I urged, begged and cajoled her to go home immediately.

Nora promised, "Sis, I will be home as soon as I have me a couple more drinks." Nora informed me, "My oldest daughter Betty, who you raised, lives at your godmama Miss Doris's house. Mama lives there too. Margie and Lennie live with me. They're probably next door. I hate to say it, but I gave Darlene to one of Mama's friends. I just couldn't take care of all the children."

And the news about Darlene, who I had raised also, was more than I could take. I turned to Jimmy and said, "Let's go!"

Jimmy drove from downtown Sugar Hill near the Neuse River banks. Past the two 'Colored' projects and one White project, 'Colored' neighborhoods and White neighborhoods, and finally to Miss Doris's house which sat across the street from the Adkin Canal. It was a route set up by nature and segregation. When we arrived at my namesake's house, I hopped out the car and knocked on the door with such rigor that the doorjamb shook. When Mama opened the door, I jumped around her neck. Mama was so surprised that she screamed, "Aren't you a sight for sore eyes!"

I quickly explained to Mama and Miss Doris, "I'm back in Kinston to get Kabari from Reba. I went by Nora's. Nobody's home, but the baby. He was cold, wet and hungry. I want Betty to stay with the baby until Nora comes home."

When I stepped away from Mama, Miss Doris hugged me as I recognized my niece Betty, sitting in the corner reading. It was a habit she picked up from me. She was a little taller, more worldly and more defiant. "Aunt Doris, you left me without telling me you were leaving."

Her greeting was filled with anger and disappointment.

"I am so sorry that I had to leave so quickly. I missed you so much." I reached to hug Betty, but she turned away. Feeling her insecurity and loss, I hugged her anyway. "I promise you I will send for you when I get settled in California."

This broke the spell. She stood up, still remembering our love and our bond. My niece hugged me for a long, long time. She knew I was her mama. And I knew that her mama had been mine. Sort of.

With that promise sealed with a pinky twist, Betty agreed. "I will go and stay with the baby until Mama comes home. But I started to live with Miss Doris when I got pregnant."

"Pregnant?" I hadn't noticed, even when she stood. Then I looked closer. Yes, there was 'a hen in the oven', as Mama would say. "Get in the car. We'll take you there. We gotta talk."

Jimmy got out of the car and greeted Mama and Betty who followed me outside. He met my godmama who stood in the doorway with her walking cane. Kabari, now over a year old, shuffled out of the car to see her grandmama again. Everyone made over Kabari and I promised to keep in touch.

When we dropped Betty at the decrepit shack, I asked my niece, "What's the baby's name?" I asked, full of sorrow. And feeling, again, a little repulsion for my mama/sister, Nora. Betty paused and looked at me, from sad, hopeless eyes. "His name is Jeffrey. I will write to you about this." She pointed to her stomach. "The baby is due in a few months."

Then she was gone, entering her new life and I drove away with mine.

* * *

As Jimmy and I rode down the highway to our life together, my reflection in the rearview mirror showed me wearing a stylish, light blue jumpsuit that I bought in California. My heart was happy, but my eyes were sad about some of the changes in my new life. Then, I settled down and looked back on my old one. I realized that I was grieving the loss of family and connection to my old life. In my mind, I drew a timeline of my innocence when I was hopeful, happy and safe. A very short line. As a child, I hadn't had a chance to develop early strong relationships with healthy adults. And I didn't have the words to express my sorrows. I had been left to fend for myself. Coming back home to get my daughter was validation that it was time for me to build my life based on what I wanted.

As my midwife had advised me, "Doris, let this pregnancy be a fall forward, not a fall backward." I was determined to use this wisdom as I journeyed forward.

I turned to Jimmy. "The last episode with Nora helped me decide that I am not going to wait for others to fix my life. I've been doing the same thing my mama did. Using men to fix her life. Here I am getting married to you and I hardly know you. All my life I waited for some knight in shining armor to rescue me. I have been waiting for my 'Jim Dandy.'"

Jimmy jerked his head and gripped the steering wheel until the veins on his knuckles popped up. As he drove, he turned his head slightly toward me. "What is a 'Jim Dandy'? I think I may have heard that name before."

He continued to drive and glanced my way occasionally. I could feel him waiting for my answer.

Finally, when I had formed the answer, I told him. "In the song "Jim Dandy to the Rescue", sung by Laverne Baker, Jim Dandy rescues women. In the second song, "Jim Dandy Got Married", Jim Dandy fell in love with a woman the day he rescued her. By the afternoon, they were engaged and by night, they were married. This was a popular song when I was twelve."

By now I was crying, feeling the intensity of my uncertain life.

"I've been stranded in a world that was too limited for my compelling imagination and recurring visions! Then I was kicked out of the house, with a baby and nowhere to go. I needed a knight in shining armor to rescue me. By the time we got to your mom's house, I realized I was actually marrying a Jim Dandy."

Jimmy slowed down as he felt my pain. I was telling him some things he didn't know.

"Getting pregnant out of wedlock filled me with shame. I felt like I had failed my mama. I'm my mama's third daughter to get pregnant without being married. Mama never said anything to make me feel less, but I wanted to break the pattern. I was born in a family where the father and the mother are screwed up in their heads! I'm just realizing that this doesn't mean my life has to be screwed up, too. What I did, I did it in the name of love! There's no sin in love."

"Look, Doris, I feel the same way. My unmarried sister had a baby. I still love her. It doesn't matter to me that you already have a baby. I love Kabari and we three can be a family together."

He smiled his broad smile that always made things seem right. "We can add to our family. Kabari needs a sister or a brother to play with. You are the type of woman I have been looking for in every country I have traveled. Fine. Intelligent. Spirited. Full of love. So, what if I am the 'Jim Dandy' you've been praying for? If the truth be told, you have rescued me from some stuff too."

His generous heart warmed my icy thoughts.

"I know I haven't done anything wrong! I thought Kabari's father loved me and was going to save me from the hurt and shame in life. It wasn't his responsibility. I guess love is something that you give yourself first. In the end, he found someone he thought would save him. How could he give me what he didn't have himself? But I knew help would come from somewhere. Well, it has already come. You have come to take me to my future. I just have to convince myself that I deserve this love and grace."

As I shared all these things with Jimmy, I began to believe them. When I remembered who I used to be, before the sadness, I remembered that I was already enough. It was time to let go of the past and honor my new life. I saw myself letting go of the old stories and opening to new adventures as I settled back in my car seat. I made a vow to myself. *I will re-write me a new story and give a new name to my heroes. 'Sheheroes'. Because courageous women are always left out of the story-making and the storytelling. I am going to invent me a new self. And I am going to love me and be by own 'shehehero'."*

My unresolved tendency to express my anger and anxiety by using fire had never been examined or discussed. I guess I needed some anger control. But I surely couldn't tell 'Jim Dandy'! And I wasn't ready to tell him about my hypocritical 'daddy' either. The idea of discussing how Rabbit helped me through the hurt and the pain of the loss of my childhood had to be delayed also. Even all this, I won't hold against myself. I had told Jimmy some of the truth of my life. But like my mama, I kept my secrets until the right time...

The brilliant 1965 Chevy cruised down the highway in Texas, taking us on to our promising future. Jimmy and I were lost in our thoughts as "My Girl" by the Temptations played on the radio. Kabari slept in the back seat. Jimmy said, "Hey, girl, I'm wondering when we'll get home." He was wearing his winning smile and clutching my hand tightly to his chest.

My heart leaped! Suddenly, a caravan of men wearing white robe-like garments, riding on horses and carrying monstrous flaming crosses, lined up completely across the highway. My memories and peace were broken and scattered. Jimmy slowly brought the car to a stop. He rolled down the window, halfway. The leader rode up to the car and asked, "Where y'all niggas goin?"

Proudly dressed in United States Marine uniform, Jimmy answered in his best corporal Marine Military Police (MP) voice—exact, correct and respectful. "We're on our way back home to California."

I glanced at my new husband whose calmness, like a cocked pistol, could explode if any wrong move was made.

The Klansman muttered, "You black uppity niggers! Go back where you come from! Keep on riding and don't look back. Don't let the sun go down on your black ass again in this state!"

The 'don't look back' reminder had a threat of possible death.

As I looked through the window, I saw the burning crosses light up the sky as the calvary of hatred trailed the Chevy. It reminded me of the Christmas parade that the principal said I was too dark to participate in. Only this time my husband and I were the 'Colored' king and queen, unwillingly participating in the parade of fire and darkness that could lead to our death.

As always, the fire calmed me. For a moment I lost myself in the flames. I stilled my mind to quiet the racing terror that filled the car. Fear sharpened my memories. All of Uncle Johnson's teachings about the history of the Ku Klux Klan came back.

The legion of Ku Klux Klansmen from Texas gave us a military escort for an hour until the next state's welcome sign that said, "Welcome to New Mexico." The image of the Ku Klux Klansmen and their burning crosses looked back at me in the rearview mirror until the hate riders disappeared in the far horizon. We were safe.

When we had been in New Mexico about fifteen minutes, I glanced out the back window. My mouth flew open! A gigantic cross lit up the sky and spread across the vast heaven, like an expansive rainbow. Along with the great vision, a voice spoke. *A cross can mean death and life.* When I turned around, I asked Jimmy. "What are we going to do?"

Instead of fears and troubles, I felt strongly full of wonder.

Jimmy, the most optimistic person I had ever encountered, answered. "We're going to keep on moving toward our dreams. I don't exactly know how, but this I do know. I love you. Our life going forward will be different and better than the one we're leaving behind." Then he lifted his gun-a M16 rifle. He smiled a new life for us.

Choosing my words with great thought, I said, in a pleased whisper, "Looking back, I can see that a limited life was not to be my destiny. Now, I can begin to measure the difference between my old life and my new one. In California, I realized that life extends beyond the narrow views of the South. Meeting you presented an ocean of possibilities of going backward and moving forward at the same time. My life is a constant pattern of crossing boundaries and changing roles. I still can't see where I am going, but I know it will be a long way from where I started."

I squeezed my purple mojo bag in its brocade cover inside my pocketbook. With the other hand, I rubbed my reading charm necklace from Cousin Babs. *Whew! I knew surviving the Ku Klux Klan—my worst nightmare—any other chains could be broken!* After a long sigh, I set my face and dreams toward the West.

References

1. Rainer, Tristine, *Your Life as Story: Discovering the New Autobiography and Writing Memoir as Literature.* (1997). Jeremy P. Tarcher/Putman. New York, N. Y. p. 2.
2. Hurston, Zora Neale. *Dust Tracks on a Road: An Autobiography.* Harper-Collins Publishers. (1942) New York, N. Y. Pp. 212-213
3. Gutkind, Lee. *You Can't Make this Stuff up: The Complete Guide to Writing Creative Nonfiction–from Memoir to Literary Journalism and Everything in Between Nonfiction* (2012). Da Capo Press/lifelong Books a Member of the Perseus Books Group p. 6.

Reading Group Study Guide

These questions encourage readers to take a close, in-depth look at childhood sexual trauma. Group discussion of the psychological, and social effects of sexual abuse can evoke a healing environment for survivors. Most importantly, these questions provide a guide for any reader to witness the struggles of a young girl as she creates meaning in her life.

1. Describe the incident that changed the course of Doris's childhood. Describe a time growing up when a major problem became a turning point in your life.
2. The experience of abuse by a child is devastating. Discuss the ramification of Doris's abuse. Who did Doris tell? If she didn't tell anyone, what were her reasons?
3. What was the significance of the Adkin Canal?
4. Did you grow up in a family with secrets? Have you broken the silence?
5. There are many layers to Doris Love. Discuss how Doris deals with the secrets in her house?
6. Discuss the progression of Mrs. Love's depression and its disruption of the family. What were the possible reasons for her mental imbalance?
7. Doris's Aunt Naomi played an important role in Doris's development. Discuss their relationship.
8. What effects did racism and television have on Doris's sense of her identity and her people?
9. Discuss Doris's use of the words 'Color', 'daddy' and 'Reverend love'.

10. The 'secret arts' is also called 'hoodoo', 'voodoo' and 'witchcraft' by the uninitiated. What do the people who practice the ancient spirituality of AfRaKa call it? How is it like and different from Christianity?
11. Doris was dark-skinned, female, poor and lived in the projects. How did this affect her growing up? Have you been affected because of skin color, social economic status or gender? Explain.
12. Compare and contrast Doris's parents' personalities. Discuss her relationship with both of them and her siblings.
13. How did Milton help Doris deal with the inappropriate behavior of her minister 'daddy'? What was the role of the marine 'Jim Dandy'?
14. Today, incest and child molestation are public issues. In the 40's, 50's and the 60's they were private, family secrets. Do you know someone who has been sexually violated? What did you do? Or didn't do?
15. Doris's imagination and her love for words led her to write down her experiences in old notebooks and diaries. Describe the development of her reading and writing.
16. Who was Rabbit? How did she come to Doris's life?

About the Author

Dr. Queen Shamala Bessie Davis Fayemi Smith has lived in Los Angeles since the 60's, migrating from North Carolina. She earned a Bachelor' s degree in Psychology from the University of Southern California, a Master's in Psychology from California State University, Los Angeles, a Doctorate of Theology from Christ is the Answer Unity in Florida and is completing a PhD in AfRaKan Spiritual Science from the University of Creative Life Initiation System (UCLIS) in Los Angeles. Queen Shamala is executive director of this learning center.

Reverend Shamala is also an ordained minister, a metaphysical practitioner, a spiritual counselor and an anger management facilitator, an ancestral seer, an Ifa aborisha (studies nature and life in the tradition of the Yoruba people of West Africa), and a heartful writer. In 2017, Queen Shamala published her first book, *Blackbutterfly Soul Songs*, which deals with the author's soul transformation in poetry. Her second book, *Breaking the Cycles of Pain: Soul Secrets* is Volume I of a memoir trilogy. The next two books, The *Journey Let Us Cheer the Weary Traveler* and *The Books of Love Healing the Secrets* complete the trilogy. These creative nonfiction memoirs are autobiographical looks at Queen Shamala's healing from early childhood abuse, systemic racism, male-domination and its resultant low-self-esteem, anger and defiance.

Queen Shamala is the mother of two daughters, Yealang Jarrice Fayemi Smith Shakir, an acclaimed chef in Hollywood, Renetta Roberson, a registered nurse and two grandchildren-Malik and Malika. Touching the lives of many young people, Queen Shamala worked as a secondary school counselor for over thirty years with the Los Angeles Unified School District. Queen Shamala travels her artful life path with her husband Kaliph. In her school, the University of Creative Light Systems, in Gardena, California, the ancestrally-led artist facilitates healing light sessions, distance healing, guided meditations, ancestral initiations, painting classes, rites of passages and autobiographical writing sessions.

Resources

The National Sexual Assault Hotline
PHONE NUMBER 800 656-HOPE (4673)

The National Sexual Assault Hotline was the nation's first decentralized hotline, connecting those in need with help in their local communities. It's made up of a network of independent sexual assault service providers, vetted by RAINN, who answer calls to a single, nationwide hotline number. Since it was first created in 1994, the National Sexual Assault Hotline (800.656.HOPE and **online.rainn.org**) has helped more than 3 million people affected by sexual violence.

The National Sexual Assault Hotline is a safe, confidential service. When you call the hotline, only the first six numbers of the phone number are used to route the call, and your complete phone number is never stored in their system. Most states do have laws that require local staff to contact authorities in certain situations, like if there is a child or vulnerable adult who is in danger.

Anyone affected by sexual assault, whether it happened to you or someone you care about, can find support on the National Sexual Assault Hotline. You can also visit **online.rainn.org** to receive support via confidential online chat.

www.ingramcontent.com/pod-product-compliance
Lightning Source LLC
Chambersburg PA
CBHW021423070526
44577CB00001B/33

SECRETS ARE OUT NOW

How a girl overcomes the world

A TRUE STORY

"God helped her."

By
Crystal Rivers